THE LIFE OF
ST EDMUND
BY MATTHEW PARIS

TRANSLATED, EDITED AND WITH A BIOGRAPHY BY

C.H. LAWRENCE

ALAN SUTTON PUBLISHING LIMITED

ST EDMUND HALL, OXFORD

First published in the United Kingdom in 1996
Alan Sutton Publishing Limited
Phoenix Mill · Far Thrupp · Stroud · Gloucestershire

In association with
St Edmund Hall, Oxford

British Library Cataloguing in Publication Data

Paris, Matthew
  Life of St. Edmund
  I. Title II. Lawrence, C. H.
  270.5092

ISBN 0-7509-1166-2

Typeset in 10/11 Bembo.
Typesetting and origination by
Alan Sutton Publishing Limited.
Printed in Great Britain by
WBC Limited, Bridgend.

Contents

Preface

Thirty-six years have elapsed since I published the Latin text of the Life of St Edmund of Abingdon by Matthew Paris. Since then, competence in Latin has become such a rare skill that a translation of Matthew's work hardly calls for explanation or apology. The earlier book was primarily a textual investigation, designed to identify and disentangle the sources of the hagiographical tradition surrounding St Edmund and to test their historicity. The preparation of a translation has provided me with the incentive and opportunity to attempt a fuller and, I hope, more coherent portrait of Edmund than was possible within the framework of the previous book.

I am conscious of the limitations imposed upon an enterprise of this sort by the character of the sources. If in some areas of thought and action Edmund remains an enigma, it is because his own literary remains are few and rather intractable. All but one of his Biblical commentaries have disappeared. His *Speculum Ecclesie*, a work that was widely read in the middle ages, is largely a catechetical treatise for the use of those in the religious life, which does not yield much biographical insight. What we lack in his case are any of the personal letters of friendship or spiritual counsel that offer us windows into the mind of an Anselm or a Grosseteste.

Apart from the public records and chronicles, the materials we possess for the study of Edmund's life all had their origin in the proceedings for his canonization in the years 1244–6. These consist, in the first place, of letters of postulation addressed to the pope by individual prelates, monasteries, and the university of Oxford, requesting Edmund's inclusion in the catalogue of the saints. Several of the letters contain personal reminiscences from former colleagues and associates. Besides these, there survive scattered remnants of the evidences presented to the papal commissioners in the course of the canonization process. The most informative of these fragments are depositions made by Robert Bacon, the Dominican theologian, and Walter de Gray, the archbishop of York, which were reproduced by Matthew Paris in his Life of St Edmund, and the testimonies of four of Edmund's servants, which were published in my earlier book under the title of *Quadrilogus*. Many of these records were deposited at Pontigny after the papal commission of inquiry had completed its work and now belong to the Trésor of Sens cathedral.

The canonization moved a number of writers besides Matthew Paris to compose hagiographical Lives of St Edmund, for which the records of the

process supplied much of the material. The earliest Life was the work of
Eustace of Faversham, a monk of Canterbury who had served as
Archbishop Edmund's chaplain. He composed it before 1246, apparently in
order to promote the cause of St Edmund. It is to a large extent a pastiche
of the letters of postulation which had passed through Eustace's hands. This
early 'biography' provided Matthew Paris with a literary frame for his own
portrait of Edmund, into which he poured a wealth of historical
information about Edmund's public life, which gives his work its unique
interest. In addition to these two works, four other hagiographical Lives
were composed in the years immediately following the canonization. One
of these, a longer and highly rhetorical Life, was written by a monk of
Pontigny and printed by the Maurist scholars Martène and Durand in the
eighteenth century. The other three Lives were the work of anonymous
authors, whom I designated respectively 'A', 'B' and 'C'. Texts of the
second and third of these were published by Wilfrid Wallace in his book
St Edmund of Canterbury (1893). The Anonymous 'A' remains as yet
unpublished. It has been necessary to refer to these sources from time to
time when writing about St Edmund. Readers wishing to pursue these
references further will find a detailed account of the Lives, their inter-
relationship, and the letters of postulation in my earlier book.

Returning to Edmund after an absence of many years has been both a
reassuring and a chastening experience. It has been reassuring to find that,
on rereading the sources with a fresh eye and taking account of the work of
others published in the interim, there seems no reason to make any radical
change in my original conclusions about his public life; in fact, in regard to
the last year of his episcopate and the myth of his voluntary exile, I found
my earlier convictions strongly confirmed. On the other hand, renewed
study has made me more than ever conscious of the difficulty of
penetrating his mind and understanding his spiritual development in some
phases of his life. New questions have suggested themselves, to which I
have been able to find only tentative and unsatisfactory answers. I doubt
whether I have yet done justice to a man whose charisma as a teacher and
spiritual guide so deeply impressed others in his lifetime. But as the great
Bollandist Delehaye remarked in a moment of disillusionment, 'heureux
quand il leur est permis de dire qu'un de ces grands amis de Dieu a trouvé
un historien digne de lui.'

Abbreviations

AA.SS.	The *Acta Sanctorum* of the Bollandists
Ann.Mon.	*Annales Monastici*, ed. H.R. Luard, 4 vols (RS, 1864–9)
Auvray	*Les registres de Grégoire IX*, ed. L. Auvray (Ecole française de Rome, 1884–1921)
Berger	*Les registres d'Innocent IV*, ed. E. Berger (Ecole française de Rome, 1884–1921)
BHL	*Bibliotheca Hagiographica Latina* of the Bollandists (Brussels, 1898–9)
BL	The British Library
BRUO	*Biographical Register of the university of Oxford to AD 1500*, ed. A.B. Emden, 3 vols (1957–9)
Canivez	*Statuta Capitulorum Generalium Ordinis Cisterciensis*, ed. J. Canivez (Louvain, 1933–6)
CChR	*Calendar of Charter Rolls*
Chartularium	*Chartularium Universitatis Parisiensis*, ed. H. Denifle and A. Chatelain (Paris, 1889–91)
Chron.Maj.	The *Chronica Majora* of Matthew Paris, ed. H.R. Luard, 6 vols (RS, 1872–84)
CPL	*Calendar of Papal Letters relating to Great Britain and Ireland*, ed. W.H. Bliss, vol. 1 (1893)
CYS	Canterbury and York Society
EHR	*English Historical Review*
Flores	*Rogeri de Wendover Flores Historiarum*, ed. H.O. Cox, 5 vols (1841–4)
Gervase	The *Gesta Regum of Gervase of Canterbury*, ed. W. Stubbs, 2 vols (RS, 1880)
Hist.Angl.	The *Historia Anglorum* of Matthew Paris, ed. F. Madden, 3 vols (RS, 1886–9)
Lawrence, St Edmund	C.H. Lawrence, *St Edmund of Abingdon: A Study of Hagiography and History* (1960)
M.D.Thes.	E. Martène and U. Durand, *Thesaurus Novus Anecdotorum* (Paris, 1717)
MGH SS	*Monumenta Germaniae Historica*
OHS	Oxford Historical Society
PL	*Patrologia Latina*, ed. J.P. Migne (Paris, 1844–55)
Potthast	*Regesta Pontificum Romanorum 1198–1304*, ed. A. Potthast (Berlin, 1874–5)

PRO	Public Record Office
Receuil	*Receuil des historiens des Gaules et de la France*, ed. Bouquet
RS	Chronicles of Great Britain and Ireland published in the Rolls Series
Sarum	*Charters and Documents illustrating the History of the Cathedral,*
Charters	*City and Diocese of Salisbury in the Twelfth and Thirteenth Centuries*, ed. W.H.R. Jones and W.D. Macray (RS, 1891)
TRHS	*Transactions of the Royal Historical Society*
Wallace	W. Wallace, *St Edmund of Canterbury* (1893)

Part I: Edmund of Abingdon

1
The Early Years

St Edmund of Abingdon was a schoolman bishop. He was one of a small but growing company of thirteenth-century prelates who came from relatively humble and obscure families, and for whom the schools opened a road to high preferment. For this period we rarely have any information about the birth or early life of prominent churchmen; but with Edmund the case is different. Thanks to the process of canonization that was set in motion less than four years after his death, we possess, in addition to the hagiographical Lives, a plethora of letters and personal testimonies from those who knew him, some of which report his own reminiscences of his early years, which he had communicated to intimate friends and colleagues.

He was born in Abingdon, a small town on the Thames, six miles south of Oxford, one of those bustling trading communities of Wessex which had begun life as the economic satellite of an ancient abbey and had grown prosperous on the proceeds of the English trade in woollens. He was the child of an otherwise obscure urban family with property in the borough. The authors of the Lives have much to say about the piety of his parents, Reginald the Rich (Dives) of Abingdon and Mabel his wife. They do not, however, tell us the date of his birth, nor do they say anything about the status or occupation of his father. Their silences on this subject prompt questions to which we shall later return.

As will shortly appear, Reginald of Abingdon was a man of some means, and the name 'Rich' may have signified no more than the reputation he had gained among his less prosperous neighbours. At any rate, it is certain that neither Edmund nor his brother Robert ever used the name as a patronymic. In medieval records both of them are designated solely by the toponymic 'of Abingdon'. The practice of attaching to them the name 'Rich' has no medieval authority. As for the date of Edmund's birth, we can venture a surmise based upon the chronology of his academic career. If, as will be argued, he went to the schools of Paris to study the arts at, or shortly before, the year 1190, his birth is to be placed in or about the year 1174.

From the confused and conflicting statements in the Lives it emerges that Edmund was the eldest child of a fairly large family. They report a conversation between him and his mother when she was dying, in the course of which she asks him to convey her blessing to all his brothers. Matthew Paris, who had the most accurate information, refers to three brothers. He names Robert, who was to follow Edmund in an ecclesiastical career and later became his brother's trusted assistant in the administration of the Canterbury diocese, Nicholas, who took the Cistercian habit at Boxley abbey, and a third brother, unnamed, who entered the Benedictine abbey of Eynsham, ten miles from his home town.

Matthew's reference to this third brother who became a monk offers a solution to a puzzling conundrum. Two of the hagiographers state that Edmund's father had obtained his wife's consent to retire from the world and had taken the monastic habit at Eynsham. But this act of fugitive piety is not confirmed by any other independent source, nor did the monks of Eynsham make any reference to it when they later wrote to postulate Edmund's canonization. Moreover, one of the writers who sponsored the story is wrong about the father's name, which he gives as Edward. The mistake suggests the writer has confused the father with the son.

A fourth brother can almost certainly be added to those named by Matthew Paris. Edmund had two sisters, Margery and Alice, whom, after the mother's death, he placed in a small convent at Catesby in Northamptonshire. Among the Catesby charters in the Public Record Office there is an early deed given by one William, who was also a son of Reginald of Abingdon, assigning the nuns of Catesby a rent from an Abingdon property occupied by Rondulf the mason.[1] It is reasonable to suppose that William's interest in the distant nunnery of Catesby and his wish to provide it with an endowment arose from the fact that he had two sisters there.

Having failed to find a suitable marriage for either of her daughters, Mabel of Abingdon had directed Edmund to place his sisters in a convent. It was only after he had travelled a considerable distance and had met with several rejections, that he secured their admission to the small Benedictine convent of Catesby.[2] According to the hagiographers, the reason for his choice of this relatively poor establishment was a scruple about promising the dowry that was demanded by the other houses he visited. It was a well established custom to offer a monastery a gift of property or a rent to help meet the cost of feeding and clothing a recruit; but the canonists insisted

---

1. PRO, Anc.Deeds, E 326/B5.
2. The religious affiliation of Catesby is not entirely clear. In M.D. Knowles & R.N. Hadcock, *Medieval Religious Houses of England and Wales* (1953), p. 222, it is listed as a Cistercian nunnery. It has also been claimed as a Gilbertine house on account of its having a community of resident canons. It seems, in fact, to have been a Benedictine convent, see Sally Thompson, *Women Religious* (1991), p. 110.

that it was not allowable to demand such a gift as a condition of admission. Superiors who made such a demand were guilty of simony. The Fourth Lateran Council of 1215 singled out nunneries as common offenders: 'the stain of simony has so infected many nuns that scarcely any are received without a price.'[3] Nevertheless, whatever the canonists said, many women's foundations of the twelfth century were poorly endowed, and they could not afford to accept new members unless they brought additional income with them.

In due course Edmund and his brother William settled a number of endowments on Catesby, but he may have refused, as the hagiographers said, to give any prior undertaking. Such scrupulosity was in character. On the other hand, his difficulty in placing his sisters may have had more to do with snobbery than simony. The larger women's houses recruited mainly from landed families of armigerous stock, and perhaps they were disinclined to look with favour on the two humble postulants from the vill of Abingdon.

Whatever the considerations that led Edmund to select Catesby, the nunnery was to derive unexpected profit from his sisters, quite apart from the properties he and his brother had settled on the house. In 1245, five years after Edmund's death, when the process of his canonization was well advanced, Margery of Abingdon was appointed prioress by Grosseteste, who as bishop of Lincoln intervened and quashed a previous election.[4] As a result of its being the home of the sisters of Saint Edmund and the possessor of some of his personal effects which he had bequeathed to the house,[5] Catesby became a centre of his cult and a focus for pilgrims. Margery of Abingdon died in 1257 with a reputation for sanctity, as was proper in the sister of one whom the Church had raised to its altars.[6]

The failure of the hagiographers to describe the status or occupation of Edmund's father leaves a gap in the story of his boyhood. Referring to the circumstances of his parents they use the word *mediocris* – middling or moderate. If this is a description of their social status, it means only that they were of free birth, occupying a middle position in the social scale between landowners or 'gentry' of the armigerous class and the ranks of servile or free peasants. As an account of their wealth, it could be understood to mean 'average' or 'fair'. Although the writer of the Pontigny Life insists that Edmund's father was rich in nothing but good works, there is documentary evidence to indicate that Reginald was by no means a poor

3. Mansi XXII, *c.* 1051; *c. 40 X de Simonia V,3.* On the problems of enforcement see J.H. Lynch, *Simoniacal Entry into Religious Life, 1000–1260* (Ohio, 1976), pp. 203–24.
4. *Rotuli Roberti Grosseteste*, ed. F.N. Davis (CYS, 1913), p. 222.
5. He sent them his grey cloak and silver diptych, described by Matthew Paris in the Life, below p. 156 and in the *Chron.Maj.*, iv, pp. 102, 324.
6. *Chron.Maj.*, v, p. 621.

man. He owned several properties in the town; and he left enough money
to support his widow and to send two of his sons to the schools.

One of Reginald's properties, which was apparently the family
residence, was disposed of by Edmund after his mother's death. In a deed,
which is undated, in the Abingdon cartulary, Master Edmund recorded the
conveyance in free alms to the hospital of St John the Baptist outside the
east gate of Oxford of 'a house with all its appurtenances, which was that
of Reginald Rich (*Divitis*), in West Street in the vill of Abingdon',
reserving only a rent of two shillings a year to Alditha of the same town.[7]
This house stood in the commercial area of the town, not far from St
Helen's wharf, where the river-borne merchandise was unloaded. It was
recognized by the townspeople as Edmund's birthplace. As such it was
acquired in 1288 by Edmund, earl of Cornwall, who erected a chapel on it
for the devotees of the saint.[8]

The following entries in the cartulary show that the brethren running the
hospital assigned the rent to Andrew Halegod of Oxford. Halegod in turn
assigned the rent to Abingdon abbey for the support of a hospital in
Abingdon.[9] Matthew Paris, alone of all the hagiographers, recorded this
transaction, in syncopated form, in a couplet of his French Life of St Edmund:

et tout son patrimonie donne
A l'hopital d'Abbendone.[10]

Edmund's disposal of the paternal house as a charitable gift to a hospice
for the poor and sick was a characteristic act of the reckless generosity that
frequently impoverished him in later years.

Other properties of the family are described in another charter recording
the endowment Edmund settled on Catesby for the support of his sisters.
By this he granted the nuns of Catesby a house in Abingdon with a garden

7. *Two Cartularies of Abingdon Abbey*, ed. G. Lambrick & C.F. Slade, 2 vols (OHS, 1992) I,
    pp. 187–8. For the Latin text, see Lawrence, *St Edmund*, p. 315.
8. On the chapel, which was served by two priests supplied by Abingdon abbey, see
    Accounts of the Obedientiars of Abingdon Abbey, ed. R.E.G. Kirk (CS, new series, 51,
    1892), pp. xxxix–xl. The site of the chapel and house is commemorated in the
    name of St Edmund's Lane, which runs between West St Helen's Street and Ock
    Street.
9. *Two Cartularies of Abingdon Abbey*, ed. Lambrick & Slade I, p. 188. For the Latin text, see
    Lawrence, *St Edmund*, p. 316. Halegod acquired the rent by an exchange. He owned
    other property near the east gate of Oxford, where the hospital stood: H.E. Salter,
    Cartulary of the hospital of St John the Baptist, Oxford (OHS, 1916), i, pp. 220–1. His
    assignation of the rent to Abingdon must be dated 1234–41.
10. *La vie de S.Edmond*, ed. A.T. Baker in *Romania* 55 (1929), l. 115.

and croft, reserving an annual rent of two pence to the kitchener of Abingdon abbey.[11] In this deed he is not yet using the title of Master, which suggests he had not yet incepted as a teacher of arts. It is therefore unlikely that he had acquired the property himself, and it must have formed part of his inheritance. If to this be added the house occupied by Rondulf the mason, out of which his brother William endowed Catesby, Reginald of Abingdon emerges as a man of some means. Under the relatively free tenurial arrangements of the town, he had been able to invest in property.

What then was the source of Reginald's wealth, which left his widow and family well provided for? The writers of the Lives have plenty to say about Edmund's boyhood, which makes their uniform silence on this subject all the more striking. Their taciturnity would be explicable, however deplorable, if Reginald was a merchant or tradesman. A long tradition of hagiographical writing associated noble birth with virtue and trade with villainy. Such notions were reinforced by the Church's prohibition of usury and the censuring of profit-taking. Although by the thirteenth century these attitudes were being eroded by the expansion of international commerce based upon capital and credit and by increasing social mobility, disparagement of merchants continued to be a commonplace of monastic hagiography. The persistence of this form of snobbery can be seen in Thomas of Celano's Life of St Francis, who was a contemporary of Edmund. Francis was the son of a prosperous cloth merchant of Assisi. In his first version of the Life of St Francis, Celano denigrated the saint's father, Bernardone, as a greedy hard-hearted worldling, and vilified the morals and manners of the bourgeois society in which Francis was brought up. The men who wrote the Lives of St Edmund were monks and traditionalists, like Matthew Paris, whose snobbery was blatant and unashamed. They would have regarded trade as an unsuitable occupation for the father of a saintly bishop.

Abingdon was a monastic township which in the last decades of the twelfth century housed a thriving commercial community. In the thirteenth century it was twice yearly the location for a fair. It was a regional centre for the wool trade and cloth production. Possibly Reginald of Abingdon was, like the father of St Francis, a wool merchant or a draper. This would account for the comparatively comfortable circumstances of the family. It would also explain the discreet silence of the hagiographers. For merchants, basic literacy and numeracy were necessary tools of their trade. Such men, too, appreciated the value of education for their children and had the means to secure it.

11. PRO, Anc.Deeds, E 326/B4. Latin text in Lawrence, *St Edmund*, p. 316.

Whatever Reginald's occupation, he appears to have died while the children were still young. The task of bringing them up thus fell to the mother alone. Mabel of Abingdon was a devout and strong-minded woman, whose personality was the single most dominant influence in Edmund's life. She trained her sons in the habit of prayer and inculcated the harsh forms of mortification that she practised herself. Edmund recalled how, when he and his brother Robert were youngsters studying at Paris, she sent them parcels of linen in which she enclosed hair-shirts with an earnest request that they should use them. This premature and over-rigid discipline imposed on him in childhood left a permanent mark on Edmund's character. There was something of the Manichean in his dread of the senses and the fierceness with which he avoided any conviviality. It was evidently her decision that he and Robert should go to the schools and become clerks.

It was partly in response to the needs and aspirations of merchants that schools sprang up in many towns of England during the twelfth century. Some of them were the property of monasteries or collegiate churches, which claimed an exclusive right to possess a school within the territory of their jurisdiction and appointed the schoolmaster. Many were independent enterprises set up by individual teachers or guilds. All were open to any pupils whose families could afford to pay the master's fees. What they offered was not higher learning, but the elements of Latin grammar – the syntax and vocabulary of the language, taught from the *Ars Minor* of Donatus and practised on the Latin psalter. There is no trace of a school at Abingdon at this date, but Oxford was already noted for its grammar schools, which were drawing pupils from other areas, although we know nothing of the teachers at this period.[12]

It was to the Oxford schools that Edmund was sent as a boy to learn his letters. He probably made the journey daily on foot. The school would have taught him French as well as Latin. In twelfth-century England an ability to speak French was a necessary accomplishment for an ambitious lad, for, more than a century after the Norman settlement, it was still the language of the aristocracy and the language of the courts. At the upper levels England was still a bilingual society, ruled by kings who were Frenchmen and who possessed huge continental dominions. French was also the *lingua franca* of merchants in most parts of Western Europe.

Several hagiographic anecdotes became attached to this stage of Edmund's life. One of these was the story of his encounter with the Christ-child when he was wandering alone in the meadows during a

---

12. Nicholas Orme, *English Schools in the Middle Ages* (1973), pp. 73–4, 95–6; R.W. Hunt, 'Oxford grammar masters in the middle ages' in *Oxford Studies presented to Daniel Callus* (OHS, 1964), pp. 163–93.

school holiday. In any age, the form taken by the religious experience of individuals is shaped by the collective mentalities of society. Apparitions of the infant Jesus were not uncommon in Cistercian hagiography of the thirteenth century. Ida of Nivelles saw the holy child move down the refectory of La Ramée and present himself to each of the nuns in turn.[13] At Himmerod a lay brother saw the Blessed Virgin enter the choir during the night office carrying the Christ-child in her arms and proffer the baby to those of the brethren who were rapt in prayer.[14] These para-mystical phenomena were the manifestations of a new orientation of Western religious sentiment, marked by a devotion to the humanity of Christ and a compassionate identification with the episodes of his earthly life.

Another anecdote of Edmund's boyhood describes how he took a vow of perpetual chastity in the presence of his confessor. He sealed the vow by a mystical espousal of the Blessed Virgin Mary, as a token of which he placed a ring on the finger of her statue in the church where the episode took place. When he endeavoured to remove the ring, the statue proved recalcitrant, and he had to leave it there. The Franciscan author of the Lanercost chronicle, who was in Oxford some twenty years after Edmund's death, identifies the statue and speaks of the story as common knowledge in the university.[15] Aside from the accidental features of the story, it is perfectly comprehensible that a devout youngster who had reached early adolescence, and who was aware that he was bound for the clerical life, should have made a resolution to embrace celibacy. As he must have known, the Church would require it of him if he proceeded to major orders.

Edmund's childhood ended when he set out with his brother, Robert, to attend the schools of Paris. This was probably in or shortly before the year 1190. He would have been about fifteen years of age or rising sixteen. In medieval society youngsters matured early. Their Oxford schoolmasters had equipped the brothers with a command of Latin and spoken French, but probably could take them no further. It seems that there were not yet any teachers at Oxford offering an advanced education in logic and the other liberal arts of the sort that was available in some of the cathedral schools of northern France. For some time to come, English lads with intellectual aspirations would find it necessary to go abroad to get what they wanted.

---

13. Simone Roisin, *L'hagiographie cistercienne dans le diocèse de Liège au XIIIe siècle* (Louvain, 1947), p. 173.
14. C.H. Lawrence, *Medieval Monasticism. Forms of Religious Life in Western Europe in the Middle Ages*, 2nd edn (1989), p. 181.
15. *Chronicon de Lanercost*, ed. J. Stevenson (1839), p. 36. A.G. Little showed that the part-author of the chronicle was Richard of Durham OFM, who was in Oxford after 1260: 'The authorship of the Lanercost Chronicle' in *Franciscan Papers, Lists, and Documents* (1943), pp. 42–54.

Edmund had now reached a stage of his life when he would have to make a personal decision. Men were drawn to the schools by a variety of motives – the fame of great teachers, an enthusiasm for learning and an awareness, which was infectious in the last years of the twelfth century, of an expanding intellectual universe, and not least the lure of promising career prospects. For growing numbers of schoolmen were being absorbed by the bureaucracies of church and state. Edmund was not a young man who calculated worldly advantages, but there is one question that forces itself on the attention of anyone who studies the records of his life. For a deeply religious youngster like him, the monastic life must have presented itself as a compelling alternative. Why did he not choose it, either now or later?

Monasteries were a familiar part of his social landscape. He had grown up under the shadow of the Benedictine abbey of Abingdon, which possessed seignorial rights over the town. Two of his brothers were to become monks. There can be no doubt that he felt the attraction of the cloister. In after years he would frequent monasteries. Before incepting as a theologian at Oxford, he stayed for more than a year in the Augustinian priory of Merton; and the canons later testified that he provided them with a model of fervent observance, meticulously keeping their horarium and never missing any hours of the divine office. At other times, he spent vacations at Reading abbey or stayed at Stanley with the Cistercians, where the abbot was his old pupil, Stephen of Lexington. As archbishop he was to speak with envy of the tranquillity and ordered life of the cloister. It is a striking fact that several of his pupils and a number of the young clerks who served him in later years were moved by his conversation and life-style to become monks or friars.

He cannot have been untouched by the traditional assumption of monastic theology that the Christian life could only be fully lived in the cloister. The call was presented as an imperative for all who were concerned for their salvation. For St Bernard, the most eloquent recruiting officer for the reformed monasticism of the twelfth century, there was no safe alternative: the new world of the schools, the profession of teaching and study, was just as much a distraction from the single-minded search for God as was any other worldly occupation. Master Walter of Chaumont, who lingered too long in the schools, received a frightening remonstrance: 'I grieve to think of that subtle intelligence of yours and your gifts of erudition being worn out in vain and futile studies, of you, with your great gifts, not serving Christ, their author, but transitory things. O what if unexpected death should strike and snatch them from you? . . . What will you answer at the dread tribunal for having received your soul in vain?'[16]

16. *S.Bernardi Opera*, vii, ed. J. Leclercq & H. Rochais (Rome, 1974), pp. 261–3.

By Edmund's time, the common assumptions underlying this appeal were being eroded by fresh and alternative forms of religious vocation, in particular by the idea of the Apostolic Life[17] – a devout life of service modelled on that of the Apostles and lived fully in the secular world. The concept of the Apostolic Life was to achieve its institutional apotheosis in the orders of mendicant friars which appeared in the first decade of the thirteenth century. But although the old assumptions were giving ground, they continued to haunt the university classrooms of the thirteenth century and lingered in the jeremiads that preachers addressed to academic audiences. In response to this appeal some of the leading schoolmen abandoned teaching to take the monastic habit, like Peter the Chanter, long the doyen of the theology schools of Paris, who ended his days as a monk at Longpont.

Edmund was clearly conscious of the traditional belief that monasticism represented the highest form of the Christian life. The literary work for which he became best known, *Speculum Ecclesie* or *The Mirror of Holy Church*, was a treatise on 'perfect living', and in its earliest version it was a spiritual guide designed for those who lived in the cloister.[18] By his decision to follow a career in the schools he evidently recognized that the pursuit of learning and teaching, the intellectual life, was an authentic Christian vocation. But his choice did not in his case involve rejecting the tradition of monastic theology. As a schoolman he lived the personal life of a monk, retreating, whenever his circumstances permitted, to live in a monastic community. If there is such a thing as 'a monasticism of the soul', as was claimed by David Knowles, Edmund exemplified it. Our sources do not allow us to probe the secrets of his heart. It is possible that he would have chosen to spend his last years as a fully professed monk, had he not been thwarted by his election to the archbishopric. That he had some such intention would in part explain his consternation on receiving the news of his election. If he had been born twenty years later, he would doubtless have found the reconciliation and fulfilment of both his intellectual and religious aspirations in the Order of Preachers.

We do not know who inspired Edmund's ambition to go to the schools of Paris. Since the days when John of Salisbury sat at the feet of Abelard on the Mount Ste-Geneviève, the fame of the masters of Paris had grown and spread throughout Europe. The two Abingdon brothers may have heard it from their Oxford schoolmasters, from clerical contacts of the family or even from their

17. On twelfth-century ideas of the Apostolic Life see M.-D. Chenu, *Nature, Man and Society in the Twelfth Century*, transl. J. Taylor & Lester K. Little (Univ. of Chicago Press, 1968), pp. 202–38; C.H. Lawrence, *The Friars* (1994), pp. 15–17.
18. *Edmund of Abingdon, Speculum Religiosorum and Speculum Ecclesie*, ed. Helen P. Forshaw (1973), pp. 18–24.

parents. For merchants and other well-to-do townspeople, who were ambitious for their children, were aware that the schools were becoming the highroad to fine careers in church and state, and they knew something of the geography of learning. It was an observable fact that every English scholar of distinction had studied in France, and as yet it was a one-way traffic: few continental scholars thought it worthwhile to come to study in England. In the intellectual commonwealth England was a colony of France.

In the last twenty years of the twelfth century, there was a proliferation of masters at Paris who were offering instruction in the philosophy and science of the new learning, and they were attracting a swelling flood of students from all parts of Europe, not least from England. Some of these, when fledged, would stay and open schools themselves or proceed to the study of law or theology. Of the masters teaching at Paris in the thirty years prior to 1215 whose names are known, it has been calculated that 38 per cent were of English nationality.[19] It was a London merchant who in 1180 endowed the simple hospice of the Dix-huit for impoverished students, the earliest collegiate foundation in the nascent university of Paris.[20] The intellectual excitement that lured so many young men to the schools of France is immortalized in the rhetorical encomium with which Guy of Bazoches urged a friend to come and join him at Paris: 'On this royal island philosophy has of old planted her seat and, with science for her companion, has trodden under her victorious foot the withered flower of the aging world. Here on this island seven sisters, namely the liberal arts, have made themselves an everlasting dwelling-place. Here is the fountain-head of learning.'[21] We do not know who was the recipient of Guy's letter. About the time when he wrote it, Edmund and his brother were preparing to set out for Paris.

In these years when Edmund was young, England's relationship with the French-speaking lands of the continent was a close and complex one. King Henry II was a Frenchman by birth and education, the son of Count Geoffrey of Anjou. Birth, marriage and conquest had made him head of a vast agglomeration of lands stretching from the Scottish border to the Pyrenees. As duke of Normandy and count of Anjou, he controlled access from the north and west to the French royal domain – the territorial heartland of the Capetian monarchy, which lay in the Paris basin. Almost all the ports of France, from Rouen in Normandy to Bayonne in Gascony, were situated in his territory. The Channel was not so much a barrier

19. J.W. Baldwin, 'Masters at Paris from 1179 to 1215' in *Renaissance and Renewal in the Twelfth Century*, ed. R.L. Benson & Giles Constable (1982), pp. 138–72.
20. *Chartularium Universitatis Parisiensis*, ed. H. Denifle & A. Chatelain (Paris, 1889–91) I, p. 49. At this date the hospice was only a dormitory in the Hotel-Dieu.
21. *Ibid.*, I, pp. 55–6.

between England and the continent as a highway, by which the king, his court and his servants, were constantly transported to his overseas dominions. In England, although a process of racial and cultural assimilation had been at work since the Norman Conquest, an aristocracy of French extraction continued to look to France for its religious and cultural standards as well as its manners.

Before Edmund completed his academic apprenticeship, much of this was to change. Philip Augustus, the greatest of the Capetian kings, launched a prolonged and determined assault upon the Angevin possessions in France. His strategic skill and military daring defeated John's poorly co-ordinated efforts to defend his lands, and with the fall of Rouen, the ducal capital of Normandy, in 1204, the entire continental inheritance of the Angevins was, with the exception of Gascony, absorbed by the French monarchy. This drastic change in the political geography of northern Europe had important consequences for the government of England. The organs of royal administration, the Exchequer and the law courts, which had developed to ensure governance in the absence of a king who was constantly abroad, now worked under the immediate direction of a ruler who was continually present. The aristocracy, whose family ties with Normandy had long since grown distant, ceased to offer its support to the military adventures of the king on the continent, and began to acquire a new sense of obligation to the community of the English realm. Knights, who had learned French from their parents, found it necessary to employ tutors to teach French to their sons and daughters.

For all this, the cultural and economic links between England and France remained strong. English merchants continued to enjoy exemption from tolls at the port of Rouen, and continued to frequent the international fairs of Champagne. The 'court style' of Gothic architecture, which originated in the Ile de France, was quick to penetrate England. English students continued to flock to the schools of Paris and Orleans and English scholars, among others, taught at them. Throughout the thirteenth century, the English Church recruited many of its prelates from men who had received their academic formation in France. The two brothers from Abingdon would find plenty of compatriots at Paris and much else that would be familiar to them.

2
Paris and Oxford

The Paris where Edmund was to spend the next five years or more of his life, and to which he was later to return, was a city in the process of transformation. From being a periodic royal residence, Philip Augustus was converting it into a political and administrative capital. Its northern and southern areas were separated from one another by the Seine. Its ancient nucleus lay in the centre, on the narrow island – the Ile de la Cité. At one end of this, the soaring Gothic choir of the new cathedral ordered by Bishop Maurice de Sully had recently been completed, and alongside it a grand évêché was rising on the riverside. During Edmund's first residence in the town, work was proceeding on the nave, and that end of the island was a large building-site enveloping the cloister and residences of the canons. At the other end, work was just beginning on the massive royal fortress of the Louvre.

The most densely populated area lay on the right bank, which was joined to the island by the Grand Pont. This area was the commercial district of the city, served by the Grève – the line of timber wharves where ships and barges unloaded the merchandise that travelled up and down the Seine. As yet, the left bank was more sparsely settled. The faubourg growing up round the abbey of Saint-Germain was still a separate village surrounded by meadows.[1] On the long slope stretching from the river up to the abbey of Sainte-Geneviève at its crown, dwellings were interspersed with fields and vineyards. Along the river further eastward, another rural suburb clustered round the abbey of Saint-Victor, a house of Augustinian canons and home of the famous school of ascetical theologians.

During the last decades of the twelfth century, the rapidly growing population of Paris was beginning to overflow on to the left bank. Here, in the houses that were springing up round the little romanesque church of Saint-Julien-le-Pauvre and on the Petit Pont, which connected the left bank with the island, some masters were hiring rooms for their lecture courses in the arts. This was the area destined to become the chosen patria of letters – the home territory of the university of Paris. Its chrysalis was the cathedral school, which was held in the parvis and was under the jurisdiction of the cathedral chancellor. He had the sole authority to license new masters – the studium was, after all, a function of the Church – and his hand lay heavily

---

1. J. Boussard, *Nouvelle Histoire de Paris*, I (Paris, 1976).

upon the island. In the early years of the thirteenth century, a body of masters, by now grown large enough to challenge his monopoly, successfully contested his right to withhold the licence from any scholar whom they had examined and approved. They thus controlled admission to their number.

The university of Paris, like the universities of Bologna, Oxford and Montpellier, was an association or syndicate formed by scholars in order to organize their studies and to protect their interests. It was not 'founded' or created by any sovereign power. It originated in the obscure arrangements between nameless masters – teachers of arts in the first place – who formulated their own statutes to regulate their teaching, elected their own rector, and bound themselves by oaths to observe corporate decisions. The schools of Paris owed their fame to the intellectual genius and charisma of a number of great teachers; but genius is always rare, and the charismatic has to be translated into institutions if it is to survive. The nameless masters who created the academic corporation in the last years of the twelfth century, and later won its autonomy from the cathedral body, perpetuated the position of Paris as the intellectual capital of medieval Europe.

While he was a student, and later a teacher of arts, Edmund may have been a party to the discussions that led to the organization of the university. Certainly, as a student and doctor of theology in the first decade of the thirteenth century, he witnessed the early tussles between the magistral body and the chancellor in its bid to gain control of the studium. We do not know where he resided or who his teachers were in the early stage of his academic career.

In the first century of its existence, the university possessed little or nothing in the way of buildings or 'plant'. Masters conducted their schools in rooms rented from the townspeople, not always in salubrious surroundings. Jacques de Vitry, who had known Paris at the beginning of the century, complained that some teachers hired rooms in brothels, where their lectures were disturbed by the shrieks of the *filles de joie* in the rooms below.[2] For faculty meetings and solemn disputations the university used the churches of the left bank or, in cold weather, the taverns. Some years after Edmund's time, the masters of the English Nation – one of the four groups into which the arts faculty was divided – were keeping their archives and funds in a chest housed in the church of SS. Cosmas and Damian, and were holding their congregations in the church of the Mathurin Friars.

Students likewise lived in rented accommodation. Halls and colleges did not yet exist. The hospice of the Dix-Huit was no more than an endowed dormitory containing eighteen beds, situated in the Hôtel Dieu. There

---

2. *The Historia Occidentalis of Jacques de Vitry*, ed. J.F. Hinnebusch (Spicilegium Friburgense, 17, Fribourg, 1972), p. 91.

were aristocratic students, like Thomas of Cantilupe, the son of a great Midland dynasty, who rented a whole house while studying at Paris and kept a menage of servants. But then, as now, the majority of students were poor, and Paris was expensive. Besides the cost of food and rent, there were lecture fees to be paid to one's master at the beginning of his course, and dues that were claimed by one's Nation. Some endeavoured to make ends meet by copying the texts of the course-books for their richer friends. Others resorted to begging. Teachers of the *ars dictaminis* – the art of letter composition – provided specimen letters for students begging for funds. Guido Faba of Bologna, a widely acknowledged master of the art, offered model letters to various addressees in a descending order of hopefulness: letters to parents, to blood-relations, to fellow students and, lastly, to godparents.[3] Some formulary collections suggest prelates as a possible source of supply, but seemingly only as a resort of desperation. A Paris letter-book of the thirteenth century offers the student twenty-one various ways of writing to an archdeacon to ask for money.[4]

Edmund and his brother had been provided with modest funds by their mother. It seems that this was enough to rent a room or a garret for his exclusive use, for it was the scene of a hagiographical anecdote about sexual temptation. He was harassed by persistent advances from his landlord's daughter until, desperate to be left alone, he offered her an assignation in his room. But his offer proved deceptive: when the girl arrived and started to undress, he belayed her with a stick and drove her away with a warning. The monastic narrator of the story, who wanted to illustrate Edmund's resolute chastity, was obviously unconscious of the sado-masochistic overtones of his tale.

The only clue to the whereabouts of his lodgings is provided by the writer of the Pontigny Life, who tells us that it was his practice to rise in the middle of the night when he heard the bells of Saint-Merri ringing for the office. He would then go to the church to hear the canons sing Matins, after which he would remain in prayer before the Lady altar until daybreak, when he proceeded to join his fellow students in the schools. From this it is apparent that he lodged in the faubourg Saint-Merri, which lay on the right bank in the commercial area of the city. There were still schools in this district in the early years of the thirteenth century. Bishop Maurice de Sully forbade the canons to let their houses in the parvis to masters, and the demand for lecture rooms to hire on the left bank had probably outrun the pace of urban development on that side of the river.

3. *Guidonis Fabe Dictamina Rhetorica*, ed. A. Gaudenzi: *Il Propugnatore*, new series V (Bologna, 1892), part i, pp. 94–108.
4. C.H. Haskins, *Studies in Medieval Culture* (1929), p. 9, 7 n.

The arts curriculum, which was taking shape in the schools, was rapidly developing under the impact of the new learning. This consisted of the newly translated works of Greek and Arabic philosophy and science which were absorbed by the West in the course of the twelfth century. At the beginning of the century scholars were familiar with the Old Logic, comprising Aristotle's *Categories* and his book *On Interpretation* together with the *Isagoge* of Porphyrius, in the Latin translation of Boethius. These books provided the logician with his basic vocabulary and concepts. Before the middle of the century, the remaining works of Aristotle's logic became available in Latin translation. These were the *Prior and Posterior Analytics*, the *Topics*, and the *Problems of the Sophists*, which became known collectively as the New Logic. The *Prior Analytics* proved especially influential in the schools, for it contained Aristotle's teaching on syllogisms, a system of inference by relating two given premises to a third, middle term, which became the favoured tool of scholastic disputation. To these works were added, later in the century, Aristotle's *Metaphysics* and his book *On the Soul*, and a wide range of Aristotelian and pseudo-Aristotelian works on natural science, which became known collectively as the *libri naturales*. With the philosophical works came also Latin translations of their Arab commentators, Alfarabi, Avicenna and Averroes.

The adoption of particular books by the schools was a gradual process, which was occasionally subject to sharp reaction and which it is difficult to date. The books of the New Logic are included in a list of prescribed texts compiled by Alexander of Nequam shortly after 1191, and he, as he writes with engaging modesty, had been 'a small pillar of the Petit Pont',[5] the playground of the Paris masters of logic. In other words, he had been one of the obscure throng of young teachers lecturing on the new Aristotle. There is literary evidence that the works on natural science were known at Paris towards the end of the century, but it is hard to tell when they were adopted as set-books for teaching the quadrivium. It is likely that in the years of Edmund's first residence at Paris the study of the liberal arts was largely confined to grammar, logic, mathematics and the Ptolomaic astronomy. We do not know to which of the many schools he attached himself at this stage; nor do we hear any more of his brother until many years afterwards.

The statutes given to the university by Cardinal Robert Curzon in 1215 required that anyone aspiring to the master's licence in arts should have attained his twenty-first year, and that he should have attended lectures and

---

5. The book-list with the incipit *sacerdos ad altare accessurus*, printed in C.H. Haskins, *Studies in the History of Medieval Science* (1927), pp. 356–76. His claim to have lectured on the Petit Pont is in *De Laudibus Divinae Sapientiae*, ed. T. Wright (RS, 1863), p. 503.

disputations for six years.[6] If Edmund fulfilled these requirements, he must have begun attending the schools of the artists at or before the year 1190. On the other hand, the ecclesiastical authorities may not have been able to impose this degree of regulation on the plethora of young would-be teachers who were offering the new learning on the left bank twenty-five years before the cardinal's visitation. All that our sources tell us is that after studying the arts at Paris, Edmund returned to England and held a school at Oxford, where he taught for six years.

Many factors could have persuaded him to return home after a few years in France. The impending death of his mother demanded his presence, and afterwards there was the need to find a convent for his sisters and to arrange for the disposal of the family properties. Apart from family responsibilities, there was much else to draw a young scholar back to England. At Paris, the swelling number of teachers struggling for a place in the sun involved keen rivalries and fiercer competition for pupils,[7] as well as pressure on the supply of rentable accommodation available for classrooms. At Paris, too, the presence of an ever growing population of students from all parts of Europe, without local roots or loyalties, was leading to frequent disorder, which in turn provoked savage reprisals from the city authorities.

By contrast to this turbulent scene, Oxford in the closing decade of the twelfth century offered practically virgin territory to scholars who were equipped to purvey the new learning. There is some evidence of the teaching of Roman and canon law at Oxford before 1190,[8] but no trace of schools offering instruction in the liberal arts. Scholars returning from abroad in search of scholastic centres where they could ply their trade, were obliged to look elsewhere. Daniel Morley, returning from Toledo soon after 1180 with a luggage of Greco-Arabic scientific works in Latin translation, found no receptive scholars in Oxford, and took himself off to Northampton, sooner than 'be a solitary Greek among the Latins'.[9] This was a gap in academic provision that Edmund and a handful of his contemporaries decided to fill.

Few of the names of this early group of masters, who were teaching in the

6. *Chartularium Universitatis Parisiensis*, ed. H. Denifle & E. Chatelain, I (Paris, 1889), no. 20.

7. On the competition for pupils, see Stephen C. Ferruolo, *The Origins of the University* (Stanford, California, 1985), pp. 262–3. According to Robert Curzon, some of the Paris masters were reduced to paying students to attend their lectures: J.W. Baldwin, *Masters, Princes and Merchants: The Social Views of Peter the Chanter and his Circle* (Princeton, 1970), ii, p. 89, 7 n.

8. R.W. Southern, 'From Schools to university' in *The History of the University of Oxford*, vol. I, ed. J.I. Catto (1984), pp. 15–20.

9. See R.W. Hunt, 'English Learning in the late Twelfth Century': *TRHS*, 4th series, xix, (1936), pp. 19–42.

borough of Oxford in the last years of the twelfth century, are known to us. Roger Bacon, complaining of the tardy reception of the New Logic by the schoolmen of the West, illustrates his point by naming two who were the first to expound the subject at Oxford. These were Edmund, who was the first to lecture on the *Problems of the Sophists*, and a colleague of his, an otherwise obscure Master Hugh, who lectured on the *Posterior Analytics*.[10] A better known colleague, who had also studied at Paris and who must have been known to Edmund, was Master John Blund. He has left the harvest of some of his lectures in a treatise on Aristotle's book *On the Soul* (*De Anima*), which he composed in the years 1197–1204. His work shows familiarity with the *libri naturales* of Aristotle, but the major source of his inspiration is the treatise *On the Soul* by the Arab philosopher Avicenna.[11] It tells us that not only the New Logic but also the newly translated works of Greco-Arabic science were being introduced into the schools of Paris and Oxford in the last years of the century. By importing the new learning, Edmund and his colleagues began the process that was to convert Oxford from a local school into an academic centre of international status, and in so doing, laid the foundation of its medieval university.

Edmund was returning to open a school in a place he had known as a child. At Oxford, as at Paris, the nascent university possessed no 'plant' or buildings of its own. Teachers and students were scattered about the town in lodgings. Masters rented houses or rooms for lectures, and for their assemblies and collective acts of worship they used the churches of the city. The only unambiguous reference to Edmund's place of residence during his regency in arts comes from the Oxford letter of postulation. This tells us that

> When he had been made a Master of Arts, although he had not yet taken holy orders, nor was under any obligation by reason of having received an ecclesiastical benefice, but moved solely by divine prompting and his devotion, he was accustomed to hear mass daily before he lectured, which was unusual among lecturers at that time. So as to do this with greater devotion, in the parish where he was then living he constructed a chapel of the Blessed Virgin, whom he always especially loved, using the fees collected in his schools and

10. *Rogeri Bacon Compendium Studii Theologiae*, ed. H. Rashdall (1911), p. 34. This passage and its bearing on the teaching of the New Logic at Oxford was elucidated in a seminal paper by Father Daniel Callus, 'The Introduction of Aristotelian learning to Oxford' in *Proceedings of the British Academy*, xxix (1943), pp. 229–81.

11. See the introduction to *Iohannis Blund Tractatus de Anima*, ed. D.A. Callus & R.W. Hunt (1970); and Callus, 'The treatise of John Blund on the Soul' in *Autour d'Aristote. Receuil d'études de philosphie ancienne et médiévale offert à Mgr. A. Mansion* (Louvain, 1955), pp. 471–95.

such other means as he had. There to this day solemn masses continue to be celebrated to her praise and glory.[12]

His sometime colleague Robert Bacon, who supplied the university with this information, adds that Edmund also induced his pupils to hear mass with him.

It has been argued with some cogency that the Lady chapel he had built is to be identified with the chapel which now stands north of the chancel in the romanesque parish church of St Peter-in-the-East.[13] According to a medieval tradition, the hall bearing St Edmund's name, which is adjacent to the church, was erected on the site of the house he occupied. The possibility that this tradition has a historical basis cannot be ruled out. Edmund's benefaction to the hospital of St John the Baptist outside the east gate, made when he was a Master of Arts, is documentary proof of his association with this area of the city.

The fact, alluded to in the Oxford letter, that Edmund had neither been ordained to the priesthood nor had received a benefice during the years of his regency in arts indicates a situation that was not uncommon among young teachers. The Third Lateran Council of 1179 had reiterated the ancient law of the Church that did not permit a man to be ordained priest or deacon without a title – without, that is, a named church he was going to serve, which would guarantee his subsistence, unless he could show he had enough property of his own to support himself. But to obtain a benefice a man needed a patron. Patronage of parish churches was in the hands of lay landlords, monastic houses and, in a minority of cases, bishops. The patron possessed the exclusive right to present a clerk of his choosing to the bishop for institution to his church. A youthful master of arts like Edmund, newly arrived on the scene and lacking useful family connections, might have difficulty in finding a patron. This was not an uncommon problem. Several young scholars of humble origins, who had managed to raise enough money to keep themselves at the schools of Paris, returned home with high expectations that were to be disappointed. At least two of them, Alexander Nequam and Samson, subsequently abbot of Bury St Edmund's, both contemporaries of Edmund, failed to get a benefice for the want of the right connections, and in the end resigned themselves to entering the monastic life.[14]

Whether or not this was Edmund's predicament, his attitude to the cure

12. Text in Lawrence, *St Edmund*, p. 191.
13. A.B. Emden, *An Oxford Hall in Medieval Times* (1927), pp. 89–93.
14. Cf. the discussion of this problem by R.W. Southern, *Robert Grosseteste: the Growth of an English Mind in Medieval Europe* (1986), pp. 50–3.

of souls would have deterred him from seeking a parish living while teaching in the schools. He took pastoral responsibilities too seriously to be a sinecurist. Non-residence, like plurality, was one of the ways by which the endowments of the medieval Church were made to support education, royal administration and other public services that fall to the charge of the modern state. Men were instituted as rectors of parish churches or prebendaries of cathedrals and received the income of their churches from tithe and glebe while they attended the schools or served the government as clerks in Chancery or Exchequer. Such men were necessarily absentees, delegating the pastoral care of their flocks to a hired chaplain, who was more often than not poorly paid and without security of tenure.

Reformers of the thirteenth century fought a long and only partially successful campaign to eradicate the abuses of non-residence and plurality. Both were too deeply entrenched in the social system to yield to facile moralization. They drew their defensive strength from a widespread acceptance of the idea – an idea shared by pope, king and many bishops alike – that government and learning, and even nobility, were a legitimate charge upon the wealth of the Church. At a later stage of his academic career, Edmund did obtain a benefice, but he refused to conform to the general practice of taking the income from it while absenting himself at the schools. 'It was an admirable practice of his,' wrote Matthew Paris, 'not to retain an ecclesiastical benefice unless he resided in it, so that when he moved to attend the schools, he resigned any benefice he had.'[15] Matthew adds that this form of self-denial was 'previously unheard of among our countrymen'. Edmund's personal scruples on the subject did not extend to an attack upon the system. As archbishop he was to accept the fact that several members of his staff, including his own brother, were absentee rectors and small-scale pluralists.[16] Edmund was a scholar and reformer in the Langton tradition, but he was not a radical like Grosseteste.[17] He was an instinctive conservative; and it is a characteristic of conservatives to castigate abuses without challenging the system that has produced them.

It is time to address the problem of fixing the chronology of Edmund's academic career. Matthew Paris and the other hagiographers recount several anecdotes about these years of his life, but they are generally unrelated to time or place. They do nothing to help us fix the date on which much else hangs: the date at which he began to teach arts at Oxford.

At least one of the clues to dating his Oxford regency proves to be a false trail. One of his personal austerities mentioned by the hagiographers

15. Below, p. 123.
16. See below, chap. 6.
17. Southern, *op. cit.*, pp. 315–22.

was his practice of sleeping fully clothed beside, but not in his bed. The letter of postulation from the university states that he had practised this form of mortification from the time he incepted as a teacher of arts. Now in his Life of St Edmund, Eustace says that Edmund had observed this practice for thirty-six years or more. If these two statements are taken to be complementary, they indicate that his inception was in or about the year 1204. Unfortunately this argument, which is plausible at first sight, does not stand up to examination. Eustace had no personal knowledge of Edmund's earlier life, and he borrowed his assertion from a letter of postulation written by Jocelin of Wells,[18] but he has 'improved' on his source. In Jocelin's letter, Edmund is said to have observed his austere sleeping habits for *thirty years*. This would make his regency in arts begin in 1210. This is certainly too late and, in fact, there is good reason to reject both of these dates.

A more promising approach to dating his regency in arts may be found in identifying some of his pupils. Two at least of his former pupils wrote letters to postulate his canonization, namely Richard, bishop of Bangor, and Walter de Gray, archbishop of York. For this purpose, Richard is disappointing. He was archdeacon of Bangor in 1236, when he was elected to the bishopric. After losing his see through war in 1248, he resided at St Albans abbey until his death in 1267.[19] But nothing is known of his career before the date of his election, beyond the fact stated in his letter that he had known Edmund from his youth and had been a pupil of his.[20] Whether he had been his pupil in arts or theology he does not say.

With Walter de Gray we are on firmer ground. In his letter he mentions that he had attended Edmund's lectures in arts.[21] The son of an influential aristocratic family and nephew of John de Gray, bishop of Norwich, Walter was marked out for a distinguished career in church and state. He was appointed royal chancellor, an office for which he paid a fine, on 21 October 1205.[22] He was to end his days in the metropolitan see of York, which he ruled until his death in 1255. Like several prelates who had been royal bureaucrats, he proved himself a conscientious and hard-working bishop. Nevertheless, it is a curious fact — one that illustrates the random patchiness of our sources for this period — that nothing can be discovered about his career before he received the Great Seal. It is certain, though, that he cannot have been an untried youngster straight from the schools when King John chose him to succeed Archbishop Hubert Walter in the

18. *M.D. Thes.*, iii, col. 1907.
19. *Chron. Maj.*, v, pp. 2, 4, 32.
20. Printed in *M.D. Thes.*, iii, p. 1,906.
21. Lawrence, *St Edmund*, p. 302.
22. *Rotuli Litterarum Clausarum* (1833), p. 53.

highest office of the state. All things considered, he can hardly have been much younger than twenty-eight or thirty. This points to the fact that Edmund must have been teaching arts well before the year 1200. We cannot be far wrong, therefore, if we assign his regency in arts to the years 1195 to 1201. On this basis, we must assume that he began studying the arts at Paris in, or shortly before, the year 1190.

According to the reminiscences of Edmund's former colleagues, which were incorporated into the letter of postulation sent by the university, he taught arts at Oxford for six years, and then gave up his school in order to take up the study of theology.[23] The same letter explains that he was persuaded to abandon the arts for theology by a dream in which he was confronted by his formidable mother, now dead. In his dream he was lecturing in the schools on arithmetic – presumably the *Ars Metrica* of Boethius – when Mabel of Abingdon appeared and asked him the meaning of the diagrams he was drawing to illustrate his lecture. Brushing his explanations aside, she seized his hand and drew three circles in it, in which she wrote the names of the Father, Son and Holy Spirit, saying 'henceforth, my dear son, make these, and no others, the subject of your study.'

Sermons of the thirteenth century addressed to academic audiences abound in anecdotes of this type, warning the master who lingers too long over the *artes* – the secular sciences – to turn to higher things: 'These are they who can scarcely be plucked from the embraces of their bondslaves, the secular sciences, and offer themselves to Lady Theology only when their sight has grown dim and they are too old to bear any offspring.'[24] Jacques de Vitry frightens a Paris congregation with the story of a Master of Arts who had a dream in which he was confronted by the tormented soul of one of his pupils who had recently died. The wretched youth was groaning under the weight of a cope of parchment which was covered with beautiful writing. He complains it is heavier to bear than the tower of Saint-Germain (under which they were standing); and in answer to the master's questions he explains 'these writings are all the vain sophisms you taught me in the schools.'[25] It was a commonplace of monastic theology that the liberal arts were valuable solely as an equipment for the study of theology. The environment of Edmund's upbringing would have disposed him to accept this assumption, which continued to haunt the classrooms of

23. Lawrence, *St Edmund*, p. 291.
24. A sermon attributed to Richard Fishacre in BL, Royal MS. 10 B VII, fo. 2; cited by M.M. Davy, *Les sermons universitaires parisiens de 1230–31* (Paris, 1931), p. 84 & n.
25. T.F. Crane, *The Exempla of Jacques de Vitry* (1890), p. 12; cited by C.H. Haskins, *Studies in Medieval Culture* (1929), p. 50.

the thirteenth century. What was distinctive about his experience of this moral imperative was that his conscience took the form of a mother-figure.

Having decided to study theology, Edmund returned to Paris. Later, he was to admit to his brother Robert and his friends that he found the transition difficult.[26] After the heady experience of conducting disputations and lecturing on the books of the New Logic, the laborious exegesis of the Bible text, which occupied the early years of the theology student, seemed tame and intellectually unsatisfying. 'His palate', says Matthew Paris, 'was still numbed by the bitter sweetness of the liberal arts.' 'Such have grown old in an alien land,' says the Paris preacher; 'when they come to theology, they can scarcely bear to be parted from their Aristotle.'[27]

The details of Edmund's second residence at Paris are as scarce as those for his first. Only two hagiographical anecdotes are clearly attached to the days when he was attending the schools of the theologians. One of these, supplied by Robert Bacon and reproduced by Matthew Paris, tells us that his old pupil and friend Archbishop Walter de Gray offered to provide him with a complete text of the Bible together with the standard gloss, but that Edmund declined the offer for fear of burdening some monastic house with the labour of copying the text. The other story, reproduced in the Pontigny Life, describes him selling his copies of the Pentateuch and the Psalms, both containing the standard gloss, in order to raise money to help impoverished students.[28] The writer records the amazement of Edmund's fellow students at his reckless generosity in selling texts needed for the course. The student attending lectures on the Bible was, of course, required to bring with him to the schools the particular text on which the master was commenting, together with the Ordinary Gloss. As yet, the Biblical lecture was the main vehicle for the teaching of speculative theology. The practice of lecturing on the Sentences of Peter Lombard only began at Paris and Oxford a generation later.[29]

Edmund's attendance at the schools during these years of his second pupilage was probably interrupted by the need to return home to restore his dwindling finances. Even for charity, no scholar sells his books except as a last resort. The theology course, as it was beginning to acquire a formal

26. In the margin of his draft Life of St Edmund, Eustace has written a note as follows: '*De difficultate quam fecit gradiendi in theologiam, Iohannes capallanus exponent, et vos, bone magister R. scitis*.': Trinity College Cambridge MS., R 5. 40, fo. 58. Cf. Matthew Paris, below p. 124.

27. Davy, p. 292.

28. A complete list of the titles sold, including a book of 'decretals', is given only in the 'A' text of this Life, viz. the Auxerre MS. 123, fo. 115rb. Cf. Lambeth MS. 135, fo. 126.

29. See P. Raedts, *Richard Rufus of Cornwall and the Tradition of Oxford Theology* (1987); C.H. Lawrence, *The Friars* (1994), pp. 141–2.

shape, was long and expensive. Curzon's statutes required a minimum of eight years of study for the doctorate, and the aspirant had to be thirty-five years old before he could qualify. It thus became common to take the course in stages. A man who had achieved the status of bachelor could retire to a benefice to finance himself for the next stage, and proceed to incept as a doctor later. That Edmund did this is suggested by Matthew's observation that he accepted a benefice only when he could reside, and resigned it again when he returned to the schools. It must have been during one of these intervals that he was ordained a priest so that he could administer the sacraments to his parishioners. He was offered several livings at this stage, but which he accepted we do not know.

There is another and more deplorable gap in our knowledge of his academic career: we do not know whose was the school to which he owed his theological formation. If we look at the teachers who ruled the schools at Paris in this first decade of the thirteenth century, we see a group of outstanding men who shared a common approach to theological problems and who were formulating a new kind of Biblical exegesis. The most distinguished of them was Stephen Langton, the future archbishop, who was removed from the academic scene in 1206 by his promotion to the cardinalate – an encouraging reminder of the glorious prospects awaiting the small elite who persisted in the schools long enough to achieve recognition as doctors of theology. The group also included Peter of Poitiers, now in his old age, and the Italian scholar Prevostin, both of them pupils of Peter Comestor, John of Abbeville, Robert Curzon, another Englishman to be elevated to the cardinalate, and, from the year 1206 onwards, Philip the chancellor of Paris.[30]

The common factor in the approach of these men was the new attention they gave to the literal sense of the Bible text and its historical context, and their concern with the practical problems of moral and pastoral theology. 'The discipline of Holy Scripture,' writes Peter the Chanter, himself the doyen of the Paris theologians, who helped to form the minds of this group, 'consists of three things: lecturing (on the text), disputation, and preaching.' The Paris masters of this period, who administered this programme, show an awareness that they were doing more than propagating a race of scholars; they had the responsibility of training in their classrooms the future pastors and rulers of the Church.

Many of the Scriptural glosses of these early masters survive to show how they conceived their task. When they expounded the allegorical or

30. P. Glorieux, *Répertoire de maîtres en théologie de Paris au XIIIe siècle*, 2 vols (Paris, 1933), pp. 235–73.

'spiritual' sense of the text, they made it the basis for moral instruction, often using lively anecdotes to press home the point, just as a good preacher would do. The academic lecture, in fact, shaded off into the sermon. At least one famous English preacher, Odo of Cheriton, drew much of his sermon material from Langton's university lectures on the Bible text.[31]

It is a natural assumption, though impossible to verify, that Edmund would have gravitated towards the classroom of an English master, where he would have found other compatriots. The fame of Langton, which he would have heard of when he was a youngster studying arts at Paris, must have exerted a powerful attraction. On the other hand, Langton left the schools on his promotion to the cardinalate in 1206, and Curzon left in 1211. If Edmund began his Biblical studies under Langton, he must have finished them under another master. Possibly he attached himself to the school of John of Abbeville, the master from Picardy who continued to teach until 1216 and who, like Langton, ended his career as an archbishop and a cardinal. Among his other works he left a commentary on the psalter consisting of moralities or moral exegesis, which may have provided Edmund with the model for his own *Moralities on the Psalms* – the only purely scholastic work of his known to survive.

Whether Edmund ever incepted at Paris in any formal sense and taught theology there is uncertain. The statute requiring new graduates to stay and teach in their faculty for two years after inception was the enactment of a later generation, when faculties were better organized and course requirements were formulated. What is certain is that after some years of study he migrated from Paris to open a school of theology at Oxford. There are several clues that enable us to date his return to England and the beginning of this last phase of his academic career.

During the first decade of the thirteenth century, events occurred in England that would have strongly discouraged him from returning home. In the autumn of 1206 a committee of the Canterbury cathedral chapter had gone to the Roman Curia to elect a new archbishop under the eye of Pope Innocent III, who had quashed the election of the king's nominee for the see. At the pope's suggestion, they chose Stephen Langton. John refused, however, to accept Langton and vented his fury on the monks of Canterbury, who were hounded out of the country. This episode inaugurated the most famous conflict between Church and monarchy in the history of medieval England. In the face of John's stubborn refusal to yield, a papal interdict was laid upon the country and published in all the

31. Beryl Smalley, *The Study of the Bible in the Middle Ages*, 2nd edn (1952), p. 209.

churches on 23 March 1208.[32] It was not to be lifted until the summer of 1214. During these five years, no services were held in the churches, the bells were silent, and the laity were denied the sacraments saving only the baptism of infants and the confession and absolution of the dying. An exception was allowed only to monastic communities, which were permitted to celebrate the office privately behind closed doors and without bells. During the first year of the interdict all the bishops, with only two exceptions, withdrew abroad, and the revenues of the Church were seized by the agents of the Crown. The clergy were thus made impotent to render their services to the laity. It was not a propitious time for a young clerk and scholar seeking to establish himself.

Under the general cloud overhanging the English Church, a local storm paralysed the burgeoning academic community at Oxford. In 1209 two clerks accused of murdering a prostitute were summarily hanged by the city authorities. In protest at this infringement of clerical immunity, which covered scholars, the masters suspended lectures and, together with their students, withdrew from the town. Oxford lay in the diocese of Lincoln. The newly consecrated bishop of Lincoln, Hugh de Wells, was sheltering in France during the interdict, and in his absence reconciliation between town and university proved impossible. The Oxford schools thus remained in abeyance until July 1214, when a settlement between the scholars and the borough was concluded by the cardinal legate, Nicholas of Tusculum.[33]

It is a significant fact that none of the sources for Edmund's academic life mentions these events or makes any reference to an interruption of his teaching at Oxford. We must infer from this that he incepted in theology in or after the year 1214, when the schools reopened. A vivid anecdote supplied by Robert Bacon described him lecturing in the theology faculty a few years later. Edmund is seated in the magistral chair, when the abbot of Quarr enters the schools. The lecture proceeds but at the end seven of the class, 'fired, it may be thought, as much by the master's eloquence as by the abbot', approach the abbot and are borne off to take the Cistercian habit. One of these seven was Stephen of Lexington.

Lexington came of an able and distinguished ministerial family. His father was a royal judge. One of his brothers became steward of the king's household, and another finished his ecclesiastical career as bishop of Lincoln. Stephen himself rose rapidly after his initial plunge and jettison of

---

32. The best account of the incidence and effects of the great interdict will be found in C.R. Cheney, *Pope Innocent III and England* (Stuttgart, 1976), pp. 301–56.
33. R.W. Southern in *History of the University of Oxford, op. cit.,* I, pp. 29–36; C.H. Lawrence, 'The origins of the chancellorship at Oxford': *Oxoniensia,* xli (1976), pp. 316–23.

secular prospects. He appears as abbot of Stanley in 1223,[34] was translated to be head of the great abbey and congregation of Savigny in 1229,[35] and in 1243 was elected abbot of Clairvaux. In that capacity he was to leave a permanent mark upon his order by setting up the college of the Chardonnet for Cistercian monks attending the theology schools at Paris.[36]

The sudden assumption of the Cistercian habit by seven Oxford scholars, including one of such a prominent family, was a sufficiently striking event to cause comment. The Dunstable annalist, Richard de Morins, noticed it as occurring in May 1221.[37] Richard was a recorder of contemporary events. He was, moreover, a well-informed and judicious observer, a former canon of Merton priory where Edmund had spent a year of retirement, and a man keenly interested in the theological studies of his time. His report on the timing of this event, therefore, deserves credit. Edmund was already regent in theology then in May 1221, and he incepted sometime between that date and 1214.

There are in fact good reasons for believing that Edmund began lecturing on the Bible at Oxford in, or very close to, the year 1214. In the first place there is the statement of Robert Bacon, the Dominican master, who describes himself as Edmund's 'most special scholar, auditor and colleague' (*specialissimus scolaris, auditor et socius*). The word 'auditor' means here, of course, one attending and hearing lectures. Bacon was already a doctor of theology in 1219. Moreover, in his commentary on the psalter he uses an authorized text of a sermon by John of Abbeville, which suggests he was studying theology at Paris about the year 1210 or earlier.[38] Since Bacon was his pupil, Edmund obviously incepted before him.

A second reason for believing that Edmund incepted in the year 1214 comes from the Merton letter of postulation. This states that before he began teaching he stayed for a year or more at the priory. Matthew Paris says that he stayed at Merton 'wishing to lecture' (*lecturiens*), the unusual desiderative form of the verb suggesting an enforced delay of his regency. The obvious explanation of this language is that the retirement was forced on him by the suspension of the Oxford schools, and that his stay at Merton fell in the years 1213–14. The Merton letter observes that he was called from this retreat to the master's chair in theology. This would have

34. *Curia Regis Roll*, xi, p. 251.
35. *Gallia Christiana*, iv (Paris, 1876), p. 806; the Savigny chronicle in *Receuil des historiens des Gaules et de la France*, xxiii, p. 584.
36. C.H. Lawrence, 'Stephen of Lexington and Cistercian university studies in the thirteenth century': *Journal of Ecclesiastical History*, xi (1960), pp. 164–78.
37. *Ann.Mon*, iii, p. 67.
38. Beryl Smalley, 'Robert Bacon and the early Dominican school at Oxford': *TRHS*, 4th series, xxx (1948), pp. 1–16.

been made possible by the reconciliation between the university and the town and the resumption of the schools in the autumn of 1214. He had probably returned to England together with the bishops and other expatriates in the summer of the previous year, on hearing the news of the king's submission to the pope. Owing to haggling over the financial terms of the settlement, a further year was to elapse before the interdict was lifted. In this distressing period, the canons of Merton offered Edmund a welcome refuge where he could hear the divine office and assist at mass.

Little of the harvest of Edmund's teaching years has been identified. Apart from a stray sermon,[39] there are only his *Moralities on the Psalms*, which survive in a single thirteenth-century manuscript,[40] and the more famous *Mirror of Holy Church*. The Moralities are a type of Biblical commentary that was common in the first two decades of the thirteenth century. They represent the old type of allegorical or 'spiritual' exegesis of the text with a practical moral bias. Edmund's Moralities are a typical classroom product of what has been called the 'Biblical Moral School' of commentators created by Peter the Chanter and Langton, but they lack the human interest or imagery of the workaday world that often enliven the commentaries of Langton and the Chanter. *The Mirror of Holy Church* or *Speculum Ecclesie* is a didactic work of an entirely different genre. In its earliest version it was written for the guidance of those who had embraced the monastic life. It is the work of a scholastic theologian well versed in the classics of ascetical theology, but there is that about it that suggests the spacious leisure of the cloister rather than the feverish intellectual atmosphere of the schools. Although it was unoriginal from a literary standpoint, it was nevertheless a personal testament that communicated Edmund's own vision of the religious life.

39. BL, Harleian MS. 325, fos. 162ᵛ–163ᵛ.
40. Worcester, Dean & Chapter Library, MS Q 67.

3
Speculum Ecclesie or *The Mirror of Holy Church*

It is clear that in its original form the *Speculum* or *Mirror* was a treatise on the spiritual life written for religious. This first version was in fact entitled a *Mirror of Religious*.[1] It opens with an exhortation to those who have embraced the monastic life, quoting with a difference the dictum of Eusebius: 'to enter religion is the height of perfection; to live in it imperfectly is the depth of damnation.' Edmund enlarges on this theme with the advice 'since by the counsel of the Lord you have entered religion, do not abandon it if you desire your salvation, but totally relinquish the world and whatever pertains to it, and apply all your effort and industry to living perfectly.' He then goes on to explain the importance of detachment from natural affections.

At many points the reader is reminded by a phrase or illustration that the writer is addressing himself to monks or nuns. When he speaks of the corporal works of mercy, for example, he deals at length with the objections raised by a monk: 'I am in religion. I have no power to give food or drink, clothing or shelter, as I possess nothing with which I can do any of these things.'[2] At a later point, Edmund proposes a programme of meditations on the life and passion of Christ, suggesting that these themes should be the subject of meditation before each office of the night and day 'which you sing in monastery or church'.[3] The probability is that the treatise originated as a series of conferences – what would now be called a 'retreat' – given by Edmund to one of the monastic communities where he was a frequent visitor. Possibly it was a product of the year of enforced leisure he spent at Merton priory in 1213–14.

In the catalogue of medieval ascetical works, *The Mirror* proved to be one of the most popular. It was translated from Latin into Anglo-Norman French and Middle English, and in due course a fresh Latin version appeared which was translated from the Anglo-Norman

---

1. This and the expanded version are edited in parallel by Helen P. Forshaw, *St Edmund of Abingdon: Speculum Religiosorum and Speculum Ecclesie (Auctores Britannici Medii Aevi* III, British Academy, 1973).
2. Forshaw, pp. 70–1.
3. *Ibid.*, p. 83.

text.[4] Although the treatise was first designed for religious, there are several passages in these subsequent versions which indicate that Edmund, or a later adaptor, reshaped it and added to it with the needs of a wider audience in mind. For instance Edmund gives some practical suggestions about the observance of the commandment to 'keep holy the sabbath day' as follows:

> You should go to church and devoutly say Lauds or hear it quietly, with mass and the other offices of the day, without chattering. And afterwards, if there be any preacher at hand who means to give a sermon, you should quietly listen to the word of God, commit it to memory, and fulfil it in your works. And when you are at lunch, distribute freely to the poor from the good things God has provided for you. And afterwards you shall not go to the tavern to watch wrestling or to carollings or other foolish and vain games, for from such things as these arise misfortunes and mortal sins, but you should visit the sick and the hapless, and thus end festive days in the service of God.[5]

This advice is obviously not directed at a religious community, even a disorderly one. It might be applicable to a parish chaplain, not in priest's orders, who could not celebrate mass but who might be expected to sing the offices in church. But it is impossible not to feel that the case best fits a lay person. After all, for the clergy, the avoidance of taverns was a matter not of counsel but of precept.

It is when Edmund comes to speak of the sacraments that *The Mirror* shows the most obvious signs of having been inflated with additional matter. His simple doctrinal explanations are capped with practical instructions for the administration of the sacraments. Thus for baptism the writer says, 'If an infant be found and it is not known whether it is baptized or not, then the chaplain shall say to the child "If you are not baptized, I baptize you etc." And let the priest take care not to immerse the child in the water again if it has been previously baptized by a layman or priest.'[6] These instructions are clearly intended for parish clergy.

---

4. The Middle English version was edited by C. Horstman, *Yorkshire Writers, Richard Rolle of Hampole,* vol. I (1895), pp. 219–61. The earlier edition of the Anglo-Norman translation by H.W. Robbins has been superseded by the definitive edition of A.D. Wilshere, *Edmundi Abendonensis Mirour de Seinte Eglyse* (Anglo-Norman Text Society, 1982). On the relationship between the Latin texts and the vernacular versions see Helen P. Forshaw, 'New light on the *Speculum Ecclesie* of St Edmund': *Archives d'histoire doctrinale et littéraire du Moyen-Age,* 38 (1971), pp. 7–33.

5. Forshaw, p. 57.

6. *Ibid.,* p. 65.

The complexity of the manuscript tradition makes it impossible to say with certainty whether these additions to the original plan of *The Mirror* were the work of Edmund himself or the work of a later compiler. One of the curious things about the treatise is that, although it purports to be a guide to spiritual perfection for those committed to the religious life, it includes a great deal of basic catechetical material of the sort to be found in thirteenth-century pastoral manuals compiled for the use of the parish clergy,[7] many of whom lacked sufficient education to instruct their rural parishioners. Thus having prescribed meditation on the Scriptures, Edmund provides a complete catechetical scheme of the doctrines to be found in the Bible following the traditional classification: the seven deadly sins, the seven evangelical virtues, the seven gifts of the Holy Spirit, the Ten Commandments, the cardinal virtues, the seven works of mercy, and so forth. The scheme of classification has been taken, with slight adaptation, from a short treatise by Hugh of St Victor entitled *De Quinque Septenis*. The treatment of these subjects is extremely simple and factual.

At the end of the sixteenth chapter Edmund actually refers to his purpose in inserting this elementary doctrinal matter in a treatise on the spiritual life:

> You have here matter for speaking with theologians, however learned they may be, and the wherewithal to talk to lay people and instruct them, be they never so untaught. When you talk to wiser people, you can offer some of this matter for conversation; but in conversation with the ignorant you must freely and kindly proffer them a sweet cup of doctrine. For you have enough material for conversation, for directing your own life, and for correcting and improving the conduct of others.[8]

In other words, the book up to this point will serve both as a personal guide to the reader's own spiritual development and as a source of pabulum for sermons or less formal instructions. Edmund has, in fact, incorporated basic doctrinal instruction of a pedestrian kind in a work on the contemplative life which advances in its later stages to teaching about the most exalted form of mystical experience. There is nothing surprising in

---

7. For a descriptive list of these, to which several items could be added, see P. Michaud-Quantin, *Sommes de casuistique et manuels de confession du XIIe au XIVe siècle* (Namur: Analecta Mediaevalia Namurcensia, 13, 1962). An English example of a basic summary of doctrine for parish clergy is Grosseteste's *Templum Domini*, ed. J. Goering & F.A.C. Mantello (Toronto, 1984).

8. Forshaw, pp. 80–2.

this. Many of the men and women recruited to monastic houses as adults can have had little or no formal theological education. But it was, of course, this elementary matter that lent the book to emendation for the use of a wider readership.

These didactic passages suggest the kind of pastoral awareness that we should expect from a scholar-bishop who had passed through the Paris schools in the early years of the century and who had been a contemporary of Richard le Poore and Thomas of Chabham at Salisbury. But we can go further than this. The handling of these doctrinal themes in many ways reflects the stage that discussion had reached in the Paris schools at the beginning of the thirteenth century. This is very noticeable in the way in which the virtues are expounded. Edmund's brief synopsis follows the lines laid out by the earlier masters such as Langton and Prevostin. It looks rudimentary by comparison with the elaborate analysis of virtue and its relation to grace that we find in the work of William of Auxerre and the masters who followed him in the second half of the century.[9] Edmund's synopsis of moral theology bears the scholastic stamp of his generation.

The essential part of *The Mirror* is a guide to the practice of contemplation, in a wider sense than is now usual; for Edmund understands by the term not only the infused contemplation of the authentic mystical experience, but also the more ordinary processes of meditation. After exhorting his disciple to embark on the life of perfection, to which his profession has committed him, he defines the essence of perfect living in a phrase of St Bernard: 'to live perfectly is to live in friendship, humility and honour.'[10] Friendship is the proper relationship between a man and his neighbour. Humility is the realistic attitude to self. Edmund passes rapidly over these and comes to honour, which he defines as a loving concern to obey the divine will; and 'this is the will of God, even your sanctification.'[11] Honour in the sense of love and loyalty to one's overlord was, of course, a feudal concept drawn from the world of knighthood and military fiefs, with which Edmund was familiar. This personal sanctification demanded by God was to be achieved by uniting the will with the will of God in contemplation, and this is Edmund's central theme.

Like all the masters of the spiritual life, Edmund teaches that the journey of the contemplative must start from the knowledge of self. At the outset, therefore, he proposes a series of points for self-examination, which will lead

---

9. The analysis of the virtues in the work of the Paris masters received magisterial treatment from O. Lottin, *Psychologie et morale aux XIIe et XIIIe siècles*, vol. 3 (Louvain, 1949), pp. 329–535.
10. Forshaw, p. 32. Cf. *S. Bernardi Opera* v, ed. J. Leclercq (Rome, 1974), p. 190.
11. *I Thessalonians*, iv.3.

to a deeper recognition of the soul's lamentable condition and of God's mercy in his dealings with it. From the self-knowledge gained in meditation the disciple has been prepared to seek the knowledge of God through contemplation. There are, says Edmund, three ways of contemplating God: the first in creation, the second in the Scriptures, and the third in the divine essence itself. These ways are, in fact, three distinct grades or levels in the ascent of the soul to God. For Edmund, the contemplative life comprehends meditation and study, which correspond to the first two grades, as well as the mystical life properly so called, which is the third grade.

When Edmund reaches the third grade, the contemplation of the divine nature in its essence, his phraseology shows a clear debt to the first book of the great treatise *De Sacramentis* of Hugh of Saint-Victor. But the Victorine influence on Edmund's work is more subtle and pervasive than the occasional verbal borrowing suggests. Edmund's whole treatment of the first grade of contemplation, the perception of God in his creation, is inspired by Hugh's vision of the created universe as a great book filled with signs which, like the words of a book, communicate to the attentive reader the ideas of the author.[12]

Edmund's second grade is the contemplation of God in Scripture. It is here that he provides the catechetical programme of doctrine, much of which bears no direct relation to the general plan of his treatise. But while providing simple dogmatic instruction, he does not lose sight of the central theme of the book. Thus he expounds the *Pater Noster* so that each petition becomes a basis for meditation. He speaks sharply of those who neglect the Lord's Prayer for 'multiple devotions' – those who 'abandon the prayer which God Himself made, and accept the prayer of some simple saint or something they find written in a book.'[13] He insists upon the importance of reciting it slowly and meditatively, a few words at a time. Frequent repetition is unnecessary. He castigates those who have a preference for prayers composed in rhythmic language according to the literary rules of the *ars dictaminis*. He seems to hint that such people confuse aesthetic pleasure in language with pure devotion. It was not a temptation that Edmund himself experienced.

In the third grade the disciple is to contemplate God in Himself, first in His humanity and then in His divinity. In order to help the disciple to contemplate the humanity, Edmund outlines a series of meditations on the life and passion of Christ, linked to the divine office. For each of the canonical hours he proposes two appropriate subjects for meditation, of which one is a 'mystery' or event in the life of Christ, and the other is an

---

12. On the Victorine sources of Edmund's work, see Helen P. Forshaw, 'St Edmund's *Speculum*, a classic of Victorine spirituality': *Archives d'histoire doctrinale et littéraire du Moyen-Age*, 39 (1972), pp. 7–40.
13. Forshaw, pp. 69–73.

incident of the Passion. Before Matins and Lauds, for example, the disciple will meditate on the Nativity and Betrayal of Christ. This practice of associating the hours with incidents in the life of Christ had behind it a long literary history stretching back to late antiquity.[14] It was not an innovation of Edmund's, but he stamped his own experience on it. His meditation consists in each case of a simple visual reconstruction of scenes. There is little moralization or introspection, but the scenes are described with vivid immediacy and great tenderness of feeling. Thus for the Nativity, the disciple's attention is directed to the crib, the ox and the ass, the cold of mid-winter, the joyfulness of Mary and Joseph over a new-born baby:

> The time was in mid-winter, when it was most cold; the hour was at midnight, the hardest hour that is; the place was in mid-ward the street, in a house without walls. In clouts was he wound and as a child was he bound, and in a crib before an ox and an ass that lovely lord was laid, for there was no other place empty. And here shalt thou think of the keeping of Mary and her child, and of her spouse Joseph – what joy Jesu sent them. Thou shalt think also of the shepherds who saw the showing of his birth, and thou shalt think of the sweet fellowship of angels, and raise up thy heart and sing with them *Gloria in excelsis Deo*.[15]

This simple pictorial freshness of the New Testament story is something that is recovered by the literal vision of the thirteenth century.

These meditations of Edmund's serve as a landmark in the history of medieval religious sentiment. An intense personal devotion to the humanity of Christ, a tender compassionate regard for his sufferings, mark a new orientation of Western piety, which had its origins in the monastic spirituality of the eleventh and twelfth centuries. It was above all the writings of St Bernard and the Cistercians that gave expression and impulse to this new kind of affective piety. Compassion, that is an imaginative identification with the sufferings of Jesus, was an important theme in Cistercian ascetical teaching. It was largely through the teaching of the Franciscans that in the thirteenth century it emerged from the cloister and became part of the religious experience of the ordinary Christian. St Francis himself became the supreme example of compassion: his experience was validated by the imprint on his body of the physical stigmata of the Crucified. This change in men's intuitive and emotional response to the story of the redemption is vividly reflected in

---

14. For the history of this practice, see Helen P. Forshaw, 'St Edmund of Abingdon's meditations upon the canonical hours': *Ephemerides Liturgicae*, 78 (1965), pp. 33–57.
15. Forshaw, pp. 84–5.

Western art during this period. In the century that separated St Bernard from St Bonaventure, the static passionless figure of the triumphant Christ, crowned and reigning from the Cross, is replaced by Cimabue's sagging contorted figure of the Man of Sorrows, which is characteristic of late medieval art.

In this path of development Edmund stands as a bridge between the monastic spirituality of the twelfth century and the popular piety of the Franciscan movement. We learn from the Lives that he was an active propagator of devotion to the Passion. He frequently preached on the subject with a crucifix in his hand and aroused powerful emotions in his audience. The Pontigny writer tells us that it was his practice to meditate daily upon the instruments of the Passion. The seven meditations on the Passion presented in *The Mirror* are a series of brief word-pictures. These sharp tableaux, in which the reader is invited to make himself a living participator, must have made a significant contribution to concern with the physical aspects of the Passion, which reached its height in the following hundred years.

An indication of the sort of influence that Edmund's meditations exerted on popular piety can be seen from an episode of the Passion which he recommends for meditation before the office of None. Here the disciple is asked to ponder upon the seven last words spoken from the Cross. The seven last utterances of Christ, conflated from the four Gospel narratives, became a popular theme of devotion in the course of the thirteenth century. Before this the history of the devotion is obscure. The earliest written evidence of it comes from the work of Ernaud, a monk of Moyenmoutier, who ended his days in 1156 as abbot of Bonneval. But his treatise on the Seven Last Words cannot have reached a very wide audience. Edmund preached on the subject to the monks of Pontigny during his last short stay at the abbey; but it was through his *Mirror* that the devotion was transmitted to St Bonaventure, and it became a favourite theme for Franciscan preachers. Through these meditations Edmund helped to form the religious experience of the thirteenth century, which produced the Office of the Passion and the sentiment encapsulated in the *Stabat Mater*.

The meditations on the life and passion of Christ are proposed as an introduction to the third stage of contemplation. After they are completed, the disciple is told to make a brief discursive meditation on the existence of God and the divine attributes. Then, with rather startling abruptness, he is confronted in the twenty-ninth chapter with the end and climax of his spiritual journey. He is led by a traditional path to the summit of mystical contemplation. Edmund describes in classical terms the process of mental preparation which some modern writers of ascetical theology call recollection and 'introversion'. The mind concentrates its powers and excludes all sensory images, shuts out the clamorous perceptions of the senses, and silences the activity of the intellect. Then, in introversion, it focuses its attention upon its own being. This exercise is, in a sense, the ultimate act of the contemplative.

According to the masters of the spiritual life, in the final stage of contemplation, St Augustine's seventh degree, the soul is no longer controller of its own faculties, but is possessed and directly fed by the power of God. This is the experience the ascetical theologians call 'infused contemplation'.

Edmund's account of the process is not, saving a brief interjection, couched in his own words. He has taken it from St Gregory the Great's *Homiles on Ezechiel*.[16] Gregory discusses the subject of contemplative prayer in the second book of the *Homilies*, building up an elaborate allegory of the Temple which was seen in Ezechiel's vision. The passage was a classical source for ascetical writers attempting to describe the mystical experience. What makes it specially interesting here is the fact that in the expanded 'vulgate' version of *The Mirror* Edmund or another has inserted at this point an autobiographical statement. In the original version – the *Mirror of Religious* – the final stage of contemplation is described as follows:

> Expel from your heart all bodily images and forms and allow your understanding to fly, above all human reasoning, up to heaven, and there you shall find such sweetness in the secrets of God as no man can know, unless he has tasted it. *And, if I, a wretched sinner, had experienced it, I could not describe such things.* For they are too deep and secret to be spoken.

The language here is inspired by St Bernard's sermon on the Song of Songs.[17] In the expanded version of *The Mirror* this diffident statement has been changed into a claim that the author has himself had the experience he refers to:

> And, although I, wretched man that I am, have myself proved it by experience, nevertheless I cannot describe it. For it is so secret that it passes all thought. Therefore it is fitting and right for me to do this, and not to teach it . . .[18]

What are we to make of this revision? We cannot rule out the possibility that the passage was doctored by a later copyist in order to place in the mouth of St Edmund a claim that he never himself made. On the other hand, it is arguable that the expansion of the treatise for the use of a wider readership was the work of Edmund himself. Perhaps it is not stretching the evidence too far to suggest that at some point between compiling the

16. *PL*, 76, cols. 989–91. Cf. Cuthbert Butler, *Western Mysticism* (1922).
17. Leclercq, ii, p. 316.
18. Forshaw, p. 109.

original conferences and reshaping them for wider use, during those endless nights of prayer witnessed by his familiars, Edmund had penetrated the third heaven of the contemplatives and heard 'the secret words which it is not given to man to utter'. The inability of the contemplative to communicate his experience is axiomatic. Even the trained schoolman was rendered inarticulate by his transcendental discovery.

It is characteristic of Edmund that in order to describe the ultimate goal of the contemplative's unitive experience he has borrowed his language from a classical patristic source. It is hardly thinkable that he was not acquainted with the mystical doctrine of the Pseudo-Dionysius, which in the twelfth century was just entering upon its remarkable career in the West for, through the writings of the Victorines, such ideas must have been in the air of Paris in Edmund's time. On the other hand, he displays no direct acquaintance with the Dionysian writings or with the elaborate map of contemplation provided by Richard of Saint-Victor in the two Benjamin treatises. He attempts no detailed analysis of the different 'states' of the contemplative life. For him the unitive experience is the looked-for consummation of the devout life of spiritual reading and meditation, the fathomless estuary of the stream of prayer which a monk entered when he made his profession. This was the traditional ascetical doctrine of monastic teachers from Cassian to St Bernard. Here, as elsewhere, Edmund shows himself to be a disciple of the traditional monastic spirituality.

4

Salisbury to Canterbury

Few men persisted long enough in the schools to acquire the status of a 'Master of the Sacred Page' – the synonym for a doctor of theology. Those who did so gained a passport to public recognition and high preferment in the Church. In the classrooms men formed useful connections which helped them to obtain the patronage they needed to secure a living. Thus it was an old pupil of Edmund's, Archbishop Walter de Gray, who provided him with a benefice, whose whereabouts cannot now be traced, in the diocese of York.[1] Possibly this was the well endowed church that Matthew Paris refers to, which was offered to Edmund while he was lecturing in the Bible at Oxford, and which he retained only long enough to refurbish its building and service-books.[2]

If our chronology of Edmund's scholastic life is right, he probably belonged to the group of distinguished men who were learning their theology at Paris in the schoolroom of Langton in the early years of the century. It was to one of this group, Richard le Poore, bishop of Salisbury, that he owed his first important advancement. Some time between January and August 1222 he was appointed treasurer and canon of Salisbury cathedral.[3] He was to hold this office, to which was annexed the prebend of Calne in Wiltshire, until the autumn of 1233, when he was elected archbishop of Canterbury.

This was an eventful time to be a canon of Salisbury. It was only two years since Bishop Richard had laid the foundation stone of the new cathedral, signifying the transfer of the see from the uncongenial site of Old Sarum. Work on the superb Gothic structure planned by Elias of Dereham was proceeding rapidly. By Michaelmas 1225 the fabric of the choir was sufficiently advanced for the bishop to dedicate the three principal altars of the chevet and inaugurate the use of the building for divine service. Meantime the area reserved for the canons' enclosure must have presented the uncomfortable aspect of a huge building site, in the

---

1. Walter de Gray's letter of postulation, printed in Lawrence, *St Edmund*, pp. 301–2.
2. Below, p. 142.
3. His predecessor in office, Abraham, attests a chapter act for the last time on 17 January: *Sarum Charters*, ed. W.R. Jones and W.D. Macray (RS, 1891), p. 121; Edmund attests as treasurer for the first time on 18 August: *The Register of St Osmund*, ed. W.R. Jones (RS, 1883–4), i, p. 339.

midst of which the canons were constructing their own houses, whipped on by William de Wanda, their dynamic new dean.

Edmund found himself in the thick of all this feverish activity. As treasurer he was, together with the dean, the precentor and the chancellor, one of the four senior dignitaries of the cathedral chapter. He was not a financial officer. The treasury, for which he was responsible, was not an office for the receipt and disbursement of money, but the repository of the precious objects – the vessels, vestments and reliquaries – belonging to the cathedral. But the treasurer was much more than a minder of valuables. He had a general responsibility for the furnishing and upkeep of the church. The customary of Salisbury, compiled early in the century when Richard le Poore was still dean, required the treasurer to provide at his own expense the lights – both oil and wax – for the altars and shrines, and bread, wine and incense for mass, and to supply rushes and mats for the floors on specified occasions. He must ensure that the linen and altar cloths are washed and the vestments kept in repair, and that the bells are properly hung.[4] For all this he had to maintain and pay a staff of guards, sacrists and laundresses.

Of necessity Edmund played an important part in the inauguration ceremonies of September 1225, when Archbishop Stephen Langton entered the new fabric and celebrated a solemn mass in the presence of a concourse of prelates and lay magnates.[5] Three days later he was present with the other dignitaries of the chapter to welcome the young king, who had come with the Justiciar, Hubert de Burgh, to celebrate the opening of the new cathedral. Clearly his office, involving care of the altars and the furnishings of the building, was no sinecure in these years.

It was specifically to meet these expenses that Bishop Richard and the chapter had allocated the prebend of Calne to the treasurership.[6] In October 1226, in obedience to a papal command, an assembly of the clergy in London voted to assist the king with a financial aid of a sixteenth of the annual value of all churches and prebends, and for this purpose the value of each of the Salisbury prebends was assessed.[7] The treasurer's office was valued at eighty marks, of which sixty came from the prebend of

4. *Statuta et Consuetudines Ecclesiae Cathedralis Beatae Mariae Virginis Sarisberiensis*, ed. C. Wordsworth and W.D. Macray (1915), pp. 42–3; *Register of St Osmund*, i, pp. 8–12. On this and the function of treasurer in other cathedrals, see K. Edwards, *The English Secular Cathedrals in the Middle Ages* (1949), pp. 220–32.
5. Edmund was listed among those present, with the dean, precentor, chancellor and 31 canons: *Register of St Osmund*, ii, pp. 37–40.
6. *Ibid.*, ii, pp. 25–6.
7. *Ibid.*, ii, pp. 70–4. On the circumstances of this clerical subsidy see *Councils and Synods with other Documents relating to the English Church*, ed. F.M. Powicke and C.R. Cheney, IIi (1964), pp. 158–9.

Calne. This placed it on the same level as the deanery. The only prebendary who topped it was the precentor, whose endowment was valued at ninety marks. Allowance must be made for the substantial under-assessment that was customary when benefices were valued for tax purposes; but even with this reservation, an income of eighty marks was on a par with that of the best endowed parish churches. Despite this, Edmund found himself in financial difficulties.

Richard of Dunstable, who served Edmund in his years at Salisbury and later testified in the canonization process, said bluntly 'he spent more than he had, and for this reason he was always in debt.'[8] The hagiographers notice that he was often impoverished as treasurer, and tided over the year as a guest of his old pupil, Stephen of Lexington, the abbot of Stanley. It was a sign of his difficulties that in 1226 he was one of seven canons reproved by the chapter for being in arrears with their contributions to the fabric fund.[9] Obviously the heavy liabilities of the treasurer's office were a major drain on his income; another was a pledge the canons had given to contribute a quarter of their annual income from the Common Fund to the building of the new cathedral.[10] An act of the chapter, allowing a temporary relaxation of the rules of residence, acknowledged the exceptional financial burdens imposed on the canons by the demands of the fabric fund and by their need to build themselves new houses.

These were unavoidable expenses. But Edmund's financial plight was clearly worsened by his own expenditure. His strict personal abstemiousness was counterbalanced by his open-handed generosity to others. His largesse to the poor was legendary. No one in search of a roof was denied hospitality. No beggar at his door was ever turned away empty-handed. He maintained young clerks like Richard of Dunstable in his household and supported others at the schools. This was the well directed generosity of a man who remembered the poverty of his own youth. Besides all this, Dunstable's recollections contain a hint of mismanagement.

Dunstable was not afraid of poverty himself. After leaving Edmund's household he joined the friars. Nevertheless, he was slightly shocked as well as edified by Edmund's unworldly indifference to the basic requirements of sound housekeeping. The master, he recalled, declined to inspect his stores, and disdained to enter his domestic offices or to hear accounts. He felt the distaste of the contemplative for business affairs. This insouciance and contempt for money matters must have posed problems for his less unworldly colleagues. Dunstable observed that he would take

---

8. The *Quadrilogus* in Lawrence, *St Edmund*, p. 188.
9. *Register of St Osmund*, ii, p. 65.
10. *Ibid.*, ii, pp. 8, 41; *Sarum Charters*, pp. 229–30.

no part in litigation and that it was only with the greatest reluctance that he could be prevailed upon to attend business meetings of the chapter.[11] He was happiest in his study or quietly ministering to the wants of his parishioners in his remote rectory at Calne.

Edmund was in his late forties when he accepted the treasurership. He was already past the age when most men retired from active university teaching and moved into more lucrative careers in the service of church or state. Had he mistaken the nature of the position he had been offered and the kind of demands it would make on him? He disliked administration. He was both an intellectual and a contemplative, an instinctive recluse. Now, if ever, was surely the time to follow the example of some other leading schoolmen and fulfil his love of the religious life by entering a monastery. Both deterrence and counter-attraction may explain the fact that he did not do so. He had discovered in himself a vocation both for teaching and for evangelistic preaching. The friars, who afforded scope for these gifts, had not yet arrived in England. The English monastic scene presented a discouraging face to a man with intellectual interests who had been trained in the dialectical techniques of inquiry. The aims and methods of monastic studies – *lectio divina*, as the Rule called it – were very different from those of the schools. By contrast, the chapter of Salisbury contained many kindred spirits. At that period it was the most learned cathedral body in England. The many canons listed as *magistri* included such men as Master Henry of Bishopstone, a canonist who had lectured at Oxford before becoming rector of the schools at Salisbury,[12] and Robert Bingham, another Oxford theologian, who was to succeed Richard le Poore as bishop.[13] Both these men must have been previously known to Edmund. Another member of the chapter was Master Elias of Dereham, the architect, who had served two archbishops and was in due course to serve in Edmund's episcopal household. The company of such men must have made a canonry highly attractive to Edmund. It also offered scope for his particular gifts.

It was not unusual for a man to hold a cathedral prebend while lecturing in a faculty of theology or canon law at a university. During the time of Richard le Poore, a roster of residence was drawn up which left members of the Salisbury chapter free to absent themselves during nine months of the year,[14] an arrangement that allowed individuals to continue teaching in the schools. But these concessions were not applicable to the four senior dignitaries of the chapter, of whom Edmund was one. Their duties necessarily involved more constant residence. Edmund's acceptance of the treasurership must therefore

11. The *Quadrilogus, op. cit.*, p. 188.
12. A.B. Emden, *Biographical Register of the University of Oxford to 1500* (1957), p. 193.
13. *Ibid.*, p. 189.
14. *Sarum Charters*, pp. 209–10.

have signified the end of his regency in the Oxford schools.[15] But his withdrawal from Oxford did not mean an end to his life as a teacher of theology. There was opportunity to continue at Salisbury.

Several English cathedral schools offered advanced teaching, and they maintained a surprising vitality in the face of competition from the rising universities. Even late in the thirteenth century, they were able to command the services of a distinguished theologian like Robert Winchelsey, who had formerly been regent in theology and rector of the university of Paris. The letter from the bishop and chapter of Salisbury postulating Edmund's canonization speaks of his inspirational powers as a lecturer and preacher.[16] The context of the statement implies that he lectured as a Biblical theologian in the cathedral school at Salisbury. Doubtless this was what Richard le Poore intended when he secured for the chapter one of the leading Biblical scholars of his generation. Edmund and Henry of Bishopstone were the starting point of a scholastic tradition which was to make the Salisbury schools increasingly like a *studium generale* or university. It was to sustain this tradition that in 1262 Bishop Giles of Bridport was to found the College De Vaux at Salisbury, with an endowment for a warden and twenty scholars studying arts and theology in the cathedral school.[17]

While canon of Salisbury, Edmund was one of a number of clergy who received a commission to preach the crusade. Before this, his gifts were known only to a select world of schoolmen and scholarly prelates and to the people of the parishes, including Calne, to whom he proved himself to be a devoted rector. It was this commission that established his national reputation as a powerful and affective preacher. In the course of the thirteenth century a series of crusades was launched with the object of defending the Latin principalities in Palestine against Muslim attack and recovering Jerusalem, which had been lost after the crushing defeat inflicted on Frankish arms by Saladin. An international crusade mounted in 1218 directed its efforts at destroying the centre of Moslem power in Egypt, but after the initial success of capturing Damietta, the expedition had ended in an ignominious retreat before the forces of the Sultan al-Kamil. Following this fiasco, a new expedition was planned for the summer of 1227 by Pope Honorius III. This was to be led by the emperor Frederick II.

Following the proclamation of a crusade, the first stage in mobilizing the necessary army and raising the required funds was the announcement of

15. In fact he attests a number of chapter acts at which he was present on dates falling within the university terms, see Lawrence, *St Edmund*, p. 123.
16. The letter is printed *ibid.*, pp. 293–5.
17. C.H. Lawrence, 'The University in State and Church' in *History of the University of Oxford*, I (1984), p. 127 & n.

indulgences for participants and the appointment of preachers with a special commission from the pope to preach the cross. Numbers of secular clergy, especially men with a scholastic training, were designated for this task. Some of these commissions were addressed to named preachers; others were sent to prelates and heads of religious orders with instructions to select preachers suitable for the task. In January 1227 Honorius III dispatched mandates to a number of prelates, including Peter des Roches, the grandee bishop of Winchester, for the preaching of the cross for the forthcoming expedition.[18] We have no record of a commission addressed to Edmund. He was presumably one of those selected by the bishop of Winchester in obedience to the papal command. He was evidently assigned a circuit that included Oxford and covered the west of England. The Anonymous A Life reported miraculous signs that accompanied his preaching in the open air at Oxford, Gloucester, Worcester, Leominster and Hereford. This roving commission must have taken him away from Salisbury for several weeks during the spring of 1227. As the Salisbury letter hints, it was evidently this that brought his rhetorical skills to the attention of a much wider public.

Richard of Dunstable, who served in Edmund's household and had ample opportunity of observing him at close quarters, has left a striking account of his way of life during the Salisbury days. His testimony was intended, of course, to further the cause of canonization, and for this reason directed attention primarily to the master's ascetical practices. He was deeply impressed by Edmund's austerity over food and drink: 'it was his custom to dine only rarely, and that for reasons of sociability; he fasted on bread and water on Fridays throughout the year, only relaxing this rule on great festivals or very occasionally when entertaining the great; he observed the Lenten fast without fish, content with eating nothing but bread and potage. He hardly ever touched delicacies – the more delicious the food or drink, the less he would take of them.'[19] Clearly cooking for him must have been a discouraging experience. From his favoured vantage point, Dunstable observed that Edmund constantly wore a hair-shirt next his skin, taking elaborate but unsuccessful pains to conceal it from others. Others besides Dunstable bore witness to the fact that Edmund had trained himself to function with little sleep. At Salisbury, when he was in residence, he always attended the night office of matins in choir, and afterwards remained in the church in solitary prayer until daybreak.

In referring to Edmund's indifference to money matters and his refusal to hear accounts, Dunstable was, of course, stressing his detachment from

---

18. *Regesta Honorii Papae III*, ed. P. Pressutti (Rome, 1888–95), no. 6157.
19. The *Quadrilogus*, op. cit., pp. 187–8.

worldly goods. The same line of thought led into a description of Edmund's reading habits: 'the first and chief preoccupation of the day for him was to have time for study – to apply himself to reading sacred works.' The expression *lectio sacra*, which Dunstable uses of Edmund's reading, comes from the Rule of St Benedict, where it means the study of the Bible and the Fathers and other works appropriate to the monastic life. He goes on to explain that in order to free himself for this Edmund invariably shut himself away in his study from early morning until lunch-time. He told Dunstable that he regarded three times as a loss – the times of sleeping, eating and riding. To these must evidently be added times in committee or chapter. It is the scholar's complaint in all ages.

Other witnesses who had served in Edmund's household enlarged on his social virtues, his affability and unfailing courtesy, his generosity to the poor and, above all, his devotion to the pastoral care of his parishioners and his 'zeal for souls'. As a canon, his parishioners were the peasants living in the parish of Calne, of which he was the rector. It was one of his favourite retreats during the Salisbury years. There, when he was not occupied with hearing confessions and sorting out the matrimonial problems of his people, he could make time for long periods of uninterrupted reading. It was there, in the last days of September 1233, that he received a deputation from the monks of Canterbury cathedral. He was in his study when they arrived. An excited domestic, wanting to be first with the news, rushed into the room only to be roundly rebuffed: 'Go away, you ass, and close the door behind you. See that nobody interrupts my studies.'[20] There is a flavour of authenticity about the story; it encapsulates Edmund's character and his sense of priorities. In due course he issued from his seclusion to greet his visitors, and learned with consternation that he had been elected archbishop of Canterbury.

The vacancy at Canterbury had been caused by the demise of Archbishop Richard le Grand, who had died in Italy on 3 August 1231, on his way back from the papal Curia. The Lives of St Edmund refer in guarded terms to the various political forces which focused upon the election of the new archbishop. After the see had been much troubled by pope and king, writes Matthew Paris, the monastic chapter elected a man 'in whom could be found no reasonable grounds for contradiction'.[21] In fact, Edmund was the fourth candidate to be elected. The first choice was the chancellor and bishop of Chichester, Ralph Neville. This was an obvious and safe nomination by the young king. Neville had already been mentioned at Rome as a possible successor to Stephen Langton and had

20. The Anonymous 'A' Life, Lambeth Palace, MS. 135, fo. 127v.
21. Below, p. 130.

hopes of the primacy.[22] Educated as a Chancery clerk, he had grown accustomed to office during the king's minority and had shown himself well able to adopt an independent line. Wendover states that the scrutiny of the election was delegated by the pope to Archdeacon Simon Langton, brother of Stephen Langton, who had been in Rome since the death of Richard le Grand, and that the archdeacon reported Neville to be a courtier (*curialis*) and unlettered.[23] Understood in a literal sense, the statement is obviously a travesty. Nevertheless, the election was disallowed.

The canon law governing the election of bishops allowed the secular power no role in the process. All the same, what prevailed in practice was a fragile compromise between the canonical procedure and the long established claims of the king to make a nomination. The obvious objection to Neville's nomination was the fact that he had combined his secular office with his tenure of the bishopric of Chichester. Although two of his immediate predecessors at the Chancery had provided a precedent, it was an arrangement that was offensive to churchmen whose mind had been permeated by the Gregorian principles of hierocratic government and the spirit of reform. Men like Neville tended to treat their bishoprics as sinecures and to neglect their pastoral duties to their dioceses. Gregory IX was a zealous pope in the reform tradition, and it is understandable that he took the view that Neville's record disqualified him from the task of leading the English Church.

A new licence to elect was issued on 7 March 1232,[24] and this time the monks chose their prior, John of Sittingbourne.[25] By now there was some anxiety at court lest the election should be reserved to Rome by the canon law of devolution, which required the electors to choose a bishop within three months of a see falling vacant.[26] Royal assent was therefore granted in haste – John probably promised to be an accommodating archbishop – and the elect set out for Rome on 4 April. Apparently he was persuaded without difficulty to resign into the pope's hands. He was not a strong enough man for the job.

In the meantime, English affairs had reached a crisis. The dismissal and imprisonment of the Justiciar, Hubert de Burgh, in the same summer signified the accomplishment of a ministerial revolution that was to bring the country to the verge of civil war. For the moment the bishop of

22. See the letter from Master Philip of Arden to Neville: W.W. Shirley, *Royal Letters* (RS, 1862), I, p. 339; J. Boussard, 'Ralph Neville évêque de Chichester' in *Revue historique* clxxvi (1935), pp. 217–33.
23. *Chron.Maj.*, iii, p. 207.
24. *Patent Rolls, 1225–32*, p. 465.
25. He was elected on 16 March: Gervase, ii, p. 130.
26. The monks were warned against sending a *compromissio* or electoral committee to Rome: *Patent Rolls, 1225–32*, p. 465.

Winchester, Peter des Roches, and his kinsman, Peter des Rievaux, held an unchallenged position in the royal counsels. It was to be expected that the next nomination to Canterbury would reflect the influence which was now dominant at court. In these circumstances, the chapter elected Master John Blund, canon of Chichester. The political cross-currents that underlay the choice can be discerned in the bitterly partisan accounts of the chroniclers. He could hardly be described as a curialist. He was first and foremost a scholar and theologian, a contemporary of Edmund's in the schools. At the time of his election he was regent in theology at Oxford. He had, however, performed services for the king, enough to earn him the style of king's clerk (*dilectus clericus noster*),[27] and he stood high in the bishop of Winchester's favour. The chapter received the royal *congé d'élire* on 12 August 1232, and Blund was elected on the 26th. The king gave formal assent on the 30th, and the archbishop-elect embarked for Rome. But this election was also quashed.

Roger of Wendover explains Blund's discomfiture by the fact that he had received a thousand marks from Peter des Roches after his election, and had been credited with a thousand more to assist him in gaining papal confirmation. Matthew Paris adds that Peter des Roches had sought the emperor's co-operation, and that all this had led the pope to suspect Blund of simony and ambition. Also, according to Matthew, Blund had admitted to holding two benefices with cure of souls, contrary to the decrees of the councils.[28] This is obviously a partisan account. Whatever the canonical definition of simony, it could hardly extend to a gift made by a patron to a successful candidate in order to cover his recognized expenses at the papal Curia.

The various accounts are, however, unanimous on two points: that Blund's chief opponent was Simon Langton, who throughout the process served as the pope's chief informant about English affairs, and that the ostensible reason for his rejection was the fact of his being a pluralist.[29] The French annalist William of Andres is a fairly reliable guide to the stories and apologies of the disappointed parties owing to the fact that his monastery in the Pas-de-Calais lay on the customary route between England and the continent and was a favoured haven for sea-sick travellers. He describes Blund as an upright and learned man, and reports that he was rejected at Rome because he held two benefices and 'on a number of other frivolous counts'.[30]

Understandably William was surprised that an otherwise exemplary

---

27. He served as royal proctor to the Roman Curia in 1228: *Close Rolls, 1227–31*, pp. 80, 118. His place in Aristotelian scholarship was described by D.A. Callus, 'The introduction of Aristotelian learning to Oxford' in *Proceedings of the British Academy*, xxix (1943), pp. 229–81; and see Emden, *BRUO*, p. 206.
28. *Chron.Maj.*, iii, pp. 243–4.
29. Thus the Dunstable annalist in *Ann.Mon.*, iii, p. 132.
30. *Chron. Willelmi Andrensis*, ed. Heller, *MGH.SS*, xxiv, p. 772.

candidate should have been rejected on the sole ground of pluralism. But Henry of Avranches, who is Blund's apologist, confirms that this was the most important objection raised, and argues that the fault, if it is a fault, is generally prevalent and approved by custom.[31] Blund clearly belonged to that class of 'sublime and literate persons' to whom the Lateran Council allowed the privilege of holding more than one benefice. It must have been his omission to get the necessary papal dispensation that tripped him up. Pluralism was a live issue at the time. It was an abuse that was coming under mounting attack from articulate sections of the clergy. Only a year before Blund's election a preacher addressing the university of Paris invoked the curse of Habacuc on those who multiplied prebends.[32] On the other hand, a less rigorous view was taken at Rome. If unlicensed plurality hindered Blund's confirmation, it was conceded that it should be no impediment to his receiving any other bishopric.[33]

This concession suggests that pluralism was only a pretext, used because the real reason for Blund's rejection could not be voiced: the suspicion that he was committed to a royal policy that was deeply unpopular with the king's subjects. In fact, as Matthew Paris says, the patronage of the bishop of Winchester had done him more harm than good.[34] That he was the favoured candidate of Peter des Roches is shown by the metrical broadside of Henry of Avranches, for Henry was a court poet and wrote for his patron. The papal Curia mistrusted Peter's influence on the young king when he was acting as his guardian,[35] and the pope's suspicion of Peter's intentions must have been sharpened by what Simon Langton told him about the English scene. At any rate, the nomination of Blund to the see of Canterbury was a worthy one and must be placed on the credit side of Peter's political balance.

Having quashed the third election, Pope Gregory nominated a candidate of his own to the representatives of the chapter who had accompanied Blund to Rome. As Wendover put it, euphemistically, 'Since, after the quashing of three persons elected to the church of Canterbury, the said church had by now been long widowed of a pastor, he [i.e. the pope] gave the monks, who had come with the unsuccessful candidate, the power to elect Master Edmund, canon of the church of Salisbury.'[36] The monks did not, however, constitute an electoral committee to whom the chapter had

31. *The Shorter Latin Poems of Master Henry of Avranches*, ed. J.C. Russell and J.P. Heironimus (Cambridge, Mass., 1935), p. 133.
32. M.M. Davy, *Les sermons universitaires parisiens de 1230–31* (Paris, 1931), p. 412; also the strictures of Master John of St Giles, *ibid.*, p. 275.
33. Auvray, i, p. 777; *CPL,* i, p. 135.
34. *Chron.Maj.,* iii, p. 243.
35. D.A. Carpenter, *The Minority of Henry III* (1990), p. 243.
36. *Chron.Maj.,* iii, p. 244.

legally delegated its powers. It was necessary for them to return home and place the new proposal before the rest of their brethren. After a papal nomination, the election by the chapter can have been only a formality, and this was completed by 20 September 1233.[37] It remained to obtain Edmund's consent to his elevation and to secure the assent of the king. The former proved to be the more difficult task of the two.

It was not the first or last time in the course of the thirteenth century that a pope was to impose his choice on Canterbury by a direct exercise of his authority. He was afforded the opportunity by the canonical principle that required the election of any prelate to be examined and ratified by his ecclesiastical superior; and the only superior of an archbishop was the pope. For much of the century the power was used in an effort to secure the appointment of metropolitans who would be loyal instruments of papal policy and who would be conscientious in implementing the reform programme of the Lateran Councils. Edmund apparently owed his nomination to Simon Langton, who had been the pope's mentor throughout the affair. He was known to the Langton circle, and he had probably been brought to the notice of the Curia by his prowess as a preacher of the crusade in 1227.

Custom expected a bishop-elect to protest his unworthiness of the proffered honour: *nolo episcopari*. Edmund's refusal of his election went far beyond the demands of liturgical protocol. His resistance was genuine and prolonged. When he at length issued from his study at Calne to confront the envoys from Canterbury, his reaction surprised them. He insisted that they had been misled about his alleged merits and his learning, and begged them to reconsider the decision and transfer their vote to someone else. As he appeared to be immovable, they persuaded him to go with them to Salisbury to seek the advice of his bishop, Robert Bingham. The bishop and Edmund's fellow canons urged him to accept the appointment. Bingham even went to the length of commanding him to consent under obedience to himself. But Edmund still demurred. It was only on the third day, after he had returned to Calne accompanied by the monks, that he was argued into acceptance of his election.

In the Life, Matthew Paris says that Edmund's resistance was overcome by the pleading of the monks and by the pressure of his friends, and he places in their mouths an argument he though particularly telling:

> Unless you consent and are installed without delay, the king's council will procure the substitution of some alien, utterly unworthy of such a great honour, and have him intruded into the place where God has

ordained so many saints. An unwillingness to assent to just requests is
a kind of folly. Do not refuse to be moved by the entreaties of good
men. If you are not careful, your pusillanimous resistance will be the
cause of great confusion in the most noble church of Canterbury.[38]

Following this impassioned plea, Matthew has the monks on their knees
begging Edmund to accept: 'we have had three or four rejections; do not
allow us to be confounded yet again.'

Like most of the dramatic dialogues Matthew inserted in his historical
works, this expresses his own prejudices and preoccupations of the
moment. His chauvinistic dislike of foreigners is constantly displayed in his
chronicles. At the time of writing the Life of St Edmund, his quill was
envenomed by the fact that the see of Canterbury was occupied by
Boniface of Savoy, the queen's uncle, whose appointment had been
procured by the king. Boniface was a mitred aristocrat from abroad, whose
continental interests took him abroad for long periods, and whose
appointment and style of government aroused Matthew's fierce animosity.
He had also seen one of the king's Poitevin relatives, another 'utterly
unworthy alien', thrust into the see of Winchester. Edmund's advisers are
made to voice Matthew's indignation.

All the same, the fictitious dialogue had a basis in reality. A Poitevin
candidate for Canterbury was not inconceivable in 1233. More important,
the dialogue represented Edmund's dilemma as a conflict between personal
preference and his duty to the English Church. The biological urge of
ambition may be mortified by the saints; but they cannot be impervious to
the call of duty. Edmund's inclinations, his intellectual interests and his own
spiritual aspirations would clearly have made him reluctant to accept his
election. If his expectations of a quiet scholarly retreat at Salisbury had
been disappointed, he can have entertained no illusions about the kind of
life he would be forced to lead as an archbishop. As primate of England
and first councillor of the realm, he would be catapulted into the centre of
the political arena. Besides the unrelenting spiritual and administrative
responsibilities that would press upon him as a metropolitan, as a tenant-in-
chief of the Crown with a great territorial lordship, he would have to
concern himself with all the tiresome duties of estate management and
with safeguarding the temporalities of his see. It was bound to be a
daunting prospect for a man whose love of learning and his desire for God
inclined him to the life of a recluse. Possibly his consternation was
deepened by a long cherished intention to end his career by embracing the
monastic life. The suggestion that the Church would be damaged by his

38. Below p. 130.

refusal, that his election was the will of God, a proposition reinforced by the command of his own bishop, was the one argument calculated to prevail over his disinclination. And it succeeded.

The royal assent to Edmund's election was obtained without difficulty on 10 October.[39] As he was the approved papal candidate, it was intimated to him that his personal presence was not required at Rome for confirmation. Instead, a delegation was dispatched from Canterbury to fetch the pallium – the yoke-shaped band of white wool worn by the pope and conferred upon metropolitans to signify their share in the care of St Peter's successor for all the churches and their jurisdiction over their own provinces. It was collected from the tomb of St Peter by a party of three consisting of a monk of Canterbury, Simon of Leicester, Master Henry Tassine, a canon of Salisbury, and Master Nicholas of Burford, a canon lawyer who was to be an important member of Archbishop Edmund's staff. The three were given the pallium on 3 February 1234,[40] with instructions to carry it to the bishops of London and Rochester, who were to confer it upon the archbishop-elect. On 4 February the royal agents received orders to release the estates into the hands of the archbishop's bailiffs. It remained to consecrate Edmund and enthrone him. This solemn ritual was to be accomplished at Canterbury on Laetare Sunday, 2 April 1234. Edmund was consecrated by the bishop of London, Roger Niger, in the presence of the king and court and the suffragans of the Canterbury province. Before this event, however, the archbishop-elect had been forced to come to grips with a grave political situation.

39. *Cal.Patent Rolls, 1232–47*, p. 27.
40. Auvray, no. 1742.

5

A Political Apprenticeship

Edmund had been called to Canterbury at the height of a national crisis. The ministerial changes and the methods of government adopted by the king following the dismissal of the Justiciar, Hubert de Burgh, had provoked a rebellion. The leader of the dissidents, Earl Richard the Marshal, was raising armed resistance to the king in the Welsh Marches. Personal antipathies were no doubt an important factor in the breakdown of trust between the king and the magnates, but the xenophobia of the St Albans chroniclers, who represented the rebellion as a protest against foreigners at court, gives a false twist to the picture. Baronial animosity was directed not against foreign birth, but against Peter de Roches, the bishop of Winchester, and his nephew, Peter des Rievaux, and the system of government they represented.

After the long eclipse of the king's minority, the royal household had suddenly resumed direction of the state. Returning from his adventures abroad, Peter des Roches had urged Henry to get rid of the Justiciar and be a king. In place of his baronial advisers, the king elevated domestic bureaucrats. As a preliminary to reorganizing the administration and resuming lapsed sources of royal revenue, all the reins of administration were concentrated in the hands of Peter des Rievaux, until then an obscure household clerk, who had been brought to power by a palace revolution. While he ruled the royal household as keeper of the Wardrobe and treasurer of the Chamber, Rievaux controlled the Exchequer as treasurer, and held the key to the secretariat as keeper of the Privy Seal. He was also temporarily appointed sheriff of twenty-one counties and keeper of escheats and wardships, a role in which he touched the baronial class at its most sensitive point.[1] In perspective, these arrangements appear less sinister than they seemed to contemporaries. But Rievaux's activities in dealing with escheated lordships in the Marches aroused baronial fears and memories of the unpredictable and uncontrollable demands of King John.

Hostilities had broken out in the Marches in August 1233, when the royal army had turned aside to lay siege to the castle of Richard the Marshal

1. For Rievaux and his offices, see T.F. Tout, *Chapters in Medieval Administrative History* (1937), i, pp. 216 ff. and F.M. Powicke, *Henry III and the Lord Edward* (1947), i, pp. 84–122, and the reinterpretation of these events by D.A. Carpenter, *The Minority of Henry III* (1990), pp. 394–412.

at Usk. By the time the king accepted Edmund's election in October, the breach between the royalists and the Marshal's party seemed irreparable. A strong lead from the Church was necessary if civil war on a large scale was to be averted. Saner counsels were anxious for conciliation and peace. The chief obstacles to understanding had been boldly pointed out by the Dominican theologian Robert Bacon, Edmund's former pupil and associate. Preaching before the court in that tense summer of 1233, he urged the king to reconsider his council. According to Matthew Paris, a wag who was present made a daring pun on the name of Peter des Roches – the rocks on whom the ship of state was foundering.[2]

Edmund was not by temperament an ecclesiastical statesman. He had a scholar's instinctive distrust of the court milieu, which must have been largely incomprehensible to him. His attitude is indicated by the surviving fragment of one of his sermons. In this he draws out the allegorical sense of a passage in the third Book of Kings, where Achab, the King of Israel, debates whether he should go up and recover Ramoth-Galaad from the king of Syria. False prophets urge him on with promises of victory, but he is defeated and killed in battle. By the prophets Edmund understands 'false counsellors, grasping persons, flatterers, the hard hearted and oppressors of the poor. With such people the court of every prince and great man is filled. Whoever, therefore, wishes to lead a good life, let him depart from court.'[3] The sermon cannot of course be related to a particular political context, but it illustrates Edmund's attitude to politics and his distrust of the *curiales* – those who made their careers in the royal bureaucracy. He can have had little sympathy for a man like Peter des Roches or his nephew.

As archbishop-elect, he worked steadily with his suffragans to bring the situation under control. He dispatched mediators between the king and the Marshal, one of whom was the Provincial of the English Franciscan province, Brother Agnellus of Pisa. Wendover has a dramàtic account of the interview between Agnellus and the earl, which took place on the night of 22 December in Margam abbey.[4] At the same time efforts were being made by Edmund to persuade the king to revise the basis of his council. At the beginning of February the bishops, assembled in a council at Westminster, urged on Henry the dangers of retaining Peter des Rievaux in his existing position. They pointed to the discrediting of the king's authority caused by Rievaux's indiscriminate use of the Privy Seal. On this occasion, Edmund's powers of conciliation were severely tested by a heated

2. *Chron.Maj.*, iii, pp. 244–5.
3. BL, Harleian MS. 325, fo. 163ᵛ.
4. *Flores*, iv, p. 262. Eccleston says that the journey in mid-winter proved fatal to Agnellus: *De Adventu Fratrum Minorum*, ed. A.G. Little (1953), p. 76.

altercation between the king and Alexander Stavensby, the bishop of Coventry.[5]

Preliminary negotiations had now proceeded far enough to make a truce possible, and Edmund dispatched Stavensby with Henry Sandford, bishop of Rochester, to the Marches. By this time the Marshal had left for Ireland, where he had gone to defend his Leinster estates, and the bishops were met by Prince Llewelyn and the earl's representatives at the Shropshire village of Brocton. Here a truce was concluded on 6 March.[6] The surveillance of the truce was the responsibility of the archbishop, and it was agreed that there would be a meeting at Shrewsbury on 2 May to formulate terms of peace.

The clerks of the earl and Llewelyn returned in the company of the two bishops and made their way to the court to obtain the king's ratification of the truce.[7] This was not signified until 12 April.[8] This was a long interval. Why did Henry hesitate? Was he waiting for the assembly of the council he had summoned for Passion Sunday, 9 April? Or was he waiting for news from Ireland? At all events, eight days before the truce was ratified, Richard the Marshal was fatally wounded in an obscure battle on the boundaries of Meath and Leinster.

Edmund's consecration strengthened his hands, and at the Easter council he directed all his efforts to securing the dismissal of Peter des Rievaux and the bishop of Winchester. This time he was apparently successful. On 28 April letters were issued revoking Rievaux's authority,[9] and in the course of the following weeks he was stripped of his offices and summoned to render account at the Exchequer.[10] Lashed by the king's reproaches, Peter des Roches withdrew from court and returned to his diocese.

With the chief stumbling-block to peace removed, Edmund could address himself to guarding the truce and preparing the ground for peace negotiations. With this in view, he set off for the Marches at the end of April, and he was continuously employed there during the spring and summer. The king set out to join him, stopping en route at the palace of Woodstock, where he was in residence from 6 to 13 May.[11] According to Wendover, while Henry was there he received the news of the Marshal's death. The chronicler depicts him unexpectedly prostrated with grief and having the clerks of his chapel sing the Office of the Dead for the earl's

5. *Chron.Maj.*, iii, p. 270.
6. *Cal.Patent Rolls, 1232–47*, p. 43.
7. *Ibid.*, p. 41.
8. *Ibid.*, p. 43.
9. *Close Rolls, 1231–34*, p. 412.
10. *Ibid.*, p. 419.
11. Vid. Chancery enrolments, *passim*.

soul.[12] Then proceeding to Gloucester, he published an amnesty to all who should seek his peace by 29 May. Under cover of this, Edmund escorted the rebels to make their peace with the king – first Gilbert, the Marshal's heir, who was pardoned, then Hubert de Burgh, whom the rebels had released from custody, and then Gilbert Basset, Siward, and the other dissidents. At this point, the St Albans chronicle reports an extraordinary confrontation between the archbishop and the king.

In the presence of bishops and magnates, Edmund is said to have produced a letter dispatched by the king to Ireland, inciting the Irish magnates to attack the Marshal and promising them a share in his confiscated fiefs. The chronicler describes a heated colloquy, the archbishop accusing the king of having treacherously contrived the Marshal's death, and King Henry parrying with the implausible excuse that he had no knowledge of what the letters contained, and that the bishop of Winchester and Rievaux had forced him to affix his seal to it. If there is any truth in the story, the seal referred to must have been the small seal of which Rievaux was the keeper, since Ralph Neville, the chancellor, was not involved in the scandal. But no such letter is known to survive; the curious story rests upon the unsupported testimony of a single chronicler.[13]

The facts of the Marshal's death, so far as they can be ascertained, are as follows. He had left Wales for Ireland at the beginning of February, evidently with the purpose of defending his earldom of Leinster. Whether or not at the king's suggestion, the earl's enemies were taking advantage of his conflict with the king to launch an attack on his estates. The lead was taken by Maurice FitzGerald, the justiciar of Ireland, and the Lacys. The Lacy honour of Meath was contiguous with the north-western boundary of the Marshal lands, and there were grounds of long-standing hostility between the two families. A meeting was arranged between Earl Richard and the Anglo-Irish baronage on the Curragh of Kildare on 1 April, with a view to discussing a truce. But fighting broke out and the Marshal was carried off the field mortally wounded. He died on 16 April, and was buried in the Franciscan church which his brother had founded at Kilkenny.

Wendover explains the Marshal's death as the outcome of the 'bloody writing' which the king's counsellors had, with unheard-of treachery, sent to Ireland early in January, and which had now come into the hands of Archbishop Edmund. He quotes the concluding part of the letter and asserts that the Poitevins had compelled the king to affix his seal to it. With this authorization, the Irish barons invaded the Marshal's lands in order to

12. *Flores*, iv, pp. 309 ff.
13. *Ibid.*, p. 293. The story is also to be found in narratives that are dependent upon the St Alban's chronicle at this point, eg. the Annals of Oseney, *Ann.Mon.*, iv, p. 78.

draw him over to Ireland, where he was lured to his death. There are serious improbabilities in this account as well as some demonstrable inaccuracies.[14] It is inconceivable that the Keeper of the Wardrobe could have forced the king to seal a letter against his will. In any case, the text of the letter cited by Wendover is so much at variance with the forms used by the royal Chancery that its authenticity cannot be sustained.[15]

Edmund's accusation of the king, as narrated by Wendover, also fails to carry conviction. It is possible that instructions were sent to the Irish justiciar, but even if they were as drastic as the chronicler suggests, this would hardly be a reason for accusing the king of treachery. If such a letter was sent, it must have been dispatched in January, when the Marshal was an outlaw who had raised his standard against the king. If the archbishop had a genuine grievance it was that he had been placed in a false position during his efforts to negotiate the truce in March. This was probably the substratum of fact underlying Wendover's highly coloured and partisan account: the archbishop reproached the king because he had not taken steps to call off the royalists in Ireland while he was engaged in making a truce in the Welsh Marches, and the king, in a panic, threw the blame on to his discredited ministers.

These doubts about the authenticity of Wendover's narrative are strengthened by what we find in Matthew Paris's Life of St Edmund. Here we find Edmund's mediation described in very different terms.[16] The Marshal is killed in battle as an enemy of the king. The archbishop comes to Woodstock to plead for the earl's brother, Gilbert Marshal, and with tears 'pleaded with the king that the brother should not have to expiate and bear the wrong that his brother had done, and that the fault of the guilty should not recoil upon the innocent'. His prayer is heard, and in the same way he obtains pardon for the other rebels; from which, adds Matthew, all sinners may derive encouragement since they have such a strong and merciful intercessor. We catch here an echo of the words the king is said to have used about Earl Richard five years later: 'a bloody traitor, a rebel against me and my realm, whom I caught making war on me in Ireland.'[17] Significantly the incident of the letter and Edmund's reproach of treachery does not appear in the Life. That Matthew should have discarded an incident of such high dramatic effect must throw doubt on the authenticity of Wendover's report; all the more so since it would

14. Thus Wendover's assertion that Maurice FitzGerald and the Lacys were treacherous vassals of the Earl Marshal is untrue: they held no lands of the Marshal: G.H. Orpen, *Ireland under the Normans* (1920), iii, pp. 66–71.
15. See discussion of the document in Lawrence, *St Edmund*, p. 135.
16. Below, pp. 132–3.
17. *Chron.Maj.*, iii, pp. 523–4.

have looked good in a hagiographical portrait of St Edmund, illustrating his courage and forcefulness in the cause of justice.

It is equally significant that Matthew omitted the incident from his *Historia Anglorum* – the shorter history that he began writing in the year 1250. Perhaps advancing years, bringing with them recognition and royal patronage, had modified Matthew's political views. When he came to rewrite the story of 1234, Wendover's interpretation no longer seemed acceptable; and the heated colloquy between the king and the archbishop appeared for what it was, a product of the passions and prejudices of the moment, working on the material supplied by rumour.

What was not in doubt was Edmund's tireless activity in restoring peace. He was in the Marches from May to July, occupied in reconciling the rebels. Henry Sandford and Alexander Stavensby gave constant assistance. While the case was in doubt, Sandford assumed custody of the Braose lands and castles, to which the Marshal had laid claim. Gilbert Marshal's castle of Striguil was held by the archbishop's men until it, along with the rest of the Marshal inheritance, was restored to Gilbert Marshal on 22 August.[18] The pardon of the rebels and the revocation on 8 June of the sentence of outlawry they had incurred marked the triumph of Edmund's pacification.[19]

When the barons had been reconciled, there remained the question of making terms with Llewelyn, the prince of Snowdon, and pacifying the March. A promised meeting to formulate terms of peace had been postponed until the reconciliation of the magnates. On 31 May the king issued powers to Edmund, Sandford and Stavensby, to proceed with negotiations, and Llewelyn was warned to be at Shrewsbury on 19 June to meet them.[20] The negotiations were actually conducted at Middle, between Shrewsbury and Ellesmere. A truce was made for two years, establishing the territorial status quo which had existed before the war. This was concluded on 21 June, and ratified by the king on 7 July.[21] It was to be periodically renewed during the following years and efforts were made to arrange a meeting between Llewelyn and the king to formulate a definitive peace treaty. The truce of Middle completed Edmund's labours in the Marches, but it did not end his worries. The thorny task of supervising the truce was left in his hands, and it was not long before he received allegations of infringement.

Edmund's political apprenticeship had been exceptionally taxing. An archbishop was rarely called on so quickly to assume such a critical and difficult role in politics. It was not a role for which he had been prepared

18. *Cal.Patent Rolls, 1232–47*, pp. 48, 65.
19. *Close Rolls, 1231–34*, p. 564.
20. *Ibid.*, pp. 564–5.
21. *Cal.Patent Rolls, 1232–47*, p. 59.

by his academic career or by his family background. Yet he emerged from the trial with conspicuous success. Within a few months of his election he had averted civil war by his efforts and had brought about an important reorganization of the king's council, thereby earning the gratitude and respect of an important section of the magnates. He had the assistance of an exceptionally able and loyal body of suffragans, but it was he who had dominated the situation. In time of war inspirational leadership comes into its own. This was something that Edmund, a mystic and a fervent preacher, could supply. The vexing problems of everyday administration and the demands of fractious subordinates would prove a more exacting test of his political acumen.

6

The Archbishop's Staff

Even before Edmund had been consecrated, the appointment of his senior administrative staff was an immediate claim upon his attention. The archbishop's government of his diocese and ecclesiastical province was carried on for the most part through clerks or secular clergy, who staffed his chapel, the secretariat of his Chancery, and his courts. These men were resident members of his household – what was called by ancient tradition his *familia*. Besides those who served as his agents in the exercise of his spiritual jurisdiction, the archbishop's entourage also included a steward responsible for the management of his estates and a treasurer entrusted with the financial management of his household and, alongside these, the chamberlains who acted as his valets, and the numerous domestic servants, the ushers, butlers, cooks, scullions, washerwomen, grooms, and marshals of the stables, who staffed the household of any great territorial magnate.

Of the archbishop's purely domestic servants we know almost nothing. We are reminded of this fact by a poignant incident narrated by Matthew Paris.[1] In the autumn of 1240, Edmund set out from England on what was to be his last unfinished journey with a somewhat reduced household. While resting at Pontigny, he was taken ill, and the party turned back, but on reaching Soisy he was too weak to proceed any further. When it became apparent that he was dying, the servants broke into lamentations over their own plight: 'What will become of us? Where shall we go when our dear lord is dead? We are stuck here as exiles in a far-away place, impoverished and without any provisions. Alas, to dig we are not able and to beg we are ashamed; we know nothing of commerce.' When he heard of this, although he was close to death, Edmund was moved to write or dictate testimonials addressed to some of his episcopal colleagues, requesting them to take his servants into their employment. One of these letters, of which Matthew reproduces the text, is on behalf of a Robert of Essex. The letter commends Robert's honesty and loyal service. Whether he was usher, cook or groom, we do not know. He is the only member of Edmund's domestic staff whose name is known to us.

When it comes to identifying his senior administrative staff we are in a better position. Several of them were notable men with a distinguished

---

1. Below pp. 153–4.

career in front of them. But even here the evidence sometimes fails us. Although the Lives and chronicles often provide information, a reconstruction of Edmund's *familia* has to rest largely upon the lists of witnesses to his surviving charters or written *acta*, and in many ways these are unsatisfactory material. Only a small proportion of his acts are witnessed, and some of these bear no date. A single surviving account roll from the years of his episcopate throws some light on that part of his staff that was engaged in the management of his estates. This is a fragment of what was apparently a Receiver's roll, containing accounts for six manors, probably for the year 1236–7.[2] The expenses listed include allowances of provender to many of the archbishop's clerks as they moved about the estates on their master's business, and they reveal the constant itinerary of the archbishop's steward and auditors from manor to manor of the Canterbury lands.

Not unexpectedly we find on Edmund's staff a nucleus of more or less 'permanent civil servants', whom he had inherited from the regime of his predecessors. In fact, the continuity between his administration and that of the previous two archbishops was probably greater than the existing evidence reveals. The most conspicuous representative of a former regime was the archdeacon of Canterbury, Simon Langton, the man who had advised Pope Gregory on Edmund's qualifications for the archbishopric. Simon had been appointed by his brother, Archbishop Stephen Langton, in 1227, and held office until his death in 1248, thus performing his duties under four successive archbishops.

By reason of his independent and irremovable status, the archdeacon tended to be of the *familia*, but not resident in it, and Langton's experience especially set him apart. Only a rash political escapade at the end of King John's reign had barred him from higher office, and in his declining years he achieved a unique position of influence and power. He had been in Rome since the death of Richard le Grand, and it was on his advice that the pope had disallowed three elections to the see of Canterbury and had designated Edmund. There is no trace of his activity in the diocese until 1237, when he was party to an agreement between the archbishop and St Augustine's abbey.[3] Towards the end of that year, he accompanied Edmund to Rome where, being conversant with the practices of the papal Curia, he helped to conduct the archbishop's litigation.[4] To the chronicler of Christ Church Canterbury, he was the cunning foe – the *hostis callidus* – who suggested to the pope that some of the chapter's title deeds and written

---

2. Lambeth Palace, Court Rolls, 1193. For the date of this, see Lawrence, *St Edmund*, pp. 139–40, n. 4.
3. Canterbury, Dean & Chapter muniments, Chartae Antiquae, C. 257.
4. Gervase, ii, pp. 131–2.

privileges would not stand up to examination. When Edmund was faced with a rebellion of the monastic community, Langton threw his weight on to the archbishop's side, and continued the struggle even after Edmund's death, forcing the people of Canterbury to observe the interdict that had been placed upon the cathedral church. In the end the monks seem to have bought off their formidable opponent. In August 1241 the prior and chapter conceded to him personally an important part of the *sede vacante* jurisdiction which they had claimed in the diocese.[5]

Another of Stephen Langton's clerks who was retained by Edmund was Master Thomas of Freckenham. A lawyer by education, he was rector of Maidstone and had served as Langton's official – his principal legal officer and president of his consistory court – throughout his episcopate.[6] He had continued in the same position under Archbishop Richard le Grand, and was executor both to him and to Langton. He was probably one of Edmund's senior counsellors from the beginning. Edmund took him with him to Rome at the end of 1237, and for a while he acted as the archbishop's attorney in the papal courts,[7] but this was his last service, for he died in Rome.[8]

From the point of view of continuity, one of the most remarkable members of Edmund's *familia* was Master Elias of Dereham. He had been steward of the estates for Hubert Walter and Stephen Langton. He was an active canon of Salisbury from 1222 at the latest. A distinguished architect, the master-designer of the new cathedral at Salisbury and of the shrine of St Thomas Becket at Canterbury, and a clerk of the king's works, his association with the administration of the archbishopric was unbroken through four pontificates.[9] He was appointed executor by three archbishops. In his old age, he was no less active in the service of Archbishop Edmund. We catch a glimpse of him as steward of the estates in the year 1236–7, touring the archbishop's Surrey and Kentish manors and auditing the accounts.[10] His attestation of acts in 1234 and 1240[11] indicates that he served throughout Edmund's episcopate.

---

5. BL, Cotton MS. Julius D, II, fo. 113.
6. K. Major, 'The Familia of Archbishop Stephen Langton': *EHR*, 48 (1933), pp. 529–53.
7. *Annales Roffenses* in *Anglia Sacra*, i, p. 349.
8. Gervase, ii, p. 131.
9. The details of his career have been traced by J.C. Russell, 'The many-sided career of Master Elias of Dereham': *Speculum*, v (1930), pp. 378–87; A.H. Thompson, 'Elias of Dereham and the King's Works': *Archaeological Journal*, xcviii (1941), pp. 1–35; and K. Major, *op. cit.* All of them, however, believed that Elias's work for the archbishopric ceased after his preferment to the canonry at Salisbury.
10. Lambeth Court Roll, 1193, *passim*.
11. *CChR*, i, pp. 196–7; *Cartulary of the Priory of St Gregory, Canterbury*, ed. A.M. Woodcock (Camden Soc., 3rd series, lxxxviii, 1956), p. 157.

One cannot fail to be impressed by the versatile genius and extraordinary industry of Master Elias. It is a pity that no letter-book of his is known to be extant, for no man could have told us more of the ecclesiastical politics of his age. His membership of the Salisbury chapter during the time of Edmund's treasurership gains special significance from the fact that he held a high place in the council of the three previous archbishops and that as steward he had a close association with Archdeacon Simon Langton, the pope's adviser during the Canterbury vacancy of 1231–3.

Another link with the past was represented by Master Aaron, the parson of Wimbledon, who attests five acts of Archbishop Edmund as a member of his household. This was Aaron of Kent, who had served as a clerk to both Langton and Hubert Walter.[12] How many more of Edmund's clerks had served a previous archbishop is a matter of conjecture. A Walter of Somercote attests acts in 1237 and 1240,[13] and he is to be found among the witnesses to a Canterbury charter of Langton's in 1227.[14] Another possibility is William, the rector of Bekesbourne, who was instituted to the living by Langton, when he is described as the archbishop's clerk.[15] Apart from these surmises we are left with a conviction that the permanent element in the *familia* of Edmund must have been greater than the archdeacon and the three elder clerks whose antecedents can be definitely established.

With Edmund's own appointments we reach firmer ground. Master Nicholas of Burford, whom he appointed as his Official, makes his first appearance as one of the trio who bore the archbishop's pallium from Rome in February 1234. We cannot be sure when he began to preside over the archbishop's provincial court, as he does not appear as witness to any datable act earlier than 1237.[16] In two documents originated by himself he used the title of Official of the Canterbury province. One of these, recording the institution of a parson to the church of Seasalter, bears the earliest extant reference to a seal of the officiality.[17] Small indicators such as these signify the parturition of new departments able to function independently in the ecclesiastical bureaucracy. Nicholas makes his last datable appearance as Official in a document of July 1238.[18] Apparently later that year he was replaced by Master Richard of Langdon. Langdon

---

12. *Acta Stephani Langton*, ed. K. Major (CYS, 1950), p. xlviii and *passim*. He was presumably dead by 18 July 1241, when the church of Wimbledon was vacant: *CPR, 1232–47*, p. 255. For his attestations see Lawrence, *St Edmund*, p. 142, n. 3.
13. Lawrence, *St Edmund*, p. 142, n. 5.
14. *Acta Stephani Langton*, p. 121.
15. *Ibid.*, p. 68.
16. *CChR*, i, pp. 238–40.
17. Canterbury, Dean & Chapter muniments, Register A, fo. 320.
18. Lambeth Palace, MS. 241 (Dover Cartulary), fo. 176ᵛ.

had been employed as a royal proctor at Rome,[19] and doubtless had legal training. He remained in office until the end of Edmund's regime. He was very active in Edmund's prolonged dispute with the chapter of Canterbury, and we find him executing mandates and issuing citations, publishing a sentence of excommunication and licensing penitentiaries. Whatever underlay this reshuffle of personnel, Nicholas of Burford did not retire from the archbishop's household. He attests three acts of 1240.[20]

We sense the importance of these men and their closeness to Edmund in the routine work of the archbishopric, but they remain for us little more than faceless names. There were, however, two members of his *familia* about whom we have more personal information. One of these was his brother, Robert of Abingdon. It was no uncommon thing for a thirteenth-century bishop to use his position to help his relatives. Nepotism of this kind was not stigmatized as an abuse where the beneficiaries had genuine merit. Two nephews of St Hugh of Lincoln became prebendaries of his cathedral chapter. In the case of Canterbury, Stephen Langton's appointment of his brother to the archdeaconry provided Edmund with an obvious precedent for associating his brother with the government of his diocese and province.

Because he attracted the attention of the hagiographers, Robert is better know to us than most of his colleagues. He was only a year or so younger than Edmund, for as boys they had set off together for the schools at Paris. There is no reason to think that he proceeded to a higher faculty after incepting in arts. He was in England in 1214,[21] and he evidently played an active part on the loyalist side during the political turmoil of the year 1216–17, which won him the approval of the papal legate, Cardinal Guala. For this he was rewarded with a dispensation to hold an additional benefice in plurality.[22] He appears as rector of Bocking in Essex in 1225,[23] but he had relinquished this living by November 1232,[24] probably on being presented to the more important rectory of Wingham in Kent.[25] Both these churches

19. *CPR, 1232–47*, p. 109.
20. Lawrence, *St Edmund*, p. 143, n. 9.
21. In that year he was involved in litigation over land in Isleworth: *Curia Regis Rolls, 1213–15*, pp. 236–7.
22. The dispensation refers to his 'loyalty to the Roman Church' (*fides erga Romanam Ecclesiam*) during the disturbances of the kingdom: *Regesta Honorii Papae III*, ed. P. Pressutti (Rome, 1888), I, no. 761. On 25 April 1217 he was granted safe-conduct anywhere in the king's power: *Patent Rolls ,1216–25*, p. 60.
23. *Acta Stephani Langton*, p. 93.
24. *Cal.Patent Rolls, 1232–47*, p. 2.
25. As rector of Wingham, he performed an institution of a rector in 1237–8: Canterbury, Dean & Chapter muniments, Register A, fo. 320.

were in the archbishop's patronage. Wingham, which was situated on one of the demesne manors of the Canterbury estates, was a favoured residence of the archbishops, and its church was usually reserved for those holding an important place in the archbishop's administration. A letter from the Franciscan Adam Marsh shows that Robert was also holding the rectory of Risborough at the time of his death.[26] This occurred in 1243 or 1244.[27]

Robert's position in Edmund's *familia* was unique. Protocol required the names of witnesses to the archbishop's acts to be listed in order of rank. In these documents Robert takes precedence over all except mitred heads. He appears to have held no specific office or title in the administration. In the *acta* he is simply designated 'our brother, rector of the church of Wingham'. Consanguinity with the archbishop alone gave him precedence over all ranks in the household. When he wrote to the cardinal legate Otto on diocesan business, the only title he used was 'brother of the lord archbishop' (*germanus domini archiepiscopi*).[28] Edmund, who had no taste for the mundane details of administrative routine, evidently relied upon his managerial capacity and trusted his judgement of other men. He seems to have had a better head for business than his brother. The extent of Edmund's dependence on him is suggested by the wide powers with which he invested him. During Edmund's absence abroad in the first half of the year 1238, when he was visiting the papal Curia, Robert and Nicholas of Burford were left in charge of the affairs of the archbishopric. Robert was invested with the powers of a vicar-general. The most striking of these powers with which he was entrusted was that of exercising the archbishop's ecclesiastical patronage – the authority to collate men to parish livings and institute them, one of the most important and sensitive of a bishop's functions. Besides this, he shared with the Official, Master Nicholas, the authority to visit, and implicitly to correct, the non-exempt monasteries of the diocese.[29] Although he attests only four of the archbishop's acts, he was clearly his brother's most trusted councillor and confidant throughout the episcopate. In the last years he was called on to act as his brother's spokesman in the conflict between the archbishop and the monks of the Canterbury chapter.

After Edmund's death Robert disappears into obscurity. At the end of 1240 he was the object of royal proceedings in the legate's court, but how he fared it is impossible to say.[30] In any case he only outlived his brother by

26. *Monumenta Franciscana*, ed. J.S. Brewer (RS, 1858), p. 247.
27. Wingham was vacant by 27 September 1243: *Cal.Patent Rolls, 1232–47*, p. 396. Matthew Paris reports miracles at his tomb in the annal for 1244: *Chron.Maj.*, iv, p. 378. Emden included him in *BRUO*, i, p. 8, but there is no evidence that he ever studied in the university of Oxford.
28. PRO, Ancient Correspondence of Chancery and Exchequer, xi, 159.
29. Canterbury, Dean & Chapter muniments, Register A, fo. 320.
30. *Cal.Patent Rolls, 1232–47*, p. 241.

three or four years. Eustace, Edmund's chaplain, who wrote the earliest Life of his master, sent the draft of his work to Robert for his inspection and emendation,[31] but it is not possible to identify any contribution he made to the finished biography. Possibly he was dead before the draft of the Life reached him. 'The Lord raised him up,' writes Matthew Paris, 'and gave him a rich reward, brilliantly endowed as he was with gifts of holiness, generosity, urbanity and profound learning.'[32] When due allowance has been made for the inflated language of the encomiast, it is evident that Robert of Abingdon was not dependent solely upon the family connection for his advancement in the Church.

Besides Robert, the most conspicuous and ultimately the most famous of Edmund's servants was the man he chose to be his chancellor, Master Richard de Wych, later the bishop of Chichester who, like Edmund, was to find a place in the calendar of the Church. Born at Droitwich, from which his name derived, he belonged to the baronial family of Chandos, holders of the honour of Snodhill in Herefordshire. The chronology of Richard's career before he entered Edmund's service is largely a matter of conjecture.[33] We have it on the authority of his confessor and biographer, the Dominican Ralph Bocking, that he incepted as a Master of Arts at a university, which may had been either Paris or Oxford, and that he then proceeded to study canon law. In due course he was elected chancellor of Oxford. In this office he attracted the attention of both Edmund and Grosseteste, the bishop of Lincoln, who both made a bid to get him as their chancellor. It was Edmund who secured him. Although the earliest acts attested by him date from 1237, he probably joined the archbishop's *familia* a year to two earlier than that.

The organization of the archbishop's Chancery at this date is obscure. It has not yet proved possible to construct a continuous list of archiepiscopal chancellors for the first half of the thirteenth century, and even where the existence of the man is undoubted, the precise nature of his functions remains uncertain. In the later middle ages the legal aspect of his office became more pronounced, and his secretarial functions were increasingly allocated to a registrar. But in the early thirteenth century this differentiation

---

31. The best copy of the Eustace Life carries a rubricated subtitle, written in the same thirteenth-century hand as the text, which runs as follows: 'Here begins the Life of the glorious confessor Edmund, archbishop of the church of Canterbury, set forth at Pontigny and dispatched to Master Robert of Abingdon, so that his labour may illuminate what is obscure, temper what is superfluous, fill in gaps and supplement what is lacking.': BL, Royal MS. 2 D VI, fo. 181. For Latin text, see Lawrence, *St Edmund*, p. 203.
32. Below, p. 118.
33. His family and career are described in C.H. Lawrence, 'St Richard of Chichester' in *Studies in Sussex Church History*, ed. M.H. Kitch (1981), pp. 35–55.

had hardly begun, and the chancellor acted as both head of the secretariat and judge. We find Richard de Wych acting in both capacities. He was a trusted confidant of Edmund's and a continuous resident in the archbishop's household. To support him in his office Edmund collated him to the rectory of Charing in Kent – a location of one of the archbishop's palaces – and the prebend of Deal in St Martin's Dover,[34] both benefices which he was to hold until his election to the see of Chichester.

Richard attests six of Edmund's surviving acts. He appears to have been the member of his inner council most constantly at the archbishop's side. He accompanied him on his journey to Rome in 1237–8, and went with him again on his last journey that ended at Soisy in November 1240. In a moving passage Matthew Paris describes Richard assembling the members of the household the morning after the archbishop's death, breaking Edmund's seal in their presence, and dispersing the *familia*. This account indicates that the chancellor personally supervised the imposition of the archbishop's seal and that letters were only issued from the writing office with his authorization:

> On the morning of the first day after he had fallen asleep, he who performed the office of chancellor sealed the aforesaid letters, which were sealed with his last seal, and handed them to those who had been granted them by the saint . . . Then, when everyone had been called together, in their presence the seal was broken, as is the custom, on account of the risk of fraudulent counterfeit.[35]

Richard remained with the small group of clerks who escorted Edmund's body back to Pontigny for burial. Bocking, who knew him intimately, describes his relationship with Edmund in terms of a close spiritual friendship. Like many others who served in Edmund's household and observed him at close quarters, Richard was deeply moved by the archbishop's transparent sanctity. After Edmund's death, he decided to step aside from the race for preferment and took up the study of theology at Orleans as a pupil of the Dominican friars, whom he purposed to join. Thirteen years later, as bishop of Chichester, his last recorded act was to dedicate a chapel at Dover to his former master and friend.

The chancellor, the Official, Robert of Abingdon, and a few senior clerks like Thomas of Freckenham and Elias of Dereham, occupied a privileged position in the *familia* by reason of their closeness to the archbishop. They were all men of academic distinction – *magistri* who had attended and in many cases taught in the schools. They surrounded their

34. *CPL,* i, p. 215. *AA.SS, April I,* 295.
35. Below, p. 157.

master with a net of watchful care that only the greatest of the land could penetrate. To this group belonged also the stewards of the estates, Simon of Seinliz and Brother Walter of Ferriby, and Edmund's chaplain, Eustace of Faversham. Simon of Seinliz had been steward to Bishop Ralph Neville of Chichester before he passed into the archbishop's service.[36] He appears on the receiver's roll of 1236–7, often in the company of Elias of Dereham, with whom he toured the archiepiscopal manors, auditing accounts.

It was a long established tradition that an archbishop chose his personal chaplains from among the monks of his cathedral priory. Edmund's chaplain, Eustace of Faversham, appears to be the only member of the monastic chapter who was taken into his service. Unlike his predecessors, he seems to have employed no other chaplains. Eustace attests only one of the archbishop's acts.[37] The evidence of his constant presence at Edmund's side comes from his own account of himself in the *Quadrilogus* and from the invidious references of the Canterbury chronicler. He was, it seems, chamberlain or *camerarius* of the cathedral priory,[38] though he can hardly have carried out the duties of an obedientiary while he followed the archbishop's court. His earliest appearance in the records is in 1237, when the monks observed that he had gone with the archbishop to Rome without having sought the leave of his monastery.[39] When the chapter summoned him from the archiepiscopal residence on the manor of Teynham to take part in the election of a new prior, Edmund excused him on the ground that he had no other chaplain.[40]

It is obvious that the rebellion of the Canterbury chapter involved Eustace in a distressing conflict of loyalties. His abortive nomination to be prior of St Martin's Dover in March 1240 probably represents an attempt on Edmund's part to extricate him from an intolerable position.[41] At all events the appointment came to nothing, as Robert, the existing prior, survived and continued in office for another eight years. Edmund made a final effort to protect him against reprisals with a letter, given at Soisy three days before his death.[42] Eustace's services to the archbishop did not end with Edmund's death. He became an enthusiastic promoter of his master's canonization and key witness in the canonization process. He was the first

36. His letters addressed to Ralph Neville were published by W.H. Blaauw in *Sussex Archaeological Collections*, iii (1850), pp. 35–76. He was in Neville's service as late as 21 June 1232: *Close Rolls, 1231–34*, p. 77.
37. *Cartulary of the Priory of St Gregory, Canterbury*, p. 157.
38. Gervase, ii, p. 146.
39. *Ibid.*, p. 131.
40. *Ibid.*, p. 145.
41. Canterbury, Dean & Chapter muniments, Chartae Antiquae, D. 76.
42. Sens Cathedral muniments, no. 3; text in Lawrence, *St Edmund*, p. 319.

to compose a Life of St Edmund – a highly rhetorical piece which had an unfortunate and lasting impact upon the hagiographical tradition.

The archbishop could delegate his jurisdiction to others, but not his sacramental order. Acts that required bishop's orders, such as ordinations, confirmations, the consecration of chrism and the dedication of churches, would demand the services of an auxiliary bishop.[43] It is probable that in Edmund's absence these duties were performed in the Canterbury diocese by John, formerly bishop of Ardfert in the Irish province of Cashel. A Benedictine monk, he had been removed from his see by papal mandate owing to the irregularity of his election,[44] and since 1224 bore the title of bishop *in universali ecclesia*, a designation used for prelates bereft of their sees. His habitual residence was St Albans abbey, where, as a venerable and respected figure, he ended his days.[45] He had already acted as an auxiliary in the Canterbury diocese under Langton. He appears in Edmund's service in 1238 and 1240,[46] both years in the course of which the archbishop made journeys abroad.

An archbishop's household offered a ladder as well as an administrative training to men of talent. The point is illustrated by the history of three of St Edmund's clerks who, although they never attained episcopal rank, had subsequent careers of distinction. These three men, Robert of Stafford, Geoffrey of Ferring, and John of Offington, were all men who had been to the schools and had attained the style of Master. They had apparently already been co-opted to serve in Edmund's *familia* by 1234, for the compiler of the *Liber Pilosus* of St Paul's London singled them out for notice among the throng of clergy present at the archbishop's consecration in Canterbury cathedral.[47]

Master Robert of Stafford, who attests four acts dating from the early years of Edmund's regime, presumably left his service in 1237 on being appointed archdeacon of Stafford.[48] Master Geoffrey of Ferring, who appears only intermittently among Edmund's clerks, passed after his death into the service of William Ralegh, bishop of Winchester, whose Official he became.[49] It was, no doubt, the association with Ralegh that brought

---

43. In the early thirteenth century, Irish bishops who had lost their sees through war, were frequently used as auxiliary bishops in English dioceses. See A.H. Thompson, *The English Clergy in the later Middle Ages* (1947), pp. 48–50.
44. *CPL*, i, pp. 68, 98, 100.
45. *Chron.Maj.*, iii, p. 394; iv, pp. 324, 501; v, p. 2.
46. Gervase, ii, p. 139; *The Register of St Augustine's Abbey*, ed. G.J. Turner and H.E. Salter (1924), p. 538.
47. *Early Charters of St Paul's Cathedral*, ed. M. Gibbs (Camden Soc., 3rd series, lviii, 1939), p. 142.
48. *CPL*, i, p. 167.
49. *CPL*, i, p. 221. He first appears in that capacity on 16 May 1245: *The Cartulary of Winchester Cathedral*, ed. A.W. Goodman (1927), p. 395.

him into the orbit of the royal service. In 1246 the king acknowledged his services by entering into a bond to provide him with a benefice to the value of fifty or sixty marks, and empowered the provost of Beverley and the chancellor of St Paul's to provide him with livings worth this amount.[50] The record of his benefices, though incomplete, suggests the picture of a pluralist on a fair scale.[51] In 1245 he received a papal indult permitting him to hold three benefices involving the cure of souls. He finished his career as dean of St Paul's and apparently died in 1268.[52]

Master John of Offington, the third of this group of distinguished *magistri*, was evidently a trained lawyer, for he had been commissary to the chancellor of Oxford before entering the archbishop's service.[53] While serving in Edmund's *familia*, he was a canon of Wells and later, in 1243, following the death of Jocelin of Wells, he represented the chapter as their proctor at the papal court. After Edmund's death Master John's services were secured by Grosseteste and he became a member of the bishop of Lincoln's *familia*. A papal dispensation from the canonical impediment of illegitimacy, obtained in 1247, indicates that he was marked out for a bishopric,[54] but he died in 1251 without having attained the purple.

For men like these, ecclesiastical administration was a profession, just as the Civil Service is for modern men, only the prizes might be higher. Generally they were clergy only in the legal sense that they had been tonsured and enjoyed the privileges of clerical status at law. They tended to remain in minor orders until the possibility of elevation to an archdeaconry or a bishopric made it expedient for them to be ordained to the priesthood. It is noticeable that Edmund's chancellor, Richard de Wych, the future bishop of Chichester, whom the Church was to canonize nine years after his death, was ordained a priest at Orleans only after the archbishop's death. For several years he had been rector of Charing and chancellor to the archbishop without feeling it necessary to seek priestly

---

50. *Cal.Patent Rolls, 1232–47*, p. 484.
51. He was admitted to the rectory of Denham on 3 September 1236: *Rotuli Roberti Grosseteste*, ed. F.N. Davis (CYS, 1913), pp. 341, 343. He held a portion of the church of Elham for life: Merton College record, no. 957. He was authorized in 1245 to hold three benefices with cure of souls: *CPL* i, p. 221. In addition to his prebends in Beverley Minster and St Paul's, he was precentor of Chichester not later than 1256: *Cartulary of the High Church of Chichester*, ed. W.D. Peckham (Sussex Record Soc., xlvi, 1946), p. 261.
52. C.N.L. Brooke, 'The deans of St Paul's, *c.* 1090–1499': *Bulletin of the Institute of Historical Research*, xxix (1956), p. 239.
53. *The Cartulary of Oseney Abbey*, ed. H.E. Salter (OHS, 1929–36), i, p. 137. Matthew Paris says of him 'there was no more famous clerk in England than he': *Chron.Maj.*, v, p. 230. For his career, see K. Major in *Robert Grosseteste, Scholar and Bishop*, ed. D.A. Callus (1955), and A.B. Emden, *BRUO*, iii, pp. 1927–28.
54. *CPL*, i, p. 238.

ordination. Edmund evidently accepted this as the normal case with his administrative staff.

The *magistri* or university 'graduates' were highly prized by the bureaucracies of church and state. They moved with ease from the service of one diocese to that of another, as we have seen in the case of Robert of Stafford, Geoffrey of Ferring and John of Offington. Besides these three, two other clerks of Edmund's found similar employment elsewhere after his death. Master John de Wich, who may have been a relative of Richard de Wych, was another lawyer, who acted as Edmund's proctor at Rome in the dispute with the chapter.[55] He was one of the archbishop's executors.[56] Later, as canon of South Malling, he appears in the *familia* of Bishop Richard of Chichester. Master Roger of Burwardiscote, who appears in the household in 1240, had by August 1242 joined the service of Grosseteste.

The bishop of a secular cathedral could draw upon the learning and administrative skills of his canons to help him in running the diocese, but a bishop with a monastic chapter like that of Canterbury was less favourably placed. He had no cathedral prebends at his disposal to which he could appoint his clerks. Edmund's chaplain Eustace appears to have been the only monk in his service. He had therefore to look elsewhere for means to support the members of his substantial *familia*. The Official may have been a stipendiary, but to maintain the rest the archbishop resorted to the same methods as were used by the king and the pope to meet the costs of their bureaucracies: he provided them with benefices.

The exempt parishes, which were in the archbishop's patronage, offered one valuable source of remuneration. Thus Robert of Abingdon was collated to the parish and deanery of Bocking by Stephen Langton, and to Wingham probably by Edmund. Richard de Wych was collated to the rectory of Charing. Elias of Dereham was rector of Harrow in the archbishop's patronage as well as a canon of Salisbury. Aaron of Kent was appointed to Wimbledon, one of the archbishop's peculiars situated in the diocese of Winchester. Another of Edmund's acts shows him providing for Master Geoffrey of Ferring out of the revenues of the church of Elham.[57] Whatever personal scruples Edmund may have had on the subject of pluralism and non-residence, they evidently failed to withstand the hard pressure of administrative necessity. Master Robert of Stafford was already holding two benefices with cure of souls when he was appointed archdeacon of Stafford in 1237; and Edmund's brother, his most trusted

55. Gervase, ii, pp. 183–4; he attests two of the archbishop's *acta* in 1240: *Cartulary of St Gregory*, pp. 156–7.
56. *Close Rolls, 1237–42*, p. 280.
57. Merton College record, no. 957.

confidant, was also, as we have seen, a pluralist on a limited scale. In 1240 Edmund received a papal faculty to license five of his clerks to hold an additional benefice each, with cure of souls.[58] It was clearly this problem of providing for his staff that underlay his attempt to revive the plans of his predecessors for the endowment of a new collegiate church in the Canterbury diocese which, as we shall see, was to be foiled by the resistance of his cathedral chapter.

A bishop had one reservoir of cheap yet highly skilled labour, provided he was in a position to tap it, in the orders of Mendicant friars. Their superior education and pastoral training made the friars valuable auxiliaries in diocesan work. Their help was greatly appreciated by reformist bishops like Grosseteste, who constantly pressed the provincial chapter of the Dominicans to send him friars to assist in the Lincoln diocese. Although no friars appear among the witnesses of Edmund's acts, it is clear from other sources that they were often to be found in his household. The Mendicant ideal, which combined monastic observance with an evangelical mission to the world, would have strongly appealed to him as a perfect paradigm of the Christian life. Trivet, the Dominican annalist, remarks that as archbishop Edmund constantly had friars in his retinue.[59] A number of his former associates of the Oxford days joined the Dominicans. It was two of these, Robert Bacon the theologian, and Richard of Dunstable, prior of the Oxford Dominican house, who were to supply the university with the information needed to postulate Edmund's canonization. Edmund used the Provincial of the Franciscans, Agnellus of Pisa, as his envoy when he was working for peace in 1234. How far he used friars for more routine tasks in his diocese it is impossible to say. Matthew Paris refers to the fact that friars were to be found lunching at Archbishop Edmund's table, and remarks that he liked to perform the role of the Master and determine theological questions in their practice disputations. Whether these were held in one of the Mendicants' priories or in the archbishop's household he does not tell us. It is during his episcopate that we first hear of the Friars Preachers building their priory at Canterbury on an island in the river Stour, a site donated them by the king.[60] Perhaps this was the location of the disputations in which Edmund was invited to participate. The friars attracted many of the best minds of the thirteenth century. Had Edmund been born a generation earlier he would probably have joined them.

58. *CPL*, i, p. 189.
59. *Nicholai Triveti Annales*, ed. T. Hog (1845), p. 228.
60. W.A. Hinnebusch, *The Early English Friars Preachers* (Rome, 1951), pp. 76–8.

7

Edmund the Archbishop

When his election to Canterbury received the king's approval, Edmund entered into a high spiritual office which possessed a very secular base. Centuries of endowment had provided the see of Canterbury with a huge territorial lordship, concentrated largely in Kent, Sussex and Surrey, which placed it on a par with the wealthiest landowners of England. Accounts rendered by the royal bailiffs for their stewardship during the vacancy of the see prior to Edmund's election show the estates of the archbishopric producing an annual net income of £1,788.[1] In the thirteenth century this was an income comparable to that of an earldom. Among English bishoprics it was exceeded only by that of Winchester. For this great barony the archbishop owed the king the military service of eighty-four knights, an obligation which by Edmund's time had normally been commuted for the occasional levy of the tax called scutage.

The preservation of the properties of his see from encroachment or dilapidation was recognized to be a solemn duty laid upon every bishop at his consecration, one for which he would have to answer to God and the patron saints of his church at the day of judgement. Although the supervision of the estates was delegated to his steward, Elias of Dereham, and an army of bailiffs, it remained one of Edmund's constant preoccupations. From time to time it involved him in bruising litigation with other landowners like William de Warenne, the earl of Surrey, and with his own chapter.

Like that of the king and other territorial magnates, the life of a thirteenth-century archbishop was spent in a perpetual itinerary. The coronation of the queen, a royal council, or more humdrum business of state, took him to Westminster. Less frequently, ecclesiastical business called him to his own cathedral city, where he stayed on the sufferance of the most cantankerous chapter of England. Neither place was his normal habitat. As a rule, he resided on the demesne manors of the archbishopric, passing with his retinue of clerks, household knights and domestic servants, from one to another of his Kentish and Sussex manor houses. Although the record of Edmund's day-to-day movements is incomplete, it is full enough to indicate that his most favoured places of residence were the Kentish manors of

---

1. PRO, Pipe Roll, 76, m. 5d, cited by F.R.H. DuBoulay, *The Lordship of Canterbury* (1966), p. 243.

Wingham and Aldington and the Sussex manors of South Malling and Teynham. One of his written acts is dated at Lambeth, and it was probably there that he stayed, in the palace built by Archbishop Hubert Walter, when business of state required his presence at the royal palace of Westminster.

Edmund's chamberlains testified that in the midst of this busy life of constant movement, despite the daily social and political demands made on him, as archbishop he continued to adhere to the austere personal regime he had followed since he was a young man. They observed that he continually wore a hair shirt, ate sparingly even when he entertained the great at his table, and managed with little sleep. His clerks, who felt obliged to attend him for the recitation of the night office in his oratory, complained of his interminable prayers which left them nodding off to sleep with the office unfinished before it was time to begin the dawn service of Lauds. He maintained in his household and chapel the monastic regime of the great silence: no one was permitted to talk following the office of Compline until dawn. This practice caused his clerks some embarrassment when they were in Rome in the spring of 1238. One evening the pope sent for him after the hour of Compline but he showed no willingness to go. Eventually he was persuaded by members of his household that he must obey the summons, but on coming into the pope's presence he registered his protest: 'O holy father, why have you troubled me at such an hour?'[2] Pope Gregory, who had befriended St Francis of Assisi and was familiar with the foibles of holy men, received the reproof with good humour.

The turbulent events of 1233–4 had called into play one of the capacities that fell to Edmund as archbishop. By long tradition, the archbishop of Canterbury was the foremost councillor of the realm and the spiritual director of the king. In this role he had taken the initiative in mediating between King Henry and the rebels and had boldly appealed to the king's conscience. In his spiritual capacity he was both a bishop with his own diocese and a metropolitan with jurisdiction over an ecclesiastical province. The title of Primate of All England gave him the moral authority to act as spokesman for the whole English Church, but in practice his metropolitical powers were confined to the southern province of Canterbury. He had no authority in the province of York, which was presided over by his old pupil and friend, Walter de Gray. These powers that set him above his suffragans or episcopal colleagues had long been defined in canon law, but their exercise was sometimes hindered by local tradition. They included the duty to examine and confirm the election of other bishops and to consecrate them. The law sanctioned the archbishop's right to visit the dioceses of his suffragans and to exact procurations or expenses for doing so; and the Councils exhorted him to convene his suffragans annually in a provincial synod.

2. The Life by Matthew Paris, below p. 135.

The itinerary that can be worked out from Edmund's surviving *acta* is too patchy to show whether or when he exercised the ancient right of metropolitan visitation. Luckily there is other evidence. In November 1239 Robert Grosseteste wrote a letter to Simon of Arderne, his proctor at Rome,[3] explaining the obstacles he had encountered as bishop of Lincoln when he had set out to visit his cathedral chapter and the prebendal churches of his canons. Resistance had been carefully co-ordinated and successful, and Grosseteste had responded by suspending the dean, precentor and subdean. The rebels were now offering to treat. There follows a page of anxious heart-searching. Should he force them with excommunication? – a dangerous course which might lead to a public outcry, 'for it has not been customary for an English bishop to attempt anything of this sort.' Few bishops, he adds, would wish to pronounce unreservedly in favour of visitation, for they hate having their own churches visited by the archbishop; moreover the action over visitation between the archbishop of Canterbury and the bishop of London is still pending.

In his dilemma Grosseteste reveals how far the English clergy of his time were from regarding regular visitation as a normal state of affairs. He seems, however, to indicate that metropolitan visitation was an evil with which his fellow bishops were not unfamiliar. Hubert Walter, certainly, had visited his province,[4] but Langton seems to have been negligent in the matter.[5] Evidently it was Edmund's visitatorial activity that Grosseteste had in mind. The dispute that he mentions between the archbishop and Bishop Roger Niger occurred in 1239 over Edmund's claim to visit religious houses in the diocese of London.[6] But earlier than this there is clear evidence that Edmund undertook a provincial visitation. On 8 May 1237 the pope sent him a rescript empowering him to use ecclesiastical sanctions against certain unnamed prelates and religious who had impeded him when he was visiting his province.[7] There is a gap in the record of Edmund's movements between the end of July 1236 and January of the following year. On 11 July we know that he was at Tewkesbury negotiating with Llewelyn. He is last recorded in the West Country on 23 July, when he attested a royal charter at Worcester.[8] His activities at Worcester are illuminated by two letters, chance survivors copied on the fly-leaf of a

3. *Roberti Grosseteste Epistolae*, ed. H.R. Luard (RS, 1861), pp. 253–60.
4. C.R. Cheney, *Hubert Walter* (1967), pp. 68–70.
5. *CPL*, i, p. 86; see also C.R. Cheney, *Episcopal Visitation of the Monasteries in the thirteenth century* (1931), p. 32.
6. *Ann.Mon.*, iii, p. 151.
7. Auvray, no. 3646.
8. PRO, Charter Roll, 29, 20 Henry III.

manuscript now in Clare College Cambridge.[9] These show that he proposed to visit the cathedral priory of Worcester on the feast of St Mary Magdalen, 22 July. The bishop, William of Blois, wrote pleading with him to call off the proposed visitation on the grounds that it was unprecedented – the cathedral had not been visited by the archbishop's two predecessors. Edmund evidently took advantage of his political engagements in the Marches to visit the western parts of his province during this period.

In the course of his short episcopate, Edmund was called upon seven times to examine the election of one of his suffragans and consecrate the bishop-elect. It was usual for the archbishop to obtain the assistance of two of his suffragans for the apostolic laying-on of hands. The ritual was an occasion for the demonstration of metropolitan authority: before consecration, the elect made a canonical profession of obedience to the see of Canterbury, which was committed to writing by his own hand and placed upon the altar. The whereabouts of such consecrations had long been a subject of contention between the interested parties.

The monks of Canterbury claimed that their legal privileges required all episcopal consecrations to be performed in the cathedral church. In practice, the venue was determined by the convenience of those involved in making the arrangement; but Edmund seems at one stage to have been willing to admit the claim of the monks, at least in principle. In the spring of 1235, after Grosseteste had been elected bishop of Lincoln, he visited Canterbury and was told by the monks about an alleged charter of St Thomas Becket which forbade episcopal consecrations anywhere other than Canterbury except by permission of the chapter. On the strength of this he wrote to Edmund begging that his consecration should take place at Canterbury.[10] Edmund in fact ignored Grosseteste's request and consecrated him bishop on 17 June 1235 in Reading abbey. Nevertheless, he was anxious to maintain good relations with his chapter; and he issued a *cautio* or notification to say that Grosseteste's consecration at Reading was not to prejudice the liberties of the church of Canterbury since it was done with the consent of the chapter.[11] Later he was to issue a similar letter when he consecrated Hugh to the see of St Asaph's in the church of Boxgrove priory in Sussex.[12] The wording of these letters appears to concede the claim of the monks. Possibly Edmund, like Grosseteste, was deceived by the alleged charter of St Thomas, which subsequently proved to be an *ad*

9. Clare College Cambridge, MS. Kk.5.6, fo.1ᵛ.
10. *Epistolae*, pp. 54–6; see the discussion by R.W. Southern, *Robert Grosseteste* (1986), pp. 251–2.
11. Lawrence, *St Edmund*, appx B, no. 8.
12. Printed in W. Wallace, *St Edmund of Canterbury* (1893), appx, p. 518.

hoc forgery.[13] His profound charity made it difficult for him to doubt the good faith of others or to enter into the minds of men more worldly than himself.

The archbishop's duty to examine the election of a suffragan prior to his consecration involved studying the 'decree' or report of the electoral process drawn up and attested by the chapter concerned, to ensure that the canonical procedure had been followed. If all was in order he would confirm the election of the candidate. All the cases that came before Edmund were ratified by him with the sole exception of the election to Rochester. This case was to be a thorn in his side for three years. The see of Rochester was unique in being a satellite of Canterbury. Since its creation by Lanfranc after the Norman Conquest, its dependent status had been apparent from the fact that it owed military services not to the king but to the archbishop. The fact that the archbishop possessed the patronage of the see – the right, that is, of designating the incumbent – was confirmed by letters patent granted to Stephen Langton by King John.[14]

Henry Sandford, the bishop of Rochester, had given Edmund sterling assistance during the political troubles of 1234, but he died in February 1235, and the monastic chapter decided to seize the occasion to make a bid for the independence of their church. Instead of waiting on the archbishop, they proceeded on 26 March to elect Master Richard of Wendover as their bishop. Possibly they hoped that the acceptability of their candidate would persuade the archbishop to waive his rights of patronage. Master Richard was eminently suitable to be a bishop. A scholar and rector of Bromley, he had been serving the see as its Official or law officer. Perhaps they were encouraged in their hopes by the knowledge that the archbishop was a man of great charity, who appreciated scholars. If so, they were disappointed. Edmund ruled their proceedings as *ultra vires*, and refused to confirm the election. It was a question of defending the rights of the see of Canterbury of which he was the trustee. If he entertained any thought of yielding the point, there were those close to him who would be ready to stiffen his resolve, foremost among them the combative old archdeacon, Simon Langton.

Faced with Edmund's determined refusal to accept the election of Wendover, the monks of Rochester appealed to the pope to confirm the election, and sent two of their number to Rome to procure the necessary letters. They obtained the appointment of the abbot of Walden, the prior

---

13. The charter, which was copied into the registers of the cathedral, was shown by diplomatic criteria to be a forgery by C.R. Cheney, 'Magna Carta Beati Thome: another Canterbury forgery' in *EHR*, xxxvi (1963), pp. 1–26, reprinted in *Medieval Texts and Studies* (1973), pp. 78–110.
14. DuBoulay, *op. cit.*, p. 84 & n.

of Merton and the archdeacon of Northampton as papal judges-delegate to summon the parties and determine the case in England.[15] But as so often happened when appeals were made to Rome, this proved to be no more than an opening gambit in a prolonged legal game. The case was to drag on for three years. After two panels of judges-delegate had had their findings disallowed on technical grounds by the pope, the chapter sent representatives to the papal Curia to plead their case there against the archbishop's attorneys. Eventually they won, but with the proviso that the judgement was not to prejudice the archbishop's rights of patronage over the see of Rochester for the future.[16] Whatever his feelings over this failure to vindicate the rights of the archbishopric, Edmund submitted to the sentence with good grace, and consecrated Wendover at Canterbury in November 1238, with the assistance of four of his suffragans.[17] At this time he was in dispute with the monks of his own chapter, whom he had suspended from their sacred functions, and this made it necessary to perform the rite of consecration in the church of St Gregory's, Canterbury, belonging to the Augustinian canons.

In an age of ecclesiastical reform and legal definition a conscientious bishop might be hard put to it to reconcile the spiritual obligations placed on him by canon law with what he owed to the secular power. The situation was made more complex by the fact that the royal service was, like that of the Church, staffed by members of the clerical order, and senior ministers were often rewarded with bishoprics. During the crisis of 1234, Edmund had shown himself a fearless critic of government in the Langton tradition. He had a receptive pupil in the young king, who could hardly forget that he owed his throne to papal protection. Possibly Edmund felt that some concessions were worth making in order to preserve the fund of mutual confidence and good will created in the early months. He seems to have been reluctant to make a major issue of something that was disturbing the minds of radical reformers like Grosseteste and the Franciscan Adam Marsh. This was the practice of employing heads of religious houses and beneficed secular clergy in offices of state, particularly as royal judges. The practice was frowned on by canon law, and such men were the object of Grosseteste's fiercest indignation. He wrote twice to Edmund begging him to take action to curb this abuse, but later complained that he had found the archbishop unhelpful.[18] Possibly Edmund's friendship with William

---

15. *Annales Roffenses* in Wharton's *Anglia Sacra* (1691), I, pp. 348–9. On the operation of judge-delegate procedure, see Jane E. Sayers, *Papal Judges Delegate in the Province of Canterbury, 1198–1254* (1971).
16. *CPL*, i, p. 174.
17. *Annales Roffenses*, p. 349.
18. *Epistolae*, pp. 105–13. Grosseteste wrote to the legate on the subject, and said he had twice sought the archbishop's help, but had achieved nothing: *ibid.*, pp. 262–4.

Ralegh, one of the outstanding judges of his generation, convinced him that the arrangement was not without advantage to both church and state. To Grosseteste such accommodations were treason against divine law, but few others were disposed to challenge a system that was deeply embedded in the socio-economic structure of medieval society.

A more severe test of Edmund's powers of spiritual leadership was posed by a direct conflict of legal principles between the laws of church and state. Just such a conflict arose over the different treatment of bastardy in the ecclesiastical and secular courts. Since the time of Pope Alexander III, the canon law had held that a child born out of wedlock was legitimized by the subsequent marriage of its parents, provided it had not been conceived in adultery.[19] The royal courts, however, which were concerned with the inheritance of land, refused to admit this doctrine: a child born out of wedlock, even if he had subsequently been covered by the marriage mantle, could not claim any rights of inheritance against the children born after marriage. Questions of bastardy belonged to the matrimonial jurisdiction of the Church and were normally referred to the bishop. But in a case of *legitimatio per subsequens* difficulty arose, because the ecclesiastical court was bound to reach a decision about a person's legitimacy that was not acceptable in common law. Consequently, in the thirteenth century the royal courts began to abandon their practice of sending such pleas to the bishop, and instead questions as to the fact of a man's birth before or after the marriage of his parents were referred to a lay jury.[20]

Such an arrangement was doubly objectionable to zealous churchmen. It deprived the ecclesiastical courts of a sensitive part of their matrimonial jurisdiction, and it produced a result that was in flat contradiction to the law of the Church. Soon after his consecration as archbishop, Edmund moved to recover this sector of marriage law for the Church. At a council of lay magnates and bishops held at Westminster on 12 October 1234, with the support of nine of his suffragans he prevailed on the king to concede that when a litigant in the king's courts pleaded the exception of bastardy against an opponent, it should be referred to the bishop, whose court would inquire whether the person concerned had been born before or after the marriage of his parents.[21]

This concession was not enough to allay the misgivings of a conscientious bishop: he was required to supply information about a litigant which might

---

19. *Corpus Iuris Canonici*, c. 6. X. iv.7: *tanta est vis*, addressed to the bishop of Exeter. See the classical discussion of the question in F.W. Maitland, *Canon Law in the Church of England* (1898), pp. 53–5; also by Southern, *op. cit.*, pp. 252–7.
20. In 1200 Archbishop Hubert Walter submitted the facts of such a case to the justices when requested: *Curia Regis Rolls*, I, p. 335; but in 1224 and 1226 such cases were referred to a jury: *ibid.*, XII, no. 2000.
21. *Bracton's Notebook*, ed. F.W. Maitland (1887), iii, pp. 134–6.

result in his being disinherited by the secular court. The formula of 1234 may have represented a success for Edmund's diplomacy in that it had restored the jurisdiction of the Church over the question of legitimacy, but it left untouched the fundamental issue – that the English courts did not admit the canonical principle that a person was made legitimate by the subsequent marriage of his parents. Grosseteste refused to answer questions for a purpose he considered unlawful, and in due course he was cited before the royal judges for his failure to comply with their requests. In his indignation he wrote to Edmund reproaching him for having consented to such an arrangement. He also wrote a very long letter to William Ralegh, proving that *legitimatio per subsequens* was postulated by both divine and natural law. He appears to have received a somewhat barbed reply.[22]

With Edmund, at least, Grosseteste's view of the matter prevailed. At the meeting of a great council held at Merton priory in 1235, the archbishop and bishops raised the question again and sought to have the common law of England brought into line with canon law on this point. To this request the assembled barons gave the famous reply that 'they do not wish the tried and approved laws of England to be changed.'[23] Clearly the change the bishops requested could have had incalculable consequences in upsetting the descent of many estates. This refusal to interfere with the established law of property created an impasse. The account of the situation which the king sent to Ireland shows that, while the courts had not yet decided on the best way of dealing with pleas of bastardy, they had ceased to refer them to the ecclesiastical judge.[24] Eventually, they resorted to the verdict of a jury, as they had done before 1234.

Conflict between the competing jurisdictions of ecclesiastical and royal courts was not new in the thirteenth century. It was recognized that through its courts of bishops and archdeacons the Church had jurisdiction over church attendance, fasts and feast-days, marriage and matters of sexual morality, and ecclesiastical offences such as blasphemy and sacrilege. But between the acknowledged sphere of the two legal systems lay an area of disputed ground, 'that debatable land which is neither very spiritual nor very temporal'. A case in point were legal actions relating to advowsons or the patronage of churches, many of which were in the hands of lay landlords. Because these cases involved landed property they were claimed by the royal courts. But an advowson meant the right to nominate a clergyman to be rector of a parish church – a spiritual office; and the Church claimed that disputes over such rights should

22. *Epistolae*, pp. 76–97.
23. *Statutes of the Realm*, I, 4. On the sources of this version, which is a composite text, see F.M. Powicke, *Henry the Third and the Lord Edward* (1947), appx D, pp. 769–71.
24. *Close Rolls, 1234–7*, p. 354.

belong to its jurisdiction. Actions over these and similar matters could be stopped in the ecclesiastical courts by a writ of prohibition, issued by the royal chancellor at the request of one of the parties to the action. This had the effect of transferring the case to the royal courts. What aroused the anxiety of the bishops in the 1230s was that writs of prohibition were being sought in increasing numbers by clergy engaged in litigation in the church courts. In March 1237 Edmund himself was forbidden to pursue litigation before papal judges-delegate on the grounds that the case, which was brought against him by the prior and monks of Canterbury, concerned the temporalities of the archbishopric, and that these were a matter for the Crown.[25]

What was seen by the bishops as a mounting threat to the jurisdiction of the Church prompted the first organized protest against the encroachment by the royal courts. Under the year 1237, the annalist of Burton abbey records a list of clerical grievances which the archbishop and clergy asked Cardinal Otto, the papal legate, to take up with the king.[26] Prominent among them are complaints about the misuse of writs of prohibition by members of the clergy. This memorandum embodies points made by Grosseteste in a long letter he wrote to Edmund about this time.[27] Grosseteste had been in trouble with the king because he had forbidden the clergy of his diocese who were guilty of ignoring writs of prohibition to answer for their conduct in the royal courts. Although Edmund gave his support to the protest, it does not appear that he took the initiative in organizing it. Here, as elsewhere, he seems to have been prodded into action by Grosseteste. His distaste for litigation inclined him to leave it to his subordinates. His powers of conciliation were frequently tested by the radicalism of Grosseteste.

We have no record of provincial councils convened by Edmund as opposed to the periodic assemblies called by the king, which included the bishops as well as the lay magnates and princes of the blood. These were concerned with matters of state. But these councils, which assembled every year, provided Edmund with an opportunity to discuss matters of common concern with his suffragans in a place apart. Doubtless questions of clerical discipline and pastoral concern figured on his agenda. Such matters formed the subject of the synodal statutes published by many bishops. No statutes have been identified as Edmund's work,[28] but the large body of ordinances that were to

25. *Ibid.*, pp. 356, 524, 540.
26. *Ann.Mon.*, i, pp. 254–7.
27. *Epistolae*, pp. 205–34. See the discussion of this subject by G.B. Flahiff, 'The use of writs of prohibition by clerics against ecclesiastical courts in England': *Medieval Studies*, iii (Toronto, 1941), pp. 101–16, and *ibid.*, vi (1944), pp. 261–313; vii (1945), pp. 229–90.
28. C.R. Cheney, *English Synodalia of the Thirteenth Century* (1941), pp. 65–7. The statutes included under Edmund's name in Lyndwood's *Provinciale* are an abridgement of Richard le Poore's statutes for Salisbury.

be promulgated by the cardinal legate in 1238, which displayed a detailed grasp of English problems, clearly reflected Edmund's concerns and advice.

Cardinal Otto di Monteferrato was sent by Pope Gregory to England as a *legatus a latere* in 1237, at the request of the king. He landed at Dover in July. Matthew Paris, who detested all foreigners and was consistently hostile to the agents of papal bureaucracy, represents the legate as one of Edmund's adversaries, whose presence in England was a constant source of annoyance to the archbishop. An attack on the legate's household staff while he was staying at Oseney abbey outside Oxford suggests that he was not a popular figure; but it would be easy to read too much into a fracas that began as a brawl between the cardinal's Italian cook and students begging at the kitchen door. There is no evidence that he was regarded with hostility by the English bishops or that relations between him and Archbishop Edmund were bad. Modern research has tended to reveal his work in a favourable light and to emphasize the tact and restraint with which he wielded his great powers.[29]

The fact that the cardinal enjoyed the confidence of the higher clergy is indicated by their readiness to resort to him not only for justice, but also for mediation and advice. Grosseteste more than once confided to him his anxieties about the use of religious as royal judges and about other matters. Eustace, Edmund's chaplain, states in his deposition that the archbishop relied upon the legate's support, and his assertion is borne out by the history of Edmund's troubles with the Canterbury chapter.

A striking instance of his reliance upon the cardinal occurred during Edmund's absence abroad in the year 1238. He had left the oversight of the affairs of the archbishopric in the hands of his brother, Master Robert of Abingdon, and his Official, Nicholas of Burford, with instructions that in the event of difficulty they should approach the legate for help. It was not long before they had to invoke the cardinal's assistance. In a letter to him they ask him to intervene on behalf of a monk of the cathedral priory named Ralph of Orpington, who is being maltreated by the other monks.[30] The case they lay before the cardinal discloses an unsuspected can of worms. Ralph of Orpington was one of the monks involved in forging a charter of privileges allegedly granted the priory by St Thomas Becket. As the original charter had been accidentally detached from its seal, Ralph, acting on the instructions of the prior, John of Chetham, had forged a new one, in the process introducing a number of 'improvements' in favour of the monks, and had then attached to it the original seal of St Thomas.[31]

29. See Dorothy Williamson, 'Some aspects of the legation of Cardinal Otto': *EHR,* lxiv (1949), pp. 145–73.
30. PRO, Ancient Correspondence of the Chancery and Exchequer, xi, 159.
31. Gervase, ii, p. 133, presents a tendentious account of these events. The facts are clearly stated in *CPL,* i, p. 194.

Forgeries of this kind were not uncommon in the monastic world of the middle ages. The facts in this case had come to light because Brother Ralph was smitten with compunction and went and confessed all to the archbishop. As Edmund was on the point of setting out for Rome when he received Ralph's confession, he had no time to investigate, but took Ralph with him to save him from possible reprisals by his fellow monks, and lodged him at the abbey of St Bertin in Flanders, to await his return. In their letter to the cardinal, Robert of Abingdon and the official report that the monks of Christ Church had lured the penitent back with false promises and had then put him in chains.

Edmund pursued the matter while he was in Rome and obtained a papal mandate addressed to the cardinal legate with orders to inspect all the privileges in the possession of the cathedral priory, and to send any that appeared to be forged or suspect to the pope.[32] Armed with this mandate, Edmund approached the legate on his return home, and together they conducted a visitation of the priory. The forgery of the charter was exposed and the culprits were summoned to appear before the legate in London.[33] The prior, John of Chetham, having confessed his fault, resigned his office and was forced to enter a house of the Carthusian Order.

The cardinal displayed his readiness to assist Edmund in other ways. When the chapter appealed against his plans for a new collegiate church in the Canterbury diocese, it fell to the legate to inquire into the matter and report. His findings were favourable to the archbishop, who received from Rome the necessary faculty to proceed.[34] He did his best to bring about a reconciliation between the rebellious chapter and the archbishop. The picture of Cardinal Otto that emerges from these incidents is not a disagreeable one. He appears to have been a modest man.[35] He was not to be bought, even by the king: a gift of silver plate the king had had made for him was gracefully declined.[36] He was clearly unwilling to interfere in the domestic quarrels of the English Church, and he only acted if he was directly appealed to or was bidden by papal mandate.[37] He discharged his difficult mission with tact and firmness. Matthew Paris's portrayal of the legate as a time-server, ready to betray the archbishop's interests in order to curry favour at court, is an obvious distortion of the truth.

32. *CPL,* i, pp. 173–4.
33. Gervase, ii, p. 133.
34. *CPL,* i, pp. 173, 180, 182.
35. Even Matthew Paris conceded so much: *Chron.Maj.,* iii, p. 403. Grosseteste, who was not given to sycophancy, comments on the grace and humility of the legate's reply to his letter: *Epistolae,* p. 185.
36. *Close Rolls, 1237–42,* pp. 33–4.
37. Miss Williamson pointed out his reluctance to intervene in disputed elections until instructed to do so by the Pope.

The pallium sent to an archbishop-elect, which was brought from where it had lain on the shrine of St Peter, signified that the authority exercised by a metropolitan over his suffragans was delegated to him by St Peter's successor. It was a share in St Peter's care for all the churches. This close bond with the Apostolic See was cemented by the oath of canonical obedience to the pope which Edmund, like all metropolitans, had taken at his installation. It required among other things that the archbishop should, where possible, make a visit to 'the threshold of the apostles' every three years. There can be no doubt that Edmund took this obligation seriously. As the time approached, a number of other concerns made it desirable for him to seek the assistance of the Roman Curia. One of these was the case of the Rochester election, which the monks of Rochester cathedral were now pursuing at the Curia. Another was the problem posed by the intended marriage of Eleanor, the king's sister, to earl Simon de Montfort. On the death of her previous husband, William Marshal the Younger, she had sought Edmund's advice and under his spiritual direction had taken a vow of perpetual continence. Edmund was anxious to obtain a judgement against the validity of the proposed second marriage, which was unpopular with the aristocracy, on the ground that Eleanor's vow constituted a canonical impediment. The marriage, which he regarded as sacrilegious, had the king's approval, and Edmund was beginning to feel the weight of the royal displeasure. Only a papal judgement would take the pressure off him.

Edmund crossed the Channel a few days before Christmas 1237. In the thirteenth century the journey from Westminster to Rome took a courier about fifty days. Most men avoided the passage of the Alps in mid-winter. We do not know the route taken by Edmund and his party. The letter written by his agents to the legate shows that he stopped at St Bertin, a customary haven for sea-sick prelates after the Channel crossing. There is also an indication that he broke his journey at the Cistercian abbey of Pontigny in lower Burgundy. The evidence for this is a charter by which he granted the abbey an annual gift of ten marks from the endowments of the parish church of Romney in Kent, to provide a pittance for the brethren.[38] The charter bears the date 1238, but it may of course be the product of a visit on his return journey in the summer of that year. Among those of his staff who went with him were Archdeacon Simon Langton and Master Thomas of Frekenham.

From an anecdote in the Anonymous 'A' Life it is apparent that the party was in Rome by 12 March.[39] It gave Edmund no pleasure to find

38. *Le premier cartulaire de l'abbaye cistercienne de Pontigny*, ed. M. Garrigues (Paris, 1981), no. 241.
39. Recorded by the author of the Pontigny Life, BL, Add.MS. 15264, fo. 106v. On that day Pope Gregory invited Edmund to a party with other prelates. Characteristically he declined the invitation.

monks of his own chapter as well as those of Rochester waiting for him at the
Curia to engage in litigation against him. The Rochester annalist observed
that he refused to take any personal part in the proceedings, which he left in
the hands of the archdeacon and Master Thomas. Although he was repeatedly
summoned to the papal audience to hear the pope's sentence on 20 March,
he declined to attend. Judgement was in fact given against him in the
Rochester case and the election of Richard of Wendover was confirmed.[40]
The chagrin the decision must have caused him would have been alleviated
by the privilege obtained by his proctors two months later, stating that the
pope's judgement in favour of Wendover was not to prejudice the archbishop's
rights of patronage over Rochester for the future.[41] Curiously, the privilege
states that these rights of patronage had not been brought to the pope's notice.
It is difficult to avoid the conclusion that the case had been mishandled by
Edmund's attorneys. He was equally unsuccessful in his opposition to the
marriage of the Countess Eleanor. The marriage was celebrated with the
king's approval after Edmund had left England, and on 10 May the pope
pronounced it to be valid.[42] Edmund bore these failures with equanimity. He
showed no ill will towards Richard of Wendover.

Edmund was back in England by August 1238. The last two years of his
episcopate were to be clouded by a deepening conflict with the monks of his
chapter. The cathedral priory was a survival from an age of monk-bishops. In
the thirteenth century relations between a secular bishop and a monastic
chapter were seldom harmonious for very long. Edmund was engaged in
almost constant litigation with his chapter. In 1235 he had to take them to law
to induce them to shoulder their share of the expenses incurred in promoting
the unsuccessful election of John Blund.[43] In the same year they reopened the
old question of the archbishop's patronal rights in the liberty of Christ Church.
They sued him before papal judges-delegate for the recovery of the advowsons
of churches and the *exennia* which the archbishops claimed from the manors
belonging to the priory. The *exennia* were customary offerings from the
monks' manors made to the archbishop at Christmas and Easter, which they
had succeeded in appropriating for a time during Becket's regime.

The abbots of Boxley, Bradsole and Lesnes were commissioned by papal
letters to try the case, but before they could get both parties into court, the
action was stopped by a royal writ of prohibition.[44] Squeezed between

40. *Annales Roffenses*, p. 349.
41. *CPL*, i, p. 174.
42. Auvray, nos. 4889, 4330. See the discussion of the case in J.R. Maddicott, *Simon de Montfort* (1994), pp. 21–9.
43. Auvray, no. 2590.
44. *Close Rolls, 1234–7*, pp. 356, 524, 540.

papal orders to proceed and repeated royal prohibitions, the judges sought escape from their dilemma by referring the parties to Rome.[45] Meanwhile Edmund tried to negotiate an agreement out of court. He personally made an appeal for peace to the monks in chapter and initiated discussions. The outcome was a concord drawn up and ratified on 18 December 1237,[46] which left the archbishop undisputed possession of the rights in dispute, while reserving to the priory advowsons and their customary share of the *exennia* in certain specified places. This agreement was expressly made subject to papal and royal confirmation.

The sequel, which led to the bitter struggle between Edmund and his chapter, has to be disentangled from the vague allegations of Matthew Paris and the highly partisan account of the Christ Church chronicler. It appears that when the archbishop arrived in Rome in the spring of 1238, he found monks from Christ Church already there, having raced ahead of him; and when he presented the agreement for confirmation, the proctors of the chapter startled everyone by repudiating it. The explanation for this volte-face is to be found not, as Matthew Paris suggests, in a desire of the lawyers to keep the ball in play for their own advantage, but in another issue which touched the cathedral monastery very closely. The Christ Church chronicler says that when the archbishop reached Rome, he sought, against the wishes of the monks, a licence to erect a new prebendal church.[47] A papal mandate of May 1238, directing an inquiry, shows that the lawyers of Edmund and the chapter had in fact joined issue on this matter.[48]

Both Archbishops Baldwin and Hubert Walter had attempted to found a college of secular canons in the Canterbury diocese and had been defeated by fierce opposition from the monastic chapter.[49] What the archbishops chiefly sought was a means whereby they could provide canonries to support the numerous secular clerks they employed in diocesan and provincial administration. They were at a disadvantage in having a monastery for a chapter, as compared with those of their fellow bishops who had cathedral prebends at their disposal. The fears of the monks appear from the guarantee that was offered them by Hubert Walter in a vain attempt to secure their agreement. The erection of a great collegiate church in the diocese, endowed out of the possessions of the archbishopric and peopled by learned clerks who

---

45. A copy of the judges' report survives in Canterbury, Dean & Chapter muniments, Chartae Antiquae, A. 168; printed by Wallace, *op. cit.*, pp. 488–95.
46. Canterbury, Dean & Chapter muniments, Chartae Antiquae, C. 34.
47. Gervase, ii, p. 133. He makes no mention of the chapter's repudiation of the agreement they had made in 1237.
48. *CPL,* i, p. 173.
49. The dossier of this dispute in the time of Baldwin and Hubert Walter was published by Stubbs, *Epistolae Cantuarienses* (RS, 1865) from Lambeth Palace, MS. 415.

served the archbishop, might prove to be the first step in tranferring the chapter's electoral rights, and even the see itself, to the new foundation.

It was Edmund's revival of this project that provoked the monks to renew their resistance. Historically, the old question of the *exennia* and advowsons on the Canterbury manors was connected with the projected collegiate church. Archbishop Richard of Dover had granted away a number of these rights to the cathedral priory, but Archbishop Baldwin had recovered them with the express purpose of using them as an endowment of his new college.[50] The news that Edmund was planning to do the same must have thrown the monks into a panic and must have placed the agreement of December 1237 in a new and sinister light; hence their anxiety to repudiate it.

As a result of the appeal lodged by the chapter, Cardinal Otto was instructed by the pope to hold an inquiry and to inspect the site of the proposed foundation. The place chosen was Maidstone, an exempt parish in the archbishop's patronage. Plans were drawn up by Elias of Dereham for conventual buildings and a great church to contain fifty prebends.[51] In May 1239 Edmund was notified that the appeal of the chapter had failed,[52] and building on the site began. The monks, who despaired of further help from Rome, appealed to the Crown, representing that the new foundation would impoverish the temporalities of the see. The king now intervened. In November a writ was dispatched to the sheriff of Kent ordering him to halt the building operations, if necessary by force.[53] This put an end to a project which was only to be realized, on a modified scale, in the time of Archbishop Pecham. By this time the conflict between Edmund and his chapter had entered a new phase of personal bitterness and recrimination.

The conflict of interests between the archbishop and the monks was exacerbated by the scandal of the forged charter. As the astute archdeacon realized, by foolishly tampering with their documents the monks had undermined their case and destroyed trust. The episode had resulted in the deposition of the prior. In November 1238, at the convent's request, Edmund entered the chapter to supervise the election of a new prior. The claim of an archbishop, who was himself a member of the secular clergy, to appoint monastic officers was a sensitive area. The Christ Church chronicler commented acidly on the intrusion of the knot of secular clerks and friars who had accompanied Edmund into the chapter. Learning that the sub-prior had departed for Rome to prosecute a further appeal, the archbishop deposed him in his absence. This caused an angry scene which

50. *Ibid.*, pp. 8–10.
51. Gervase, ii, p. 174; *Ann.Mon.*, iii, pp. 150–1.
52. *CPL*, i, pp. 180, 182.
53. *Close Rolls, 1237–42*, p. 234.

ended in the monks walking out of the chapter-house, leaving Edmund alone with his staff. He responded to this contempt for his office by suspending the community from sacred functions. The monks, however, defied this sentence, taking their stand on the appeal they had lodged, and continued to celebrate the divine office and ring the bells as before.

The lack of a legitimate head was obviously a hindrance to the monks in prosecuting their case. So, ignoring the archbishop's repeated pleas to purge their contempt and regularize their position, they requested him to come to a full meeting of the chapter to assist in electing a prior. In an attempt to resolve the impasse, on 11 December Edmund returned to Canterbury from Aldington to resume discussions. Rather than risk another affront by entering the chapter-house himself, he sent the auxiliary bishop, John of Ardfert, his chancellor, Richard de Wych, and his old colleague and friend, the canonist Henry of Bishopstone, to represent him.[54] Their task was to explain to the monks the steps they must take to regularize their position before they could proceed to an election. But this peace overture miscarried. The monks refused to treat with Edmund's delegates, and demanded he should come in person. Finally, despite Edmund's repeated warnings, on 7 January they proceeded to elect one of their number, Roger de la Lee, as their new prior, and sent messengers to the archbishop's residence at Teynham to notify him of the fact. This brought down a sentence of excommunication, first on the group which had elected Roger de la Lee, and finally on the entire community.[55]

The monks refused to bow before the storm, and they sent a fresh appeal to Rome. It was evidently felt in some quarters that the archbishop's treatment of the chapter had been rather high-handed, for when he raised the subject at a synod convened by the legate in March 1239, he was unable to carry two of his suffragans – the bishops of Chichester and Rochester – with him. Cardinal Otto made an effort to bring about a reconciliation and sent the archbishop-elect of Armagh, Albert of Cologne, to Canterbury to negotiate with the monks. But this intervention came to nothing. The futile dispute dragged on. People were required to shun the company of excommunicates, who became 'untouchable', and Edmund's sentence left the monks of Canterbury isolated and their cathedral interdicted to the public. The town also suffered a crippling loss from the cessation of the pilgrim traffic attracted by the shrine of St Thomas the martyr. The conflict was not to be terminated until after Edmund's death. Underlying the

54. Gervase, ii, p. 165.
55. *Ibid.*, ii, pp. 168–71. The archbishop's official, Master Richard de Langdon, was ordered to publish the excommunication of the chapter throughout the diocese of Canterbury on 26 April.

struggle there was a genuine conflict of interests but, as often happens, the parties drifted into war over more personal issues that were irrelevant to the main problem. In an age of secular bishops a monastic chapter was an anomaly. The irony of the situation was that in Edmund the chapter had a bishop and titular head who was a profound admirer of the monastic life.

Edmund had other problems to preoccupy him besides the rebellion of his chapter. Relations between the bishops and the king were increasingly strained by Henry's ruthless manipulation of episcopal elections. Grosseteste complained to Edmund of the use of bribery and intimidation at Hereford to induce the canons to elect the royal candidate, Peter of Aigueblanche.[56] The vacancy at Winchester caused by the death of the grandee bishop and royal minister Peter des Roches in June 1238 opened the way to a royal intervention that was causing much anxiety. Henry wanted the bishopric for another trusted counsellor, the queen's uncle, William of Savoy, one of those Provençal relatives of his wife whom he found so congenial. Already bishop-elect of Valence, and involved in the turbulent politics of northern Italy, William was less a cleric than one of those mitred barons the higher aristocracy still produced, a man whom Matthew Paris described with some justice as 'a man of blood'.[57]

Faced with unexpected resistance from the monks of the cathedral priory, the king appointed a new prior and proceeded to pack the chapter with new monastic officers who would comply with his wishes – an unheard of extension of lay intrusion into the life of a monastic establishment. But before this cynical plan could be brought to a successful conclusion, it was aborted by the death of William of Savoy on 1 November 1239. He died at Viterbo, where he was presumably waiting on the papal Curia for his confirmation to Winchester. His initial plan having thus fallen to pieces, Henry decided to transfer his choice to Boniface of Savoy, another relative who would support the Savoyard interest.

This high-handed disregard of ecclesiastical liberties moved Edmund to make a formal protest. An assembly of the great council had been convened to meet the king at Westminster on 13 January 1240. Edmund used the occasion to ventilate the anxieties of churchmen over the king's proceedings. With the support of his suffragans and Cardinal Otto, who had also been invited, he presented the king with an itemized remonstrance. The major sources of complaint were, according to Matthew Paris, the appropriation of the goods of vacant bishoprics by agents of the Crown without subsequent restitution, and the refusal to allow free and canonical elections to vacant

56. *Epistolae*, pp. 264–6.
57. *Chron.Maj.*, iii, pp. 490–1.

sees.[58] The protest adopted the traditional protocol of placing the blame for these 'oppressions' of the Church upon 'evil counsel'; and the ritual was concluded by anathemas hurled against those unnamed persons who were guilty of such offences against the liberties of the Church, which had been guaranteed by Magna Carta.

The last days of Archbishop Edmund are wrapped in an obscurity upon which the hagiographers cast only a feeble and uncertain light. On 9 August 1240 Pope Gregory dispatched letters to all the metropolitans of the Western Church, summoning them to come with their suffragans to a council to be held at Rome the following Easter.[59] The kings of France and England were invited to send representatives. It promised to be a stormy event. The pope's primary objective was to secure the deposition of the excommunicated emperor Frederick II, and Frederick, who had gained control of much of Lombardy and the duchy of Spoleto, had made it known that his forces would deny the prelates access to Rome.

Whatever Edmund's view of the conflict between the pope and the emperor, it was unthinkable that he should disobey such a summons. He had in any case pressing reasons of his own for seeking an audience with the pope. The proctors of his rebellious chapter were at the Curia prosecuting their appeal against his sentence. He also needed the pope's support for his stance over the Winchester business – he had excommunicated the prior intruded by the king. With fish of his own to fry, he probably thought it prudent to get to the Curia early, before his business was submerged by the major concerns of the council. Unfortunately it is impossible to pinpoint the day of his departure for Rome. The Patent Rolls for the years 23 and 24 Henry III were already missing in the fourteenth century, so there is no record of his having received the usual safe-conduct. The Oseney annalist places his departure 'around the feast of All Saints' – 1 November; but the Tewkesbury annalist places it in August. The last episcopal consecration that was certainly performed by him was that of Hugh Pateshull to the bishopric of Coventry-Lichfield, which took place at Newark on 1 July 1240. A copy of the *Flores Historiarum* made at St Paul's notes that Edmund was present on 1 October, when Bishop Roger Niger consecrated St Paul's cathedral.[60] Although this is a later copy of the *Flores*, the fact that the entry was inserted by a St Paul's writer gives it a title to serious consideration. On

58. *Ibid.*, iv, p. 3.
59. Auvray, nos. 5,420–5,633. The pope reiterated the summons on 15 October, despite the emperor's declared refusal to allow the prelates through his territory. A number of bishops and abbots attempted the sea route from the south of France using Genoese transports, but were intercepted by the Pisan fleet under Frederick's instructions.
60. *Flores Historiarum*, ed. H.R. Luard (RS, 1890), ii, p. 237 & n.

this evidence we may hazard a guess that Edmund embarked in or about the third week of October. He cannot in any case have received the papal summons earlier than the last week of September.

Edmund took with him his chancellor, Richard de Wych, a number of his clerks, his chaplain, Eustace of Faversham, and a reduced corps of grooms and domestic servants. He embarked at, or near, Sandwich, and landed at Gravelines – a port chosen for its convenient access to the abbey of St Bertin, where he had rested on his previous journey to Rome. From there the party proceeded to Senlis, where they encountered the French royal court, and Edmund was graciously received by King Louis and the Queen Mother, Blanche of Castile. Continuing their journey south, the party reached Pontigny, which lay between Auxerre and Tonnerre, a few miles north of the main highway up the valley of the Yonne. In view of its associations with Canterbury, as well as its size and eminence, the abbey was a natural resting place for the archbishop. He had broken his journey there on his previous visit to Rome. For Edmund, who admired the observance of the Cistercians, the memories of Becket and Langton, who had resided there, gave the place a peculiar resonance.[61]

How long the party stayed at the abbey is a matter of conjecture. Matthew Paris says they stayed a few days. During this time, Edmund was invited to attend a meeting of the chapter and, at the request of the community he preached them a sermon.[62] He then begged for the privilege of confraternity, which was granted. This was a privilege much sought-after by devout lay people as well as by prelates. It was a form of association that made a person a participant in all the spiritual benefits of the monastery; at his death the monks would celebrate the full office of the dead for him as they did for members of their own community.

Whether Edmund planned to continue his journey after a few days of rest we cannot say. Possibly he was hoping to complete the passage of the Alps before the onset of winter made the passes too perilous. On the other hand, he must by then have heard that the Alpine passes were in the grip of the imperial forces, and he may have thought it prudent to wait until the situation in north Italy was clarified. As it was, he was taken ill after a few days at the abbey and, as his pain worsened, it was decided to turn back. His itinerary northwards suggests that he was making for Provins, and probably home. But on reaching Soisy he was too weak to go any further. It was there, under the roof of a small Augustinian priory, a cell of St Jacques de

---

61. In the Life Matthew Paris says that Edmund was assigned the house adjacent to the cloister where Becket had stayed when in exile, which gave him deep pleasure.
62. Matthew Paris appended the text of the sermon to his Life of St Edmund, printed in Lawrence, St Edmund, pp. 286–9.

Provins, that he died on 16 November. The sources do not tell us what his illness was. It was apparently an abdominal complaint, which left the clarity of his mind unimpaired. His last acts, performed only three days before his death, were to write with his own hand a letter of protection for his chaplain, Eustace,[63] and testimonials for his domestic servants.

In medieval Christianity immense importance was attributed to a man's dispositions at death. Consequently Matthew Paris gives extensive treatment to the scenario of Edmund's death, which he regarded as the triumphant consummation of the saint's heroic life. He obtained the details from Eustace of Faversham and Richard de Wych, who had both been present at the end. He records that Edmund received the sacrament of extreme unction, and that when he was brought holy communion, he startled those who were present by addressing these words to the proffered host: 'It is you, Lord, in whom I have believed, whom I have loved, about whom I have preached and taught. You are my witness that I have sought nothing on earth except you.'

---

63. Canterbury, Dean & Chapter muniments, Chartae Antiquae, D. 76; printed in Lawrence, *St Edmund*, appx D, p. 318.

8
Posthumous Glory

On the morning after Edmund's death, Master Richard, the chancellor, handed the testimonials to the servants and then broke the archbishop's seal and ordered a dispersal. He himself, together with Eustace the chaplain and the other clerks, remained to perform the obsequies. Edmund had declared it his wish to be buried at Pontigny. After the body had been embalmed, therefore, and dressed in pontificals, the clerks set off with the remains of their archbishop. The procession was the signal for one of those extraordinary outbursts of popular religious fervour that occasionally erupted and convulsed whole cities in the thirteenth century. The news that the clergy were carrying the body of a holy man spread swiftly through the surrounding villages, possibly helped by the generous alms dispensed by the archbishop on the outward journey. All along the route the procession encountered scenes of popular devotion. Some peasants who succeeded in touching the bier claimed they had received immediate and miraculous cures.

At the township of Trainel, which they reached at the end of the first day's march, they were met by the abbot of Pontigny. Here the crush of devotees became so intense and excited that the abbot began to fear for the safety of his precious freight and decided to take a strong line with the thaumaturge. Ordering the bearers to place the body in the church and excluding the crowd, he invoked the saint and commanded him in virtue of obedience (although he was an archbishop, he was a confrater of Pontigny) to desist from any further miracles until the procession reached home. Thereafter progress was better, until they reached Villeneuve-l'archêveque, where an enthusiastic crowd pushed the clerks aside and seized the bier, which they carried off and placed on the altar of the parish church. A further hazard was encountered at Coulours, where the Templars tried to lay claim to the body on the grounds that, when passing that way on his outward journey, the archbishop had expressed a wish to rest in their house. The procession, however, reached home without further mishap, and Edmund's body was interred in the abbey church on 23 November.

In these propitious circumstances no time was lost in petitioning the pope to set up an inquiry into the merits of Archbishop Edmund – the first stage in a process of canonization. The earliest dated letter of postulation was dispatched in December 1240, by the abbot of Provins, where

Edmund's entrails had been buried.[1] But the main thrust for the canonization came from Pontigny, which was in possession of the body. The Cistercian general chapter at its meeting in 1241 discussed the hopes of the Pontigny monks and in the absence of the abbot of Cîteaux, who along with other prelates travelling to Rome had been arrested by the emperor, the chapter deputed Abbot Bruno of La Ferté to write a letter of postulation to the pope.[2] The Cistercians were to be active promoters of the cause throughout its vicissitudes, and they found a willing agent at the Curia in the English Cistercian cardinal, John of Toledo.

The course of the process is described by Albert of Cologne, archbishop of Armagh, in his *History of the Canonization*.[3] As head of the papal commission of inquiry, he was able to write a first-hand account of the proceedings, and he included a selection of the letters that passed through his hands. According to Albert, it was the report of miracles at Pontigny that induced the prelates of France to assemble and draft letters petitioning for an inquiry. These letters are unfortunately undated, but an *inspeximus* or written authentication of some of them survives, and it is dated 1242. Similar letters were collected from the university of Oxford, where Edmund had taught arts and theology, and from the prelates of England. Letters are extant from Walter de Gray, archbishop of York, the bishops of Bangor, Bath, Chichester, Dunblane, Ely, Exeter and Salisbury, and the abbots of Abingdon, Eynsham, Reading and Westminster, and the prior of Merton.[4]

A textual comparison shows that, apart from those of Oxford and Merton, these letters are not entirely independent productions. The writers borrow phrases from one another freely, a fact indicating that a circular was being sent round inviting contributions. The abbots of Westminster and Eynsham, who had no personal reminiscences of their own to contribute, were content to reiterate the encomiastic statements of others. The fact that the letters were gathered in this snowball fashion gains added probability from the survival of five of them copied together in one of the cartularies of St Augustine's Canterbury.[5] All the letters sent to promote St Edmund's cause are undated with the exception of that from

1. *M.D.Thes.*, iii, col. 1897.
2. *Statuta Capitulorum Generalium Ordinis Cisterciensis*, ed. J. Canivez (Louvain, 1933–6), ii, p. 233.
3. *M.D.Thes.*, iii, cols. 1831–58, printed from the *Liber Sancti Edmundi* in the Bibliothèque d'Auxerre, MS. 123 (ancien Pontigny 165), the only known copy of Albert's work.
4. See Lawrence, *St Edmund*, pp. 15 ff.
5. BL, Add.MS. 46352, fos. 48–50ᵛ. The letters from Oxford, the bishops of Bath, Ely (the only extant text), Salisbury, and Abingdon abbey, are copied in a hand of the mid-thirteenth century. Thomas Hearne transcribed them from this manuscript into Bodleian, Rawlinson MS., B.254, fos. 86–90ᵛ.

Merton priory, which is dated 27 February 1242. The Oxford letter is addressed to Pope Gregory IX and must therefore have been written prior to the end of September 1241, when news of Gregory's death would have reached England. With this in view, we can safely place all the English letters between the summer of 1241 and the early months of 1242.

From an early period, the cultus of a new saint was officially inaugurated by a solemn translation of the relics to a place in or under the altar. This was a ritual carried out by the bishop. During the twelfth century, however, it was becoming increasingly common to seek a canonization by means of a solemn papal judgement. This prepared the way for the reservation to Rome of the exclusive right to declare somebody a saint, which was firmly established during the first decades of the thirteenth century.[6] It has been shown that the formal reservation of this right to the papacy was pronounced in the decretal *Audivimus* of Alexander III (1159–81), which became widely known through its inclusion in an official collection of canon law in the time of Innocent III (1198–1216). In this process of centralization England played an important part. Edward the Confessor was the first English saint whose canonization by the pope can be established with certainty. This was accomplished in 1161 in response to enthusiastic promotion by King Henry II and Westminster abbey. Thereafter, for England at least, the Apostolic See was the only official source of canonization, and episcopal canonization may be said to have lapsed.

With the growth of papal control came the establishment of the papal process. By the time of Urban II the commission of inquiry was regarded as a regular preliminary to canonization. An embarrassing flood of petitions in the century that followed necessitated more discrimination and a more careful formulation of procedure.[7] The evolution of procedure can be traced from the surviving records of a number of causes that were submitted to Rome between 1200 and 1240.[8] In this line of development Innocent III stands out, as the pope with the sharp legal mind who defined the conditions that a candidate for canonization must satisfy, and who imposed stricter rules of evidence. Those who wanted to promote a person for enrolment in the catalogue of the saints must establish two facts: that he had lived a life of heroic virtue, and that his intercession had caused miracles to be performed

6. E.W. Kemp, *Canonization and Authority in the Western Church* (1948); the official history of canonization is that of Benedict XIV, *De Servorum Dei Beatificatione et Beatorum Canonizatione* (Bologna, 1734–8). A modern conspectus of the subject will be found in A. Vauchez, *La sainteté en occident aux derniers siècles du moyen-âge* (Ecole Française, Rome, 1981).
7. On the development of the process, see the evidence reviewed by L. Hertling, 'Materiali per la storia del processo di Canonizzazione': *Gregorianum*, xvi (Rome, 1935), pp. 170–95.
8. See the notes on processes conducted between 1218 and 1240 by M.Bihl, 'De canonizatione Sancti Francesci'; *Archivum Franciscanum Historicum*, xxi (1928).

after his death. Neither one would serve without the other.[9] At the same time, Innocent demanded a more rigorous scrutiny of the evidence.

The written testimonials of an earlier age were no longer regarded as adequate. In 1201 the promoters of the cause of St Gilbert of Sempringham had their dossier set aside. They were told that instead of sending reports of miracles supplied at second-hand by prelates, they must take down directly the depositions made by witnesses under oath. There was to be no writing up of the evidence. Moreover selected witnesses were to be dispatched to the papal Curia to give their testimony to the pope in person.[10] This insistence on recording the actual words of the witnesses is reflected in the preface to the Miracles of St Laurence of Dublin, who was canonized by Honorius III in 1225. The writer states that he is reproducing evidence given at the inquiry, and that the inquisitors had transmitted to the Curia the simple unvarnished speech of the witnesses.[11]

The growing rigour of the rules of evidence is shown by the care taken to authenticate alleged cures by obtaining the opinion of the neighbourhood. In the course of the inquiry into the miracles of St Gilbert, a subsidiary commission visited the parishes where one of the witnesses, Ralph of Attenborough, had resided, to obtain evidence of his previous illness.[12] The commission inquiring into the case of St Hugh of Lincoln 1219, presided over by Stephen Langton, sent sub-commissioners to the villages of Cheshunt and Alconbury to take evidence of miraculous cures.[13] A further development, designed to ensure a searching investigation, was the sending of a questionnaire along with the rescript appointing the commissioners. When directing an inquiry into the life and miracles of John Buoni of Mantua in 1251, the pope added a short formulary for the use of the commissioners: they were to ask witnesses 'how they know; at what time, which month, which day; who was present; at what place; whose was the invocation; what words were used, etc'. These questions were to be put for each item or article of the inquiry.[14] The articles of inquiry were an obvious device for keeping garrulous witnesses to the point.

9. As stated in the act canonizing the Empress Kunegunde in 1200: 'two things are necessary for one to be held a saint by men in the Church Militant: the *virtus* of conduct and the *virtus* of signs, namely merits and miracles; for merits do not fully suffice without miracles, nor miracles without merits': G. Fontanini, *Codex Constitutionum quas Summi Pontifices ediderunt in solemni canonizatione Sanctorum* (Rome, 1792), pp. 37–8. Similar words were used in the act canonizing St Homobonus of Cremona: *ibid.*, p. 34.
10. R. Foreville, *Le livre de Saint Gilbert de Sempringham* (Paris, 1943), pp. xxxv–xli.
11. 'Vie et miracles de S. Laurent': *Analecta Bollandiana*, xxxiii (1914), pp. 129 ff.
12. Foreville, *op. cit.*, pp. 65–7.
13. D.H. Farmer, 'The cult and canonization of St Hugh' in *St Hugh of Lincoln*, ed. H. Mayr-Harting (1987), pp. 75–86.
14. *AA.SS.*, October, IX, 768 ff.

The thirteenth-century popes insisted on evidence of a candidate's *mores* as well as evidence of miracles because, as the canonists explained, the Devil could work miracles, a fact that could be plainly seen from the feats of Simon Magus and Moses' daughter.[15] On the other hand, miracles could not be dispensed with, for it was possible to be deceived about a man's life. Miracles provided the divine seal of authenticity, without which an apparently exemplary life might be a façade concealing sin and secret indulgence. In consequence the evidence bearing on the life of the candidate for sainthood was gradually subjected to the same critical scrutiny as that for miracles. It is possible to discern a marked advance in criticism between the process of St Hugh of Lincoln in 1219 and that of St Dominic in 1233. In the former case, the critical attention of the commissioners seems to have been focused wholly on miracles, and a short summary of the saint's life was placed at the head of the report. The depositions taken in the process of St Dominic, on the other hand, show the witnesses of the saint's virtue were being as closely controlled as the witnesses of miracles. The pressure of the questioners is often evident. The fact that most of the depositions make identical points in the same order strongly suggests that the commissioners were following a list of *capitula* or articles submitted by the promoters.[16] The documents of this process are of special interest because of its nearness in time to that of St Edmund.

During the forty years preceding the cause of St Edmund, the procedure of the papal inquiry was acquiring a common form and the rules of evidence were becoming increasingly rigorous. It was no uncommon thing during this period for the report of a first inquiry to be set aside on grounds of inadequacy or irregularity. In this respect the process of St Edmund, with its checks and repeated demands for further evidence, may be regarded as a typical one. The claim of Albert of Armagh, the president of the commission, that few saints since St Peter had been subjected to such an intensive scrutiny before elevation to the altars,[17] was a rhetorical self-advertisement rather than an exact statement of fact.

The process of St Edmund may be said to have begun with a preliminary inquiry into *fama*, meaning fame or common opinion, made by Bernard de Sully, bishop of Auxerre, in whose diocese Pontigny lay. He made this

15. Thus Bernard of Parma, *Glossa Ordinaria in Decretales* (Venice, 1504), fo. 122; cf. Innocent IV, *super libros quinque Decretalium* (Frankfurt, 1570), in lib. iii, titulus xlv.
16. *Acta Canonizationis S. Dominici*, ed. A. Walz: *Monumenta Ordinis Fratrum Praedicatorum Historica*, xvi (1935). Hostiensis, commenting on the decretal *Venerabili fratre*, lays down rules that commissioners must follow in interrogating witnesses to a man's sanctity of life: *Summa Aurea Henrici Cardinalis Hostiensis* (Lyons, 1548), fo. 188.
17. *M.D.Thes.*, iii, cols. 1833, 1851.

inquiry on his own initiative and reported his findings to the pope.[18] It was not unusual for an interval to elapse between the postulations and the setting up of a papal inquiry. In this case, delay was made inevitable by the vacancy of the Apostolic See. Gregory IX had died on 21 August 1241. Frederick II's stranglehold on the countryside round Rome, and the fact that he was holding two members of the college of cardinals in captivity, prolonged the vacancy for eighteen months. At length the cardinals assembled at Anagni, and on 25 June 1243 elected the canonist Sinibaldo Fieschi, who took the title of Pope Innocent IV. The new pope issued mandates for an inquiry into the case of St Edmund on 23 April 1244.

Two commissions were appointed, one in France consisting of Albert, archbishop of Armagh, the bishop of Senlis, and the dean of Paris,[19] and one in England consisting of the bishops of London and Lincoln.[20] The letters repeated the formulas used by Innocent III in defining the marks of sanctity, and request the commissioners to send to the Curia not only depositions but also four, or three, or at least two witnesses, who have been the subject of allegedly miraculous cures. In the absence of the bishop of Senlis, Archbishop Albert and the dean of Paris proceeded to Pontigny abbey, where they opened the inquiry on 17 July 1244.[21] The brief narrative of the opening procedure indicates that the commission followed a formulary supplied by the pope. Witnesses were summoned through their bishops, and depositions were taken which were dispatched under the seals of the commissioners to the pope. The same was done by the English commissioners, Fulk Basset and Grosseteste.[22] According to Albert, a number of witnesses were sent to the pope together with the dossier of this inquiry.

Innocent's response was cautious. He apparently found the dossier too prolix and the miracles insufficiently attested. Another inquiry was ordered in France, again under the presidency of Archbishop Albert, and in England under Edmund's former chancellor, Richard de Wych, who was now bishop of Chichester, assisted by the prior of Canon's Ashby and the Dominican theologian Robert Bacon. The new French commission submitted its returns in May 1245, but those from England were not dispatched until November.[23] The replies show the commissioners attempting to meet the pope's demand for good evidence of only four or five miracles, the essential

18. *Ibid.*, iii, col. 1837.
19. Berger, no. 622.
20. *Ibid.*, no. 619.
21. *M.D.Thes.*, iii, col. 1902.
22. The reply from England, undated, is Sens Cathedral muniment, no. 21.
23. Sens Cathedral muniments, nos. 23, 25; *M.D.Thes.*, iii, col. 1845, 1913–14, where, however, the reply from the English commission is undated.

thing being several witnesses in each case. Neither reply makes any mention of sending witnesses to the Curia. In neither case does the dossier of testimonies attached to these replies survive.

The only record of these proceedings that survives in its original form is the fragment of a procès-verbal, which now belongs to the Trésor of Sens cathedral.[24] It is a parchment roll of six membranes on which are recorded the statements made by a number of Burgundian peasants who claimed to have experienced miraculous cures at the tomb of St Edmund. The haste of the heavily abbreviated writing and the rather chaotic deletions and insertions show that the document is the original draft taken down by the notary as the inquiry was going on. Although the roll is an undated fragment, having neither beginning nor end, it is evidently a record of the first inquiry held at Pontigny in the summer of 1244. The character of the entries may be judged from that relating to one Bernard of Perrons, who produced three witnesses to support his statement:

> Bernard Perrons, being sworn and interrogated, said that while he was in a field minding four oxen, he felt a stabbing pain in the back. Feeling no further pain, he returned home, but then began to feel pain in his back. He followed his oxen, however, for eight days, and he then began to use a staff, and for fifteen days he was unable to walk without it. After this he took to his bed. He was unable to leave his bed without two crutches. Without them he could neither stand nor walk. He was in this condition for nearly a year. At the end of that year, about Easter, having confessed his sins, he made a vow to Saint Edmund and he then began to get better. So on the day of Pentecost, he set off after lunch to make the journey to the saint, and on the morrow he entered the monastery in which Saint Edmund was buried. And when he was praying at the tomb and while Vespers were being sung, he raised himself without the crutches, and he discarded them there and proceeded to walk through the monastery without any support. On the morrow he walked from the said monastery to the vill of Perrons, which is eleven leagues away, in a single day.

Whether or not Bernard's osteopathic cure was assisted by the intercession of St Edmund, his statement will command the sympathy of all who suffer from a chronic back-condition.

Besides evidence of miracles, the papal commissions had to submit evidence of the saint's virtuous life. A sole relic of this part of the inquiry is the

24. Sens Cathedral muniment, no. 26.

document referred to as the *Quadrilogus*.[25] This is a copy of the depositions made by four witnesses, of whom one had been a close acquaintance of Edmund's, and the other three had been members of his household. These were Richard of Dunstable, prior of the Dominican house at Oxford, Stephen, a subdeacon, and Robert, formerly a canon regular but now a Cistercian postulant, both former chamberlains of the archbishop, and Eustace, the monk of Christ Church, who was the archbishop's chaplain and his earliest biographer. Richard of Dunstable's statement is not in fact oral testimony; it is a letter, written from the Dominican priory at Paris and collected by Robert of Asthall, a clerk of earl Richard of Cornwall. Evidently it was dispatched at the request of the English commission of inquiry. The fact that the letter was carried and attested by Robert of Asthall indicates that Richard of Cornwall, the king's brother, was actively pressing for the canonization of St Edmund. This is in accord with the earl's subsequent devotion to St Edmund, and gives added probability to the assertion of Matthew Parish that Earl Richard was bitterly disappointed because he could not be present at the saint's translation.[26]

The dossiers compiled by the second inquiries reached the pope at Lyons, where the Curia was then residing, safely outside the emperor's clutches. The task of examining them was delegated to a committee of seven wise men, consisting of three cardinals, Hugh of S. Sabina, John of the title of S. Lorenzo in Lucina, and William of the title of The Twelve Apostles. Cardinal Hugh was the distinguished Dominican theologian Hugh of St Cher, and Cardinal John was the English Cistercian scholar John of Toledo. The other four members of the committee were Grosseteste, the bishop of Lincoln, Fulk Basset, the bishop of London, the canonist Vincentius Hispanus, and the famous English theologian Master Alexander of Hales. It was an impressive panel. Three of its members were among the most distinguished and productive theologians of their generation.

The report of the committee was favourable, but Pope Innocent was still unwilling to pronounce sentence. Albert voices a suspicion that the pope's delay was prompted by the opposition of the English court and the church of Canterbury. Although this is not improbable, the chief reason for the delay seems to have been the healthy scepticism of the Curia in face of this plethora of miracles. It was objected that witnesses who had been the subject of cures had not been presented for inspection at the right time. At this point, Cardinal John took the initiative and sent to France and England to procure witnesses. The bearer of this commission was Eustace of Faversham, 'the sole faithful Achates who', according to Albert of Armagh, carried the major burden of the

25. Printed in Lawrence, *St Edmund*, pp. 187–202.
26. *Chron.Maj.*, iv, p. 632. Richard made a visit to the shrine at Pontigny later in 1247: *ibid.*, iv, pp. 646–7.

business. He was sent with letters to the bishop of Lincoln, the abbot of Bayham and Archdeacon Simon Langton,[27] requesting the production of two or three persons who had been the subject of cures, together with suitable witnesses. The letters are dated at Lyons on 9 April 1246. Langton's replay and report is dated 6 June 1246. It throws an interesting light on the background and the problems that beset a papal inquiry.

Langton found his commission difficult to execute. On receiving the letters, he set off with Eustace for the district where the necessary proof could be obtained. This involved a journey of six days from Canterbury. On their arrival, the necessary witnesses were presented to them by the local parish clergy, and the whole neighbourhood supported their testimony to St Edmund's miracles. But when Langton urged a number of them to undertake the journey to the Curia at Lyons, there was an ugly scene, and anti-clerical sentiments were expressed in very strong language. Even the offer to pay expenses failed to overcome 'the effective excuses and canonical impediments' which the people raised against making the journey. It was no light matter for a peasant farmer to be absent from his tenement when harvest time was approaching, and the witnesses were not surprisingly angered by this example of clerical insouciance. In the end, a small but, it was hoped, convincing party of witnesses was cajoled into going.[28]

On their arrival at Lyons, the witnesses were summoned to the houses of the individual cardinals and examined, and finally they were examined in the pope's presence. This closed the inquiry. In face of the accumulated evidence, canonization could not be delayed much longer. On Sunday, 16 December 1246, a full consistory met in Lyons cathedral. Cardinal Hugh of S. Sabina delivered an address on the merits of the saint and the miracles performed at his intercession. He observed that the pope had taken counsel of the cardinals on the previous Saturday, and that they had urged him to delay no longer.[29] After the cardinal had finished his allocution, the pope pronounced sentence and declared Saint Edmund to be enrolled in the catalogue of the saints. The bull *Novum matris ecclesie*, in which his sentence was promulgated, was issued on 11 January 1247.[30] It commanded the bishops of the universal Church to

27. *M.D. Thes.*, iii, col. 1912, 1914; Sens Cathedral muniments, nos. 27–9.
28. Sens Cathedral muniment, no. 29. *M.D. Thes.*, iii, col. 1914.
29. On the two public consistories preceding canonization, as well as the committee deputed to examine the report, cf. the early fourteenth-century procedure in *Ordo Romanus XIV*: Mabillon, *Museum Italicum* II (1689), pp. 418–24. On the part played by the cardinals in the process see J.B. Sägmüller, *Die Tätigkeit und Stellung der Kardinäle bis Papst Bonifaz VIII* (Freiburg, 1896), pp. 49–51.
30. *Bullarium Romanum* (Turin, 1858), iii, 522. Copies of the bull addressed to the church of Lyons and to the English baronage are in the Sens muniments, nos. 31, 32. See the translation of the copy which Matthew Paris attached to the Life, below pp. 163–6.

celebrate St Edmund's feast annually on 16 November, the day of his death, and offered an indulgence of a year and forty days to those who, being confessed and truly penitent, visited his tomb on that day.

The apotheosis of a new saint was not completed until his remains had been translated from his grave to a special place of honour, where the faithful could come to venerate them. St Edmund's translation was carried out at Pontigny on Sunday 9 June 1247. It was a splendid event attended by King Louis, the Queen Mother, Blanche of Castile, and the princes of the blood, as well as two cardinals and a galaxy of French prelates. The English hierarchy was suitably represented by Edmund's old friend and former chancellor, Master Richard de Wych, now bishop of Chichester. He described the event in a letter to Reginald, the abbot of Bayham, who had served with him in the archbishop's administration.[31] Richard was one of a small coterie of men who had been present at the opening of Edmund's tomb the evening before the public ceremony. He was deeply moved to find his master's body intact and incorrupt and the face shining, and he tenderly combed and composed the hair on the familiar head. He understood the balm with which the face was still glistening to signify the grace that had been manifested in Edmund's life and teaching, 'for in lecturing, disputation, preaching or teaching, grace cascaded from his lips'.

The canonization and the reports of miracles aroused widespread interest and attracted to Pontigny a swelling stream of pilgrims from England and France. A second translation was made on 9 June 1249, exactly a year after the first, in order to transfer St Edmund's body from its plain stone sarcophagus to a new and more sumptuous shrine. Henry III sent a chasuble of white samite and a chalice for the first celebration of the feast, and allocated twenty marks annually from the farm of Canterbury to maintain four candles burning perpetually round the shrine. In November 1254 he made a personal pilgrimage to Pontigny, on his way back from Gascony. The popularity of the Pontigny pilgrimage among the English was reflected by a special privilege granted by Pope Alexander IV on 13 April 1255, authorizing English women to enter the abbey precinct on the feast of the translation, notwithstanding the prohibition of the Cistercian statutes. The flow of English pilgrims seems, however, to have dwindled towards the end of the thirteenth century and to have been virtually brought to an end by the outbreak of hostilities between England and France. Its renewal is one of the most remarkable religious phenomena of the late twentieth century.

31. Below, pp. 166–7.

Part II: Matthew Paris and the Life of St Edmund

9

Matthew Paris, Biographer of St Edmund

Matthew Paris was the greatest chronicler of thirteenth-century England. Yet we know surprisingly little about his own life history – nothing, in fact, other than the little he tells us himself. The name he used, 'Parisiensis', was not unknown as a patronymic in England, and everything about him, his style and his attitudes, not least his fierce chauvinism, indicate that he was of English birth.[1] He took the Benedictine habit at St Albans in January 1217 and, save for a year's absence in Norway where he was sent to sort out the affairs of the abbey of St Benet Holm, his entire life was spent in the cloister of St Albans. An entry in the Great Chronicle makes it apparent that he died in 1259. One of his brethren enlivened his obituary notice with a painting of him on his death-bed, with his chronicle propped up beside him, his inert hand holding the quill, which is still resting on the parchment.

Matthew's greatest literary work, the *Chronica Majora* or Great Chronicle of St Albans, was the continuation of a large-scale narrative history begun by his predecessor, Roger of Wendover. Wendover, who was apparently the first of the St Albans school of historical writers, called his work the *Flores Historiarum*. It was an ambitious project, extending from Creation to his own lifetime. For the later years of King John and the first nineteen year of Henry III's reign, it was a contemporary and original narrative of public events. Matthew Paris took up the narrative after Wendover's death in 1235, and continued writing an account of his own times until he died twenty-four years later. But Matthew fancied his own talents as a stylist – his Latin is vivid, racy and always readable – and felt he could improve on Wendover's more sober prose. So before continuing his predecessor's work,

---

1. See R. Vaughan, *Matthew Paris* (1958), pp. 1–20: the best account of Matthew's life and work.

he recopied the entire text, as he did so interlarding it at various points with amplifications and comments of his own.

St Albans abbey, which was a day's journey on the great road to the North from London and the palace of Westminster, was well placed to be an emporium of news. It had a large guest-house, with stabling for three hundred horses,[2] providing for a constant stream of visitors which included magnates and royal ministers and even, on several occasions, the king himself. This brought Matthew a steady flow of information about events and ensured in turn that his history of the times received wide publicity. On one of King Henry's visits, in March 1257, Matthew was invited to the king's table. Henry asked about the progress of his chronicle, suggested matters that deserved to be inserted, including the election of his brother, Richard of Cornwall, to the Empire, and for Matthew's benefit he listed the imperial electors.[3] Ten years before, when the king was seated in Westminster abbey during the solemn reception of a relic of the Precious Blood, he had Matthew sit on the step beside the throne and told him to record every detail of the event in his history.[4]

With the years, royal patronage and the growth of public recognition had their impact upon Matthew. Men of note sought him out to provide information. He designed a shorter history, abridged from the Great Chronicle, covering the years 1066 to 1253, suitable for circulation outside the cloister, in which he toned down some of his more excoriating comments on public figures. He began this shorter expurgated version, called the *Historia Anglorum*, in 1250. His autograph manuscripts of the Great Chronicle, now in Corpus Christi College Cambridge and the British Library,[5] contain marginal notes in his own hand indicating items to be omitted from the *Historia Anglorum*, in several cases because they would give offence to the king or the pope.

Although he was eager to get his facts right and was an enthusiast for collecting documents, Matthew was no merely pedestrian annalist. He was a rumbustious commentator on the events of his time; and when he came to write up his record of the year's happenings for his chronicle, he aired his personal convictions and prejudices with the freedom of a confidential diarist rather than the circumspection of an official historian. As a monk, he was intensely proud of his order and of his ancient abbey, whose aristocratic traditions he celebrated by writing a history of its abbots. He disparaged

2. *Chron.Maj.*, v, p. 344.
3. *Ibid.*, iv, pp. 617–18.
4. *Ibid.*, iv, pp. 640–44.
5. Corpus Christi College Cambridge, MSS. 16 and 26; BL, Royal MS. 14, C VII. On the handwriting of Matthew Paris and the inter-relationship of these text, see Vaughan, pp. 35–77.

other and newer monastic orders. Although he wrote about St Francis of Assisi with reverence, he was an unashamed hater of the friars, and voiced the mistrust and jealousy felt by both monks and secular clergy over the immense social success enjoyed by these newcomers on the ecclesiastical scene. Where the interests of monks were involved, whether in conflict with their bishop or in dispute with other landowners, he is fiercely partisan.

The internationalism of the medieval Church and scholastic culture can present a misleading picture of European society. It may have mitigated, but certainly did not eliminate national consciousness. In this, as in much else, Matthew voices the prejudices of the common man. He is intensely chauvinistic and insular in his sympathies. He bitterly laments the loss of the Angevin territories in France, so that the English kingdom had been 'deprived and mutilated through the cowardice and falseness of her kings'.[6] King Henry's failure to recover the lost continental empire of his father and grandfather was the primary reason for Matthew's increasing contempt for Henry's person. He mistrusts and dislikes all foreigners, but his xenophobia is at its most intense when he writes of the king's Poitevin relatives and the Savoyard relatives of the queen, who were admitted to the king's council and, in some instances, promoted to English bishoprics.

Matthew's notion of the state is simple and anthropomorphic. He regards the king as the father of his people and the protector of their rights and privileges, but his role is a secular one. Although he has been anointed by the Lord to protect the Church, the king is a layman. He usurps the role of the sacerdotal order by imposing his will in the election of bishops and by haranguing monks in chapter. Matthew is consistently hostile to the king's ecclesiastical patronage and to the exercise of regalian rights over the properties of the Church. The virtues he most appreciates in a king are those traditionally associated with lordship: military prowess and leadership in war, lavish hospitality and the generous giving of gifts.

Though he is opposed to all forms of taxation and constantly decries royal demands for subsidies, he heartily approves of expenditure on the court and the upkeep of royal pomp. He lovingly describes the splendid banquet thrown by King Henry for the marriage of his daughter, Margaret, to Alexander III of Scotland in 1252 – more than a thousand knights clad in silk, and the consumption of more than sixty oxen at a sitting. Similarly, the banquet of Henry and Louis IX held at the Old Temple at Paris is given the full treatment: it cost, he claims, £1,000 parisis, not counting the gifts. This for Matthew was a royal way to spend money: 'the king's honour and England's were much enhanced.'[7] Conversely, he records with

6. *Chron.Maj.*, v, p. 278.
7. *Ibid.*, v, pp. 478–82.

disgust the retrenchment of court expenditure in 1250, observing, rather surprisingly, that it was a deplorable departure from his father's footsteps.

Matthew had several acquaintances in the royal administration, like Alexander Swereford, a baron of the Exchequer, who supplied him with information and gave him access to some of the documents he inserted in his chronicle. Nevertheless, he had scant regard for bureaucracy and little understanding of the principles or techniques of government. His notions of public finance were those of a more primitive economy, in which the king was expected to fund political and military activities from the income of his own demesne. He did not accept the notion of taxation as a charge upon the property of the subject for services rendered by the state. He regarded the taxation of property, which was becoming increasingly common in the thirteenth century, as a tyrannical invasion of the subject's rights. The taxation of the incomes of the clergy was equally obnoxious, whether it was levied by the king or the pope. He was equally hostile to the agents of bureaucratic government, whether they came from Westminster or the papal Curia. In the latter case, they incurred the added odium, in Matthew's eyes, of being foreigners – usually Italians.

This did not mean, of course, that Matthew was in any sense 'anti-papal'. Like all Western Christians of his age, he accepted the fact that the pope was the head of the universal Church, of which England constituted two provinces. The pope was for him the 'Apostolicus' – the divinely chosen successor of St Peter. He was the holy father, the 'universal ordinary' – everyman's bishop, to whose tribunal all men, even the humblest clerk or layman, might have immediate access. By the thirteenth century, the doctrine of the pope's universal spiritual jurisdiction had brought an ever growing flood of petitioners to Rome and it had materialized in a large and complex structure of central government. But the benefits of ecclesiastical government cost money no less than those provided by the state. This was a truism that men of the twelfth and thirteenth centuries were reluctant to accept. The venality of the papal Curia was a favourite butt for medieval critics. It was in the thirteenth century that the vitriolic satire called *The Holy Gospel according to the Mark of Silver* was refurbished to include the activities of the cardinals. Matthew was not alone in his dislike for the financial expedients adopted by the papacy to fund the Curia, such as the taxation of the clergy and the use of papal provisions to provide members of the Curia with English benefices.

These political and ecclesiastical attitudes, which colour all Matthew's historical writings, are just as evident in his hagiographical works, and we shall find them in his Life of St Edmund. They are the trademark of his literary identity.

Hagiography was a recognized province of the medieval historiographer: the cultus of the saints was a theme that called for his best efforts. The saint stood at the apex of the historical process – an individual fulfilment of the divine plan of redemption and renewal. Matthew worked as assiduously in this field as he did in the writing of general history. More than a century later, looking back with pride over the literary and artistic achievements at St Albans, Thomas of Walsingham wrote of Matthew's contribution to the fame of his abbey: 'he enlarged as was necessary the chronicles of the said Roger [i.e. Wendover], and he wrote and elegantly painted Lives of Saints Alban and Amphibalus, Thomas and Edmund, the archbishops of Canterbury, and furnished many books for the church.'[8] Matthew, as Walsingham observed, was also an artist. He was a superb draughtsman, and the margins of his chronicles are enlivened with many delicately tinted drawings. His Lives of St Alban and St Edward, with half-page illustrations, are virtually picture-books.[9]

Modern research has been able to extend Walsingham's list of Matthew's writings by identifying two more of his hagiographical works – the Lives of Edward the Confessor and Stephen Langton. His Life of Saints Alban and Amphibalus is written in Anglo-Norman verse and is a translation of an earlier Latin prose passion by William, another monk of St Albans. His Life of the Confessor, similarly, is an Anglo-Norman metrical translation of the Latin Life composed by Ailred of Rievaulx in 1163 to celebrate the translation of Edward's remains. Both of these French Lives have long since been published,[10] but in each case the task of ascribing them to their actual author was left to Montague Rhodes James.[11] It was also James who identified Matthew's Life of St Thomas Becket with the fragments of an Anglo-Norman metrical Life which Paul Meyer published from a manuscript at Courtrai.[12] This too was a translation of a Latin original – in this case the twelfth-century compilation of Becket's Lives called the *Quadrilogus*.[13]

The Life of Stephen Langton was written by Matthew in Latin, and it

8. *Annales Amundesham*, ed. H.T. Riley (RS, 1870–1), ii, p. 303.
9. On the attribution of these illustrations, see Vaughan, pp. 205–34, who considers the illustrations to the Life of St Alban to be Matthew's work, but that those for the Life of the Confessor are probably the work not of Matthew but of a pupil.
10. *Vie de Seint Auban*, ed. R. Atkinson (1876); *The Lives of Edward the Confessor*, ed. H.R. Luard (RS, 1858), pp. 1–157.
11. M.R. James, *La Estoire de Seint Aedward le rei* (Roxburgh Club, 1920), and M.R. James, E.F. Jacob and W.R.L. Lowe, *Illustrations to the Life of St Alban* (1924). For a discussion of the French metrical Lives from a philological standpoint see Dominica Legge, *Anglo-Norman in the Cloisters* (1950), pp. 20–31.
12. *Fragments d'une vie de Saint Thomas de Cantorbery* (Société des Anciens Textes Français, 1885), with facsimiles. Matthew's references to a Life of St Thomas in the Great Chronicle appear to refer to a different text, possibly one written by himself, see Lawrence, *St Edmund* pp. 72–3.
13. *Ibid.*, p. 71.

survives only in fragments which were edited by Liebermann.[14] The two fragments, which are in different manuscripts of the Cottonian collection, are in fact two halves of what was originally a single folio, so that when fitted together, they form a short but continuous narrative covering the period of Langton's life from 1215 to 1220.[15] The piece is written in Matthew's own handwriting,[16] with the marginal headings and after-thoughts that are a familiar feature of his manuscripts.

Finally, there is our Life of St Edmund, which Matthew wrote in Latin in the first place, and then translated into French verse. Both versions survive and have long since been identified. The original version is of particular interest, since it is the only complete Latin hagiographical work we have from the pen of the man who was the greatest historical writer of thirteenth-century England. Besides the passage of Walsingham's already quoted, there are several references to the Life of St Edmund in the writings of At Albans. In three places Matthew mentions it himself. It will be enough to quote the notice he inserted in the Great Chronicle under the year 1253, in connection with the death of Richard de Wych. It is as follows:

> Informed by his [i.e. Richard de Wych's] declarations and also by those of friar Master Robert Bacun of the Order of Preachers, Dom Matthew Paris, monk of the church of St Alban, has written the Life of the aforementioned Saint Edmund, having diligently set in order what he learned, without reason to doubt, from those worthy of trust. Whoever wishes to see this can find it in the church of St Alban.[17]

It will be noticed that the passage refers to the existence of one Life only, that written by Matthew Paris himself. He says he used the information supplied by Richard de Wych and Robert Bacon. There is no suggestion that either of these informants ever composed a biography of St Edmund. The point needs to be emphasized as some modern authors have been over-eager to attach the names of Edmund's *familiares* to one or another of the other Lives of St Edmund.

Matthew's Life, long unrecognized, was thought to be lost until A.T.

---

14. F. Liebermann, *Ungedruckte Anglo-Normannische Geschichtsquellen* (Strasburg, 1879), pp. 319–29.

15. Thus BL, Cotton MS., Vesp. B XIII, fo. 133 fits on to the bottom of Cotton MS., Nero D I, fo. 197. The suggestion of J.C. Russell in *Dictionary of Writers of Thirteenth Century England*, p. 83, that Matthew's life of St Thomas is to be found in Vesp. B XIII is based on a misunderstanding. The manuscript contains no Life of Becket.

16. Vaughan, p. 159.

17. *Chron.Maj.*, v, p. 369. The Life is referred to in the same terms in *Hist.Angl.*, iii, pp. 13 and 135.

Baker published the French metrical version of it which he discovered in the famous Welbeck Abbey Legendary.[18] Baker was able to show that the French Life was the work of Matthew Paris and that he was translating a Latin work of his own. He correctly identified this Latin version with the Life contained in the Cotton MS., Julius D VI.[19] This is small volume of 184 folios. Like most of Sir Robert Cotton's collection, it is a composite book made up of pieces from various places brought together under one cover by him or his librarian. It contains two Lives of St Edmund, that by Eustace (fos. 161v–78v) and that by Matthew Paris (fos. 123–51v), but there is no resemblance between the hands in which they are written, nor is there anything to show their place of origin. Matthew's Life is copied in single column in a very distinctive round book-hand of the early fourteenth century. The titles in the text are rubricated and the capitals are illuminated with calligraphic decoration.

Although the Life of the Julius manuscript contains much conventional hagiographical matter, it is unique in the amount of information it supplies about Edmund's public life and in the animus that the author displays against the papal legate, Cardinal Otto, and the royal court. This enabled Baker to identify it without difficulty as the source of the Anglo-Norman metrical Life. The French is often a close, sometimes literal translation of the Latin. In the French version, however, there are indications of the author's identity which are wanting in the Latin. Thus the author of the metrical Life names himself as Matthew:

> *La dareine enselée lettre*
> *Faz ge Maheu en livre mettre*[20]

He dedicates his book to Isabella de Fortibus, countess of Arundel, patroness of Wymondham priory, which was a cell of St Albans. What is more, in the Envoi the writer states that he has written the Life in two languages:

> *Et ke chescun en seit plus sages*
> *Escritel'ay en deux langages*[21]

and that he has translated his Latin version into romance especially for the benefit of the countess.

---

18. 'La Vie de S. Edmond' in *Romania*, lv (1920), pp. 332–81.
19. The text was published by Wallace, pp. 543–88, but he failed to identify Matthew's authorship and attributed it wrongly to Edmund's chaplain, Eustace.
20. 'The last sealed letter I, Matthew, inserted in the book': *Romania*, lv (1929), 1691.
21. 'and that each person may be the wiser for it, I have written it in two languages': *ibid.*, 1975.

As it happens, the fondness of the countess for works of hagiography and her friendship with Matthew Paris are attested by another source. A note on the fly-leaf of a St Albans manuscript now in the library of Trinity College Dublin, and written in Matthew's own hand, requests her to pass on his Lives of St Thomas and Saint Edward which he had translated and illustrated and which she had borrowed.[22]

A comparison of the French and Latin Lives shows that the French follows the content of the Latin text closely, omitting only the deposition of Robert Bacon, the testimony of Archbishop Walter de Gray and a number of other documents that did not lend themselves to reproduction in the form of octosyllabic rhyming couplets. Thus the text of Edmund's last letter in favour of Robert of Essex, referred to in the couplet quoted above, is omitted from the French version but is to be found, as Matthew says, at this point in the Latin Life.[23]

In a few points of detail the French supplements the Latin text. Thus, for example, the French tells us that during his period of regency at Oxford Edmund received a benefice from the archbishop of York, but that he resigned all and gave his patrimony also to the hospital of Abingdon:

> *E tut sun patrimonie done*
> *a l'hospital de Abinedone.*[24]

These pieces of information are peculiar to this version, and their authenticity is established by other sources. For the statement about the presentation made by the archbishop of York is supported by an otherwise incomprehensible phrase in Archbishop Walter de Gray's letter of postulation, where he says he had promoted Edmund to a share in his pastoral 'solicitude' – that he had, in other words, appointed him to a parish in his diocese.[25] The reference to the fact that Edmund had given his patrimony to the hospital of Abingdon is a slightly syncopated record of the transaction documented in the Abingdon cartulary: he had, in fact, donated his father's house in West Street, Abingdon, to the hospital of St John the Baptist at Oxford, but it had afterwards come into the hands of the Abingdon hospital by a process of exchange.[26] Here, as in many other contexts, the evidence vindicates the superiority of Matthew's information, based, as it was, upon local knowledge and his extensive contacts outside, as well as within the monastic world.

Matthew, then, was translating into Anglo-Norman verse a Latin Life of

22. *Illustrations to the Life of St Alban, op. cit.,* pp. 15–16.
23. Below p. 154.
24. *Romania,* lv (1929), 115.
25. Text printed in Lawrence, *St Edmund* p. 302.
26. See above, p. 4.

St Edmund composed by himself. It is of this Latin Life that a translation is provided here. What were his sources of information and how much did he owe, writing some years after the canonization of his subject, to a hagiographical tradition that was already in the process of forming round the image of the saint?

In the passage of the Great Chronicle quote above, Matthew tells us he got his information from Richard de Wych and Robert Bacon, and that he had 'set in order what he had learned from those worthy of trust'. Bacon's contribution can be easily distinguished because it has been given a separate title in the text. It consists of a deposition made under oath in the course of the canonization process, describing Edmund's ascetical practices during his teaching years at Oxford, when Bacon was a pupil and later a colleague of his. In form it is similar to the four statements gathered together in the *Quadrilogus*, all of which provide personal testimonies to Edmund's manner of life. Matthew provides here the only known text of this stray fragment of the canonization process.

The only specified contribution made by Richard de Wych is the text of his letter to the abbot of Bayham, reporting the translation of St Edmund's body at Pontigny. But he was almost certainly the source for Matthew's account of the deathbed scene at Soisy, the breaking of the archbishop's seal, and the dispersal of the *familia*. It was also probably he who in part supplied the vivid first-hand description of the scenes that accompanied the funeral procession back to Pontigny.

Besides these named informants, Matthew had a literary source which he does not name, and which supplied him with a framework for his story. This was the earliest Life of St Edmund, which was composed by his chaplain, Eustace of Faversham, the monk of Christ Church Canterbury. Eustace's 'biography' of his master was a relatively short and rhetorical piece of hagiography, based largely upon the letters of postulation that had passed through his hands. He composed it in the years 1242–44, before the canonization process had ended.[27] He had no personal knowledge of Edmund's life before he became archbishop, and what little information he provides for these early years he derived from the depositions of Bacon and others. For the rest, he padded his narrative with the pious commonplaces that were the hagiographer's stock-in-trade. One of his less happy digressions was a forced comparison of Edmund with St Martin of Tours; another – one fraught with unfortunate consequences for Edmund's posthumous reputation – was an attempt to liken his master to St Thomas Becket, who had gone into exile to escape royal tyranny.[28]

27. For the problems of authorship and dating see Lawrence, *St Edmund*, pp. 30–47; for the text *ibid.*, pp. 203–21.
28. See below, appx A.

Matthew incorporated into his text almost the whole of the Eustace Life, with the exception of its opening paragraph. Thus the whole of Matthew's chapters 4 to 9 and much of chapters 10 to 13 are lifted wholesale from this source. So, too, is some of the narrative of Edmund's funeral procession, here reproduced as an eye-witness account written in the first person. He makes fairly free with his literary authority, altering a word here and inserting a phrase there to suit his fancy, rather in the way he treated the text of Wendover in the Great Chronicle. But, while preserving the order of Eustace, he makes a number of interpolations in his source, which grow in length and importance from the point where Edmund is elected to the archbishopric. Among these are a number of hagiographical anecdotes, such as the story of Edmund's boyhood encounter with the Christ Child in the meadows, possibly derived from the Anonymous 'A' Life.

Besides this additional hagiographical material, Matthew has expanded the rather jejune work of Eustace with a quantity of purely historical information and comment that is peculiar to his Life of St Edmund and that gives it its unique historical interest. Many of the details in these chapters display an exact and well-documented knowledge of English ecclesiastical affairs. Matthew knows the names of the three other candidates for the archbishopric who were rejected. He tells us the day of Edmund's consecration and who was present. He appreciates the part that the new archbishop played in the pacification of 1234 following the death of Richard the Marshal. He clearly knows, though he tries to gloss over, the discreditable conduct of the Canterbury monks, which led to the intervention of the papal legate and the deposition of the prior of Christ Church. He can name the executors of the papal absolution obtained by the monks after St Edmund's death. He gives us the text of one of the archbishop's last letters in favour of Robert of Essex, one of his servants, which is not otherwise extant. He also has some details of Edmund's family that are not to be found in any other source.

If he is well informed, Matthew also gives full rein here to his political and social prejudices. Much has been written about the 'constitutional attitude' of the St Alban's school, the pride of an ancient and privileged monastic corporation which caused its writers to align themselves almost instinctively with the critics of royal and papal government.[29] This attitude is apparent in Matthew's Life of St Edmund. The rebels, Gilbert Marshal

29. Cf. Hans Plehn, *Der politische Charakter von Matheus Parisiensis* (Staats-und socialwissenschaftliche Forschungen, xiv, Hft 2, Leipzig, 1897), pp. 44–5; and V.H. Galbraith, *Roger of Wendover and Matthew Paris* (1944), p. 6; and H.-E. Hilpert, *Kaiser-und Papstbriefe in den Chronica Majora des Matthaeus Paris* (Deutschen Historischen Instituts London, 9, Stuttgart, 1981), pp. 90–6, who argues that some of Matthew's hostility to the policies of Henry III were derived from Richard of Cornwall.

and Hubert de Burgh, are treated sympathetically as victims of official wrongdoing, though their rebellion is not condoned. The king's counsellors are the oppressors of the Church, who may be expected to foist an unworthy archbishop on the chapter of Canterbury. Proud of his order and his membership of a great landowning corporation, Matthew is a snob. He points out that the Canterbury monks had conferred a great favour on Edmund by electing him archbishop, thus elevating him above his very humble origins; and he suggests that Edmund was moved by the fear of seeming ungrateful to them for his social mobility (p. 144).

Here, as in his chronicles, Matthew's xenophobia is much in evidence. A friend of Edmund's is represented as pleading with him to accept the election of the Canterbury monks 'lest the king's council will procure the substitution of some alien, utterly unworthy of such a great honour, and have him intruded in that place where God has ordained so many saints' (p. 130). This was a thinly veiled attack on Archbishop Boniface of Savoy, the queen's uncle, who was in occupation of the see at the time Matthew was writing. The legate, Cardinal Otto, is condemned on both counts, as a foreigner and as a representative of the bureaucracy of Rome. He is cast for the role of the Achitophel who poses as a peacemaker, but who is really an adversary of the saintly archbishop. This is the only Life of St Edmund that depicts the legate in such an unfriendly light.

On the subject of monasticism Matthew is particularly sensitive, and his bias is correspondingly strong. He is profoundly convinced of the superiority of Benedictine monasticism over all other forms of the religious life and he has a strong sense of fraternity with monks of the same profession in other houses. The rebellion of the Canterbury monks against Archbishop Edmund thus posed a problem for him. As far as possible, he extenuates their conduct. He places the best interpretation on the destruction of the charter of St Thomas by members of the convent, and he glosses over the fact that one of the monks had forged an improved replacement with the connivance of the prior. He suggests that some of their number had voluntarily withdrawn to embrace the Carthusian life owing to contention within the community. In fact, as he well knew, the prior and others were disciplined on account of their part in the forgery and were forced to enter a severer order by the cardinal legate.[30]

One of Matthew's interpolations towards the end of the Life is especially revealing. Eustace ends his short Life with an eye-witness description of the funeral cortège from Soisy to Pontigny and the acclamation of the crowds that thronged the route. Two clerks of a sceptical disposition (*vere Didimi*) express

---

30. Gervase, ii, p. 133. That Matthew knew the true facts of the case is evident from his account in *Chron.Maj.*, iii, p. 492.

surprise at the universal acclamation of Edmund's sanctity by people who knew nothing about him. How could this acclamation of a foreign archbishop by the French peasantry be accounted for? Perhaps the monks of Pontigny had ridden ahead and engineered the whole thing. This gives Matthew the opportunity for an interpolation which he cannot resist. A heated colloquy is invented, of a kind that may well have taken place in the parlour at St Albans:

> Had he been a real saint, he wouldn't have cared to be buried in a Cistercian house. Almost all the glorious saints lie in houses of the Black Monks, few or none in Cistercian houses. In confirmation of what he had said, he instanced the houses of Canterbury, St Albans, St Edmund's, Durham, and many others in both the kingdoms of France and England (p. 160).

St Edmund's eccentric wish to be buried at Pontigny had offended Matthew's patriotism and touched his pride in his order.

Matthew's interpolations in, and additions to, the Eustace Life far exceed the length of his literary model. If these historical interpolations are compared with the related passages in his chronicles, the resemblances of matter and language are strikingly obvious. Details of St Edmund's early life and family are not included in the chronicles, presumably being unsuited to works of that scale; but it is apparent that Matthew had the same stock of information about Edmund's public life at his disposal as he had when he wrote the Life. There are many instances of verbal parallelism, but these are perhaps less striking than the identity of sentiment and interpretation. These resemblances stand out from the page sharply when Matthew's own prose is decrusted of the conventional rhetoric of Eustace in which it lies embedded.

In a number of instances we find a seminal phrase in one of the chronicles extended and developed in the Life. For example, when recording the baptism of Edward, the king's son, by the legate, Matthew observed with a venomous eye that the legate, Cardinal Otto, had been accorded precedence over the archbishop in the performance of the rite. In the Great Chronicle, a parenthesis of four words contains only a hint of reproach: 'the legate baptized him, although he was not a priest, but Archbishop Edmund confirmed him.'[31] In the Life, the point is elaborated and Matthew allows his animosity full rein: 'it was Otto, then the legate, who was chosen before others to baptize him, after putting himself forward for the office. He who was in deacon's orders, a foreigner, a man of inferior character and a pretty poor theologian, was given precedence over the archbishop of Canterbury

31. *Chron.Maj.*, iii, p. 539.

and primate of all England, who was well known to be a priest, of native birth, a man of conspicuous holiness etc' (p. 147).

Both verbally and in its interpretation of events, the Life bears a more intimate resemblance to Matthew's shorter history, the *Historia Anglorum*, than to the Great Chronicle. When it comes to the archbishop's pacification of 1234, an interesting variation appears between Wendover's treatment of the subject (incorporated by Matthew in the Great Chronicle) and Matthew's treatment of it in the *Historia Anglorum* and the Life of St Edmund. The Great Chronicle is more sympathetic to Richard the Marshal and more critical of the king. Richard goes to Ireland to defend his own property and is killed by a treacherous alliance, to which the king is party.[32] Afterwards, Archbishop Edmund produces in council the infamous letter sent to Ireland under the royal seal, and reproaches the king with having treacherously contrived the Marshal's death. Henry is stricken with remorse and turns on his scheming counsellors.

It has been suggested above that this account is suspect at several points and that it lacks a documentary basis. These doubts are strengthened by the fact that the whole incident of the letter is omitted from both the *Historia Anglorum* and the Life. The episode is one that would have reflected much credit on St Edmund as an intrepid prelate denouncing the king's wrongdoing to his face. Matthew's deliberate omission of it from these later works must shake the credibility of Wendover's narrative.

In their interpretation of these events the *Historia Anglorum* and the Life are closely allied. Here the Earl Marshal is killed in battle as a rebel against the king. The archbishop comes to plead with the king 'that the brother should not expiate the wrong which his brother had done, nor the fault of the guilty recoil upon the innocent'. The king is moved to pity by the archbishop's intercession, and agrees to temper justice with mercy. Matthew's special sympathy is reserved for Richard's heir, Gilbert Marshal, whom he seems to have admired, and for Hubert de Burgh, victim of a palace revolution engineered by Peter des Roches, the Poitevin bishop of Winchester. Not only are these events described in the same terms in the *Historia* and the Life, there is also a strong verbal similarity between the two accounts.

This resemblance of language and sentiment between the *Historia* and the Life appears again in Matthew's handling of the dispute between the archbishop and the monks of Christ Church Canterbury. On this subject Matthew was clearly divided in his feelings. He sympathizes with the anxiety of the monks to protect their privileges and their refusal to accept directions from secular clergy, but he cannot very well condone their rebellion against St Edmund. Canonization was a papal sentence against

32. *Ibid.*, iii, p. 273.

which there was no appeal and, besides, St Edmund was the hero of his story. Thus in the *Historia* he says that the monks 'were zealous for good, but acted without knowledge'[33] and in the Life that they 'were zealous for justice, but acted without knowledge' (p. 143).

Besides these resemblances of language and content between the *Historia* and the Life, a number of documents reproduced in the Life are also to be found in the dossier which Matthew called the *Liber Additamentorum*. This was an appendix of documents which he apparently decided to assemble when he was writing up the annal for the year 1247 in the Great Chronicle.[34] In it he included the bull announcing the canonization of St Edmund and the letter of Richard de Wych describing the translation, both of which he subsequently reproduced in the text of the Life. The 'Book of Additions' also contains the description of the archbishop's privy seal, which Matthew copied verbatim into the Life, and the prayer addressed to St John the Baptist, which follows the Life in the Julius manuscript.[35]

Matthew's prose style is always lively and highly idiosyncratic. But owing to its essentially rhetorical character, hagiography offered more scope for fine writing than the chronicle. Thus in the Life of St Edmund the peculiarities of Matthew's style are thrown into relief. He shows an abnormal fondness for certain grammatical constructions which can only be appreciated by a study of the Latin text. Apart from these, the most distinctive features of his style are his figures and tricks of speech, some of which are repeated *ad nauseam*. For instance litotes is used in the Life seventeen times. In certain contexts is appears with predictable regularity as when, for example, Matthew is referring to any kind of expenditure. Thus we are told that the archbishop conducted his suit at the Roman Curia 'at no little expense', and that the monks obtained papal absolution 'not without pouring out much money.' The trick of speech is so habitual with Matthew that it sometimes slips out unawares and results in bathos. This is the effect of it when he builds up to an eloquent climax with Edmund's last words in the death-bed scene, and adds that these words produced in the bystanders 'not a little surprise on account of their novelty'.

Another trick to which he is addicted is oxymoron, and where he is striving for special emphasis he often repeats the contradictory elements of a phrase in reverse; so we have such combinations as 'sad hilarity and

---

33. *Hist.Angl.*, ii, p. 411.
34. Matthew makes many references to documents in this collection, but its contents evidently was not the same as the collection appended to the Great Chronicle and published by Luard, *Chron.Maj.*, vi. For the problems relating to the *Liber Additamentorum*, see Vaughan, pp. 65–77.
35. *Ibid.*, vi, pp. 127–8.

hilarious sadness' (*tristis hilaritas et hilaris tristitia*) and 'delightful bitterness and bitter delight' (*delectabili acerbitate et acerba dilectatione*). Puns pour from his pen with extraordinary profusion, and synonyms chase one another in pairs with an exuberant garrulity that is often meaningless.

Biblical quotations and reminiscences scatter through his prose unbidden. He has a characteristic way of placing them in the mouths of his characters. Thus the legate addresses the monks of Christ Church in the words of I Peter, v.6 (p. 144). The archbishop remonstrates with them in the words of Isaiah, xlviii.22 (p. 145). He addresses the pope in the words of I Kings, xxviii.22 (p. 135), and in despair, he quotes Job, i.21 (p. 149). Like many hagiographers, Matthew sometimes uses the dramatic associations of a Scriptural quotation in order to heighten the emotive effect of a situation. The most dramatic episode in the Life and the one to which he gives the most extended treatment is Edmund's death. In this elaborate scene Matthew depicts the model of a holy death. This was the consummation of a life that all men devoutly wished. The saint forgives his enemies, writes testimonials for his servants, and when the viaticum – the consecrated host – is brought to him, he utters words that sum up the dedication of his lifetime to the service of Christ. Finally, he consoles the prior of Soisy, who is present at his death-bed, with a prophetic promise that his heart will always remain with them. At the end, Matthew explains that the prior and canons of Soisy failed to understand the archbishop's promise until after his death, and he evokes in the reader's mind the sudden revelation of Christ to the disciples at Emmaus with the quotation 'then their eyes were opened and they understood his words' (cf. Luke, xxiv.31).

When did Matthew write his Life of St Edmund? Dates within which he wrote it can be established from internal evidence. He cannot have composed it earlier than 1247 because, besides the bull of canonization reproduced at the end, it contains a reference to Edmund's canonization at a much earlier point in connection with the archbishop's consecration. On the other hand, it was not written later than 1253, for Matthew refers to the Queen Regent of France, Blanche of Castile, as still living, and she died in that year.

The evidence of the St Albans chronicles brings us closer to a date. In both the Great Chronicle and the *Historia Anglorum* Matthew states explicitly that he has written a Life of St Edmund and that anyone wanting to read it will find it at St Albans.[36] This statement is introduced rather arbitrarily in connection with the death of St Richard Wych in the annal for the year 1253. It looks as if Matthew seized on the death of Richard de Wych as the first opportunity of announcing his Life of St Edmund. The natural place to mention it, if it already existed, would have been in the

36. *Ibid.*, v, p. 369; *Hist.Angl.* iii, p. 135.

passages of the chronicles dealing with Edmund's death and canonization. A further opportunity might have been found when Matthew noticed the death of Robert Bacon, one of his principal informants, in 1248. It is impossible to say with confidence when the annals for the years 1240, 1246 and 1248 in the Great Chronicle were written up, though they were evidently completed by 1250.[37] But the absence of any reference to the Life under these obvious headings in the *Historia Anglorum* also, and its arbitrary insertion under the year 1253, suggests that Matthew had not yet composed the Life when he began writing the *Historia* in 1250.[38] This probability is strengthened by the close resemblances of language and interpretation between the two works, which we should expect to find if both were under production at the same time. In short, the Life of St Edmund was unquestionably written between 1247 and 1253, and most probably much nearer the latter than the former date.

It would be idle to complain that Matthew's Life of St Edmund fails to satisfy the demands of a modern biography. The hagiographer's purpose was to edify. Instead of personality he depicts a more or less stereotyped model of sanctity. In place of a portrait he offers us an ascetical programme. For all his talents, Matthew was not a man of profound spiritual perception. Though he was a conscientious monk, he lived on the surface of things. The inwardness of the contemplative was, one suspects, beyond his experience. Thus, although he frequently alludes to the long hours Edmund spent in prayer, he tells us nothing of his interior spiritual life and development. Nevertheless, the Edmund he presents us with is much more than a lay figure draped in the religious sentiment of his age. Alongside the chilling details of his ascetical practices, we are shown the features of a generous, compassionate but diffident man, who was by instinct a scholar and a recluse.

It is not, however, these human torches, which Matthew derived from Eustace and other witnesses, that give his Life its unique interest. Where it differs from the other Lives of St Edmund is in its depiction of him as an

---

37. Hilpert argues that the annal for the year 1239 cannot have been written up until after 1245, *op. cit.*, p. 32.

38. In another reference to his Life of St Edmund in the *Hist.Angl.*, iii, p. 135, Matthew writes that the bull of St Edmund's canonization is to be found in his Life, but this reference to the Life is an amendment in Matthew's own hand on a slip of parchment pasted over the text, which originally read 'in the Book of Additions' (*in libro additamentorum*). It is tempting to conclude from this that when he wrote the text of the *Historia* up to this point (after 1250), he had not yet composed the Life of St Edmund, and later when he had composed it, amended the reference to it in the *Historia*. But this fails to take account of many similar amendments in the text of the *Historia*. It seems that after writing it, he abandoned his plan of providing it with an appendix of documents and so went through the text obliterating his references to the Book of Additions and pointing out other sources where the documents were to be found.

ecclesiastical statesman acting on the stage of public events; and it is precisely here that the historical veracity of Matthew's portrait is open to question. For the role in which he casts Edmund is that of the just man who suffers persecution for righteousness, the eternal victim, akin to the Suffering Servant of Isaiah. The persecutors of St Edmund are the familiar figures drawn from Matthew's political demonology 'evil counsellors of the king, tax collectors, foreign interlopers, plunderers of the Church's temporalities, and the worldlings and flatterers who people the court. This image of the holy man persecuted by the world and in the end forced to flee from his persecutors was suggested to him by Eustace, the Canterbury monk, whose Life of St Edmund endeavours to depict him as the disciple and imitator of St Thomas the Martyr, whose shrine was the jewel in the crown of Canterbury cathedral.

Eustace accompanied Edmund on his last journey, and the stay at Pontigny, with its memories of the exiled Becket, must have fuelled his imagination. Taking a leaf from John of Salisbury's Life of Becket, he represents Edmund as following the example of St Thomas the Martyr and leaving England because he could not freely exercise his pastoral office or protect the liberties of the Church. This hint – and in Eustace it is no more than a hint – was eagerly seized on and developed by Matthew Paris. He has Edmund advised by St Thomas to seek relief from his troubles by flight. He sends him to Pontigny to wait in peace until the Dayspring from on high should visit him and the English kingdom, though, as Matthew makes clear, Edmund and his household stayed at Pontigny only a few days. In this picture of Edmund as the victim of demonic persecution and in the strained comparison between him and the martyr St Thomas, we have the germ of the myth that Edmund retired from the archbishopric to end his days as a voluntary exile at Pontigny. As we have seen elsewhere, this implausible story does scant justice to the historical St Edmund.

10

The Life of St Edmund by Matthew Paris

Blessed Edmund, the archbishop of Canterbury, came of very devout parents of modest wealth in the township of Abingdon. His father was Reginald, who was also called Rich, and his mother was Mabel, to whom Reginald was joined in marriage. Such a second name as theirs was indeed apt, for among their other assets the divine pleasure made them rich and blessed them with holy offspring of both sexes. Reginald's wife bore him Edmund, of whom I am now speaking, whom God afterwards called to the high office of archbishop, as will be told below. She also bore him Robert whom, like Edmund, the Lord endowed and raised to a position of rich reward as his outstanding merits deserved, for he had striking gifts of sanctity, cheerful generosity and profound learning. He also had Nicholas, who despised the sterile flower of this world[1] and took the habit of religion in the house of the Cistercian Order at Boxley. He also had two daughters, Margaret and Alice, who at an early age, preserving their virginal purity and being instructed in letters, took the veil of perpetual chastity as nuns at Catesby.[2] This was procured for them by Edmund without any reproach of simony.[3] Edmund also had a brother, a prudent and peaceable man, who took the religious habit at Eynsham. I have written this as a perpetual memorial to such a blessed progeny.

After a few years the father died. As has been said, the Lord so gladdened him in this world with his wife's undivided companionship and her fruitfulness in holy offspring that he was fittingly and truthfully called Rich. The mother persisted in irreproachable widowhood, persevering in fasting, almsgiving and prayer, so that of all the widows of Abingdon she was said to be the jewel. When her dear son Edmund, the one especially chosen among his brethren, was still studying at Paris, with motherly concern she sent him linen garments and, wrapped up with them, a very rough hair-shirt, begging him to use it for the sake of Christ. This he did

---

1. 'The sterile flower' etc. from the Dialogues of Gregory the Great: *PL,* lxvi, p. 126.
2. Catesby, Northants, a Benedictine nunnery.
3. The canonists allowed a recruit to a nunnery to bring an endowment with her, but the exaction of a dowry as a condition of entry was condemned as simony. For this reason Edmund declined to give any prior undertaking. As the canonist Gratian observed, 'it is one thing to make a voluntary offering; it is another thing to pay an exaction': *Corpus Iuris Canonici c.2 D Causae i, Q.ii.*

in obedience to her instructions. When he returned to Oxford, his mother had gone the way of all flesh in a holy death, and she left him a breastplate, which he was to use as long as he lived. In her advice to him, she had insistently implored him to follow her example and use this breastplate as a shirt for the love of Christ and in his warfare in God's service.

The good son happily complied with the prayers and counsels of the good mother; and so following in his mother's footsteps to God, he assiduously tamed his flesh; nor did she cease to inform her son and to please God even while she was dying. While she lived, she imparted to her child with his first milk the name of Christ, sweeter than milk, and implanted in him the love and fear of Christ. As he grew and progressed, she instructed him by her virtuous example, sometimes imploring, sometimes chiding, in the place of father and master as well as that of mother. It is thus a pleasure to unfold to our audience the story of his early childhood as well as that of his growth to maturity while he was studying at the schools in his mother's lifetime. For he continued to rule himself with the rod of strict discipline throughout the course of his life and governed his entire life in his learning and his conduct by the teaching of those who were the most respected and most expert in learning, using the breastplate over his bare flesh or over a crude hair-shirt.

Thus from infancy he espoused virtue, so that, as we read of St Benedict, 'from the time of his boyhood he bore the heart of an old man'.[4] For from his mother's womb, like another Nicholas,[5] he was chosen by God and from childhood he meditated on how to please God, striving while in the flesh to live above the flesh, to 'offer himself as a living sacrifice pleasing to God',[6] to gain by grace that which he could not obtain by nature, namely everlasting glory.

How he espoused a figure of the Blessed Virgin with a ring

Now Blessed Edmund, while he was yet a boy of twelve attending school under a master, was governed by the teaching of a certain holy priest to whom he frequently made his confession. In the sight of his confessor he vowed to give his intact virginity to Mary, the chaste mother of God, and promised to preserve it all the days of his life; and when he had recited these words in church before the figure of the Virgin, he quickly rose to

4. St Gregory's *Dialogi,* ii: *PL,* lxvi, p. 125.
5. Perhaps a reference to the story that as a baby Nicholas showed abstinence by sucking his mother's breast only once on Wednesdays and Fridays, see Surius, vi, p. 795.
6. Romans, xii.1.

his feet and placed on the finger of the statue a ring which he had obtained for the purpose,[7] saying 'To thee, O Virgin of virgins, most pure mother of my Lord Jesus Christ, I vow, pledge and consecrate the gift of my virginity. And wedding thee with this ring, I choose and thankfully adopt thee as my Lady and spouse, that as a virgin to a virgin I may henceforth be worthy to offer thee a more pleasing and fitting service.'

Then kneeling before the figure as if before the mother of God herself, he prayed devoutly with floods of tears, saying 'O my most serene Lady, spouse of my heart, beseech thy Son, my Lord, efficaciously that I may persevere in His service and thine and may be worthy to follow in the footsteps of St John the Evangelist.' After this prayer, he wanted to pull off the ring that he had placed on the finger of the statue, lest people should wonder at it, but, although he tried by every means in his power, he was unable to do so. At this he rejoiced, thinking hopefully that the Blessed Virgin accepted and looked with favour on his vow, and that as he in his pure boyhood had promised himself as a spouse to the most chaste mother of God, so had the Blessed Virgin herself freely promised to be the spouse of the blessed Edmund.

How the Lord appeared to him when he saw a bush in flower

He was a youngster already approaching physical maturity and associating with more advanced students, when he went with them for a walk in the meadows one day in mid-summer. He followed them so as not to be thought singular, but he did not want to take part in their games, and took himself off alone and 'meditated on the law of God'.[8] And, lo, he came upon a bush marvellously covered with most beautiful flowers, contrary to its habit and out of its proper season, scattering its fragrance far and wide all around. As he pondered on this, it occurred to him that it had some heavenly meaning, and kneeling down, he prayed, saying 'O God, who didst appear to the holy Moses on Mount Sinai in the figure of a burning bush that was not consumed, reveal to me what is portended by this miraculous thing.'

As he sank down on his knees, alone, praying tearfully, a flood of light from heaven shone round him, and in it, to his stupefaction, there appeared the infant Christ shining with great clarity, who spoke to him words of consolation: 'I am Jesus Christ, the son of Blessed Mary the Virgin, your spouse, whom you wedded with a ring and took as your Lady. I know the

7. According to the Franciscan author of the Lanercost chronicle, who was in Oxford after 1260, the statue was in an Oxford church: *Chronicon de Lanercost*, ed. J. Stevenson (1839), p. 36.
8. Cf. Psalms, i.2.

secrets of your heart, and I have been your inseparable companion as you walked alone. From now on I promise you that I and my mother, your spouse, shall be your helpers and comforters.' Saying this, he imprinted a blessing on the young man's brow with these words: Jesus of Nazareth, King of the Jews, and added 'Sign yourself often thus and repeat this in memory of me.'

He remained long in that place, praying on his knees and asking the Holy Spirit to grant him the learning that conduces to salvation with the other virtues. When he got up, his companions came hurrying up to him and they asked him what that great light was that they had seen shining beside the bush. But he carefully dissembled, not wanting to disclose that mystery to anyone. So in his youth from that time the saint happily increased in all virtue and learning; and retaining this in his memory, day and night throughout his life he made this sign upon his brow and eyes, devoutly reciting the words as he did so. There is no doubt that, like a faithful spouse, he persevered in blessed virginity until his death. Though men may doubt, thou, O Christ, dost testify to this at the present time by a multitude of miracles, and especially by the preservation of his body from decay. And 'thy testimonies are very sure.'[9]

How from that time the Blessed Edmund advanced daily in virtue

When, as a youngster of more mature years he was put to the study of liberal arts, he proceeded of his own will along the road by which he had previously been led, being – as his name signified – blessed and pure.[10] For from that time he began freely to sacrifice to God,[11] attending church more often and earlier, avoiding the vain frivolities which usually occupy those of that age, diligently applying himself to learning, not merely fleeing the pleasures of the flesh but ever bearing in his body the dying of the cross,[12] he bent all his mind upon the search for the Author of life. It seemed he had already understood that proverb which he had not yet read: 'A child, in the early way he should go, when he is old, he will not depart from it.'[13] In him this was really fulfilled. For vigils, fasts and other hard penitential practices were

---

9. Psalms, xcii.5. The reference to the preservation of Edmund's body comes from the letter of Richard de Wych describing the state of the body at the time of the translation in 1247, see below, p. 167.

10. The etymology of Edmund's name is thus described in the Eustace Life. The whole of this and the following four chapters are taken by Matthew from this source.

11. Cf. Psalms, liii.8.

12. Cf. 2 Corinthians, iv.10.

13. Proverbs, xxii.6.

from then so customary for him that, as he himself testified, at a later age he found them easy and even pleasant. He restrained the insolence of the flesh with the belt of chastity, taming it with a rough and knotted hair-shirt, for which he devised a new use, at night making it cover his hands and neck. To increase his self-imposed affliction, he wound round his body a triple cord of thick hair. Thus imitating St John the Baptist, he never defiled his flesh with any impurity. This is firmly asserted both by those who heard his confessions and by those who knew him intimately from childhood. Thus it is believed that while in the flesh he lived without concession to the flesh.

Of the wonderful austerity of his life

Truly, as he grew, he grew also in virtue. For through divine favour he so advanced in grace that in his young years, when studying the liberal arts and not yet following lectures on the Sacred Page, he looked like a doctor of Holy Scripture by reason of the distinction, maturity and holiness of his life. Thus for him not only did action precede teaching; it even preceded learning. He maintained from infancy his abstemiousness in speech, food, drink, sleep and all worldly things. When theatrical shows came round, he never went to them, nor did he 'sit with vain persons'[14] or with players. He was assiduous in prayer. At night he took only the briefest sleep, and that not in his bed but lying or sitting on the bare ground in front of the bed; and so he would rest a little, always clothed and belted. It is believed that this was his unfailing practice for upwards of thirty-six years, unless he was prevented by serious illness.

Always strict and harsh with himself, but affable and kind to others, he was conspicuous as a man of holy life, evident chastity and singular abstinence. He showed himself to be assiduous in vigils, prayer and teaching, an eminent doctor of Holy Scripture, a fervent and devoted preacher and confessor, conscientious in maintaining poor scholars, a lover of poverty, zealous for souls, an eradicator of vice and an example of all that is good. As if by some secret voice acting in the minds of everyone, all his words and works proclaimed that their author was seeking not his own ends but those of Jesus Christ.

He mortified his flesh with such harsh penance, constantly fasting on bread and water and in many other ways, that scarcely anyone considered human strength sufficient to sustain such toil. But in order to hide from men his interior austerity, he always appeared full of joy and gaiety. We considered, indeed, that among his other virtues the one that should be

14. Cf. Psalms, xxv.4.

represented as a particular model is this: that by the cultivation of a kind of simplicity in his words and actions he marvellously purged the taste for vain glory, a pestilential vice that is so troublesome to men of virtue. In a wonderful way, the more he progressed in virtue the more zealous he was to preserve humility, so much so that in public activities he preferred to be thought simple by the wise of this world than to do anything for the sake of vain display. Truly he was a refuge of the oppressed, a consoler of the wretched and a most kind comforter of the afflicted. He kept his hands uncontaminated by gifts, and, so far as he could, he eradicated the filth of avarice and impurity from those of his household.

That he was an incomparable lover and frequenter of the church

When therefore he had been made a Master of Arts,[15] although he had not yet been promoted to holy orders and was not yet under any obligation through having accepted an ecclesiastical benefice, but prompted solely by love of God and pious zeal, he used to hear mass daily before he lectured, which was more often than customary among lecturers at that time. In order to do this more devoutly, he built in the parish where he was then living a chapel of the Blessed Virgin, whom he had always especially loved, where solemn masses continue to be celebrated to her glory and honour. And since he excelled in these and many other virtues, God for his merits granted his servant this added grace that, while living, he was made illustrious by miracles, as those who have seen them with their eyes and been present faithfully assert and testify. For, according to many trustworthy men who have known him from infancy, grace so nourished this great lover of the faith that he is believed to have been free from any mortal sin, so that he could say with Job, 'from my youth mercy was brought up with me, and goodness from my mother's womb.'[16]

It was an admirable practice of his not to retain an ecclesiastical benefice unless he resided in it, so that when he moved to attend the schools, he resigned any benefice he had, which was previously unheard of among our countrymen. After he had been regent in Arts for almost six years, it pleased Him who separated him from his mother's womb[17] that in him and

---

15. This passage describing Edmund's religious observance when he was teaching arts at Oxford, including the construction of a chapel to the Blessed Virgin, is from the Eustace Life, but its ultimate source is the letter of postulation from the university of Oxford, see text in Lawrence, *St Edmund*, pp. 290–3.

16. Job, xxxi.18.

17. Cf. Galatians, i.15.

through him he might reveal his Son and that he should become a chosen vessel.[18] While he was giving cursory lectures[19] on arithmetic to some of his companions, his most pious mother, who had died shortly before, appeared to him in a dream, and said,

'My son, what are those shapes to which you are giving such earnest attention?' When he replied,

'These are the subject of my lecture,' and showed her the diagrams which are commonly used in that faculty, she promptly seized his right hand and painted three circles in it, and in the circles she wrote these three names: 'Father. Son. Holy Spirit.' This done, she said,

'My dearest son, henceforth direct your attention to these figures and to no others.'

Instructed by this dream as if by a revelation, he immediately transferred to the study of theology.

Thus he began to despise the sterility of philosophy and with eagerness to seek after the profitable fruits of theology. But because his teeth were still numbed by the sweet bitterness or the bitter sweetness of the liberal arts, he did not savour the early study of the divine page, which usually satisfies the soul's hunger with abundant food, instead of titillating the restless spirit with illusory problems. Then coming to himself, he began to be exceedingly afraid that he was sinfully entrapped by his type of learning, so much so that he might be rejected like a reprobate, recalling that text of Scripture: 'Wisdom will not enter a deceitful soul.'[20] So he had recourse to the cleansing bath of confession, and by confessing cleansed himself of all his mental scruples. From that time, with God's help, he progressed so rapidly in the faculty of theology that he either equalled or surpassed all his fellow pupils. Whether he acted in disputation as opponent, respondent or as determiner,[21] he brought light into the dark places of ignorance and resolved the objections of his opponents. For this reason, soon after a few years he was persuaded by many to assume the chair of a master.

---

18. Cf. Acts, ix.15.
19. Cursory lectures were those that took students through a text with minimum exegetical comment (in this case, apparently the *Ars Metrica* of Boethius), as opposed to the 'ordinary lectures' given by the masters in the mornings. Here the context suggests a voluntary lecture. On this nomenclature see Strickland Gibson, *Statuta Antiqua Universitatis Oxoniensis* (1931), pp. lxviii, cxxxv.
20. Wisdom, i.4.
21. Students for the arts degree were required to take part in formal disputations at various points in the course. The respondent had the main burden of meeting the argument of the 'opponens', who attacked his proposed solution of the question under debate. The determiner was the presiding master, who summed up and gave his definitive solution to the question.

How he stayed for a time at Merton

Then, before he was publicly regent in the schools of theology, the father stayed continually for a year and more in the monastic house of Merton,[22] and for a long time afterwards he often entered and left the cloister as if he were one of the sons of that church. Some of the brethren derived great pleasure from talking with him and were helped by his advice, and they admired his way of life beyond description. For, though he was living in the world, he had trampled the world under foot, and although he was young in years, he surpassed all the old in faith, learning, knowledge and wisdom. Wonderful to relate, while moving among scholars, he seemed to be not merely religious, but a perfect model of the religious life. He was assiduous in reading and meditation, very fervent in prayer, ever constant in keeping fasts and vigils. He never missed the office of matins through sleep, but came to all the offices with the brethren, as if he had been under an obligation to do so. His practice extended to the most inward as well as the exterior acts of religion, which he had learned from the Holy Spirit. He appeared, in fact, to possess the key to the whole spiritual life. He had moreover, 'made a covenant with his eyes'.[23] so much so that he scarcely knew the name of the brother who ministered to him at table for a year. In what manner he 'went from strength to strength to see the God of gods in Sion'[24] was known not only to them; it was common knowledge. He applied himself to sacred letters with such effort and with such a thirst for learning that he passed the nights almost without sleep; and the days seemed to him to be few beside the great love with which he panted for the chaste embraces of the lovely Rachel. Nor was he cheated of his desire.

He accomplished in a brief period the work of a long time, and by what he regarded as a modicum of labour he quickly plucked the blessed fruit of generations. Indeed, hearing and holding the divine Word in his heart, as it were soil drenched by the dew of heaven, he produced a crop of holy thoughts and affections and a most abundant fruit of good works. Truly, in lecturing and debating he was a distinguished and energetic sower of the Word, edifying others with, as it were, showers of eloquence and divine wisdom. Thus it happened that not a few men of religion, among whom he used to stay during vacation, whose hearts were touched by God, were edified by the maturity of his speech and by his example. Pondering on the signs of sanctity they

22. This chapter is from the Eustace Life, but its ultimate source of information is the letter of postulation from Merton priory, see text in Lawrence, *St Edmund*, pp. 297–8.
23. Cf. Job, xxxi.1.
24. Psalms, lxxxiii.8.

perceived in him, they thought themselves tepid and slothful by comparison with him who was a secular – they who were supposed to be and were religious – and they were ashamed, as in the prophecy of Isaiah: 'Be thou ashamed, O Sion . . . the sea hath spoken.'[25] And from that time they began to feel a healthy shame and strove to follow in his footsteps.

Of various aspects of his conduct

As the light of divine wisdom increased in him daily, so the exterior life of the blessed Edmund was made glorious by good works. That part of the night when he could not dispense with rest without harming his body he passed in tears, prayers and holy meditation. He kept his body chaste; he was ever modest at heart, measured in his speech, and just in his acts. Those he was going to instruct by his words he admonished by the example of his sanctity. For he was an outstanding preacher and an eminent teacher. The fire of his preaching and the eloquence of his teaching illuminated the minds of his hearers with the knowledge of the truth and kindled in them a love of the good, so that by the effect of his words upon those who heard him it was clearer than daylight that in him and through him there spoke He of whom it is written 'It is not you who speak, but the spirit of your Father'[26] and 'He is a consuming fire.' Hence he pleased the clergy, was accepted by the laity, and was to be reverenced even by princes. When he sat among the elders, he did not cease to console those who mourned. Compassion was brought up with him from infancy:[27] it caused him to embrace the miseries of others and to share as a partner in every affliction. Who was ever gentler in his piety? Who was harsher to himself in his diet? Whose speech was more charming? Whose dress more austere? Who was slower to speak, yet more fluent in prayer? Who from his youth spent less time in bed or more in reading? Who was less moved by insult or more by mercy? Who was readier to give with loss to himself? Who was more rarely preoccupied with the world or more frequently with Christ? Who in such a position of eminence thought less of himself, or who, the higher he rose by his merits, was more deflated by his consciousness of sin? We cannot adequately represent the immense charity and charisma by which he converted many hearts, as many people have known and learned by experience. For such was his love even for some of his adversaries that he seemed to prefer grave insults to the generous service of some of his friends, which did not please some rigid people.

25. Isaiah, xxiii.4.
26. Matthew, x.20.
27. Cf. Job, xxxi.18.

Of his generosity and his reverence at the altar

He was so active in offering hospitality and in other acts of generosity that whatever was within his means seemed to be at the common disposal of everyone. He made the utmost effort to avoid the vice of detraction, a failing that usually creeps into the conversation even of men who watch themselves carefully. So when an occasion occurred or words of detraction were spoken, he either changed the subject or, if the detractor persisted with his words, he would take his leave, not wanting to be polluted by listening, as he scarcely or never polluted himself in speaking ill of anyone. At the altar he was greatly given to tears, and he conducted himself in the service of the altar as if he discerned the Lord's passion being visibly enacted in the flesh. In fact he celebrated the divine sacraments with such great reverence that his ministration itself enhanced the faith and influenced the conduct of those who witnessed it. Anyone wanting to go into the kindness with which he everywhere treated subordinates and enumerate the virtues he propagated everywhere will inflict a burden on his hearers with excessive prolixity.

He was indeed specially endowed with gifts of divine grace, chaste in body, dedicated in his mind, affable in conversation, of pleasant countenance, endowed with prudence, with manifest temperance, immovable in his inner fortitude, just and firm in his judgement, constant in patience and hardy in suffering, humble, gentle and abounding in charity. Thus had the divine wisdom ordained in him the beauty of all the virtues, so that, to quote the apostle, his 'speech was always with grace, seasoned with salt'.[28] Never was anything in his mouth except peace, chastity, piety and charity. Never did anything dwell in his heart except Christ, the source of all these, who through him ministered to others the many fruits of charity, joy, peace, sobriety and continence. Like a granary at harvest, he amassed in his heart a manifold crop while he was at Merton, desiring to lecture.[29] Afterwards he proceeded to Oxford to lecture, having been called and pressingly urged by many people to do so. There he lectured and preached for some years with acclaim and bore abundant fruit, multiplying the talent he had been given.

28. Colossians, iv.6.
29. 'desiring to lecture': here Matthew uses the rare desiderative form of the verb *legere* – *lecturiens*, implying that Edmund desired to lecture but was prevented, probably because the masters had suspended the schools at Oxford as a protest against the hanging of two clerks by the city authorities. Teaching was only resumed in the autumn of 1214. The sense of the passage is that Edmund used this year or more of enforced leisure to lay up a hoard of spiritual treasure.

How he vanquished the Devil by reflecting on the passion of Our Lord on the cross

It happened one day that, after he had been in conference with a large number of people who had come to him for various reasons but chiefly for spiritual instruction, he was meditating and preparing his lectures when, in his weariness he took a little early rest and fell asleep. He was having notes made for some of his scholars so as to impress more firmly on their memory what they had previously heard.[30] At this the enemy of the human race appeared to him. The holy man endeavoured to put him to flight with the sign of the cross, but the Devil seized his right arm and held it fast in a fierce grip so as to prevent the saint from making the sign for his protection. The master therefore raised his left hand to perform the task of the right and make the sign. But, as bold as before, the enemy gripped that hand as well with greater strength and still prevented him from defending himself. But trusting in God's help in this struggle, the saint recalled to mind the passion of Christ and the shedding of his precious blood; then holding the Devil in a powerful embrace, he dashed him to the ground with a mighty crash, adjuring him by the blood of Christ, which usually confounds and repels him, to depart and come back no more. Thus he departed vanquished and confused.

How a scholar was cured of a serious illness by him

One day it happened that a scholar of his fell seriously ill with a fistula in one of his arms, so much so that his life was despaired of. As he groaned with misery, the master with great compassion for him said to him, 'Have faith, my son. I will ask God to transfer your malady to me.' And after he had prayed at length with tears and sighs, he gained what he sought, and the malady that the other had was marvellously transferred to him. The arm of the scholar, however, which had been intolerably painful for about fifteen days, was immediately and completely healed, leaving no trace of a scar, which is surprising and unusual. The physicians commonly call that disease anthrax because it leaves a cavity when it goes. The master was healed a short time afterwards, leaving the skin smooth, through the saving medicine of charity.

---

30. The Latin construction here is ambiguous. It seems to be some kind of informal note-taking that is meant rather than a *reportatio* or formal record of a lecture. On the subject of note-taking in the thirteenth-century universities see J. Destrez, *La 'Pecia' dans les manuscrits universitaires du XIII* et du XIV* siècle* (Paris, 1936).

The clouds obey him

When he had lectured in theology with distinction for many years and had taught the law in which his will was engaged night and day,[31] it seemed to him that the subtleties of disputation were bound to involve some degree of vain glory. For this reason he stopped teaching for a time and vacated his magistral chair. However, at the mandate of the Supreme Pontiff he sowed the Word on behalf of the Crusade,[32] not without abundant fruit. Often, through his invocation of the name of Christ the clouds and rain obeyed him to ensure that the faithful people were not prevented from hearing his sermon.

Of the sweet odour of his reputation

Such were the lovely flowers of virtue that flourished in the holy man, and the repute of his integrity and indeed of his sanctity began to be widely disseminated throughout England. For his teaching was so catholic and so clear that throughout the province all would say of him his 'tongue is the pen of a ready writer'.[33] And indeed he was possessed of a ready and fluent eloquence, adorned in its succinct rhetoric and matter by the Gregorian style;[34] as the poet says,
    'He who mixes sweet with utility takes away all the sting.'[35]
In fact he had a superhuman ability to bring forth without hesitation things new and old from the treasury of Holy Scripture. So, when he lectured or preached, it seemed to his hearers that the finger of God was writing in his heart the words of life that flowed from his mouth like the river of paradise.

31. This version of the anecdote is drawn from the Anonymous B Life: Wallace, p. 619.
32. Mandates for the preaching of the crusade were issued to prelates by Pope Honorius III in January 1227: Pressutti, no. 6157. Matthew Paris has misplaced the anecdote, giving the impression that Edmund's preaching of the crusade interrupted his regency in the schools, whereas he was treasurer of Salisbury when he undertook the commission.
33. Psalms, xliv.2.
34. The masters of the *ars dictaminis* − the art of formal prose composition − expounded four styles, the Gregorian, Tullian, Hilarian and Isidorean, according to the arrangement of the stressed syllables in a sentence; see the exposition of John of Garland's *Poetria de arte prosaica* in Rockinger, 'Briefsteller und Formelbücher des elften bis vierzehnten Jahrhunderts': *Quellen und Erörterungen z. bayerischen u. deutschen Geschichte,* ix (Munich, 1863), p. 501.
35. Horace, *Ars Poetica,* p. 343.

How he was made Treasurer of Salisbury and how he was deemed worthy to be a bishop

A prebend of the church of Salisbury was therefore conferred on him, so that he was called and was the custodian of the treasure.[36] It was fitting and expedient 'for such [to be] a high priest, holy, innocent, undefiled and separate from sinners';[37] thus, on the vacancy of the see of Canterbury, in the year of the Incarnation twelve hundred and thirty four, by divine inspiration and after the said see had suffered papal and royal vexations unworthy to be told, he was solemnly elected archbishop. For the convent of Canterbury, to whom, as is well known, the right of election has pertained since ancient times, said, 'Let a man be chosen in whom can be found no just grounds for objection and whose merits will silence all the carping detractors.' So, after they had invoked the Holy Spirit and had prayed devoutly, and after they had carefully weighed the merits of many candidates in the balance of reason, the opinion of all the electors finally settled and rested upon Master Edmund of Abingdon, the lecturer in theology. This was undoubtedly according to the will of God.

Having therefore sung the angelic hymn, namely the Te Deum, the electors themselves went to Edmund – they find him reading – and begged him for his gracious assent. But for two days the elect would not at all consent to the election that the community had canonically performed and agreed. Then under pressure of prayer and persuasion from many people and in bitterness of spirit he began to hesitate. Some of his friends secretly told him 'unless you consent and are installed there without delay, the king's council will procure the substitution of some alien, utterly unworthy of such a great honour, and have him intruded in that place where God has ordained so many saints. An unwillingness to assent to just requests is a kind of folly. Do not refuse to be moved by the entreaties of good men. If you are not careful your pusillanimity and resistance will be the cause of great confusion in the most noble church of Canterbury.' The monks also pressed him, imploring him on their knees with clasped hands and many tears to give his gracious assent, saying 'Sir, you who are said to be and are so good, we have had three or four rejections; do not allow us yet again to be confounded.'

---

36. The prebend was that of Calne (Wilts). Edmund first appears as treasurer of Salisbury in a chapter act dated 18 August 1222: *Register of St Osmund*, ed. W.H.R. Jones (RS, 1883–4), i, p. 339.
37. Cf. Hebrews, vii.26.

With reluctance he consents to his election

Moved and disturbed by these prayers and arguments, the blessed Edmund at last, but with reluctance, consented. Hence what we read of the blessed Gregory can be said of him:[38] he is seized, dragged, and by happy outcome and with the greatest devotion he is created metropolitan of all England in the name of the Holy Trinity. But having been made the shepherd and leader of the people of God, he did not put aside his old humility, but by continual abstinence, rough clothing, frequent vigils and devotion to prayer, he compelled his flesh to serve the spirit and, like Eve to Adam, subjected his sensuality to reason. His mind was wholly uncorrupted by any pomp or pride in his exalted episcopal rank.

Of his first acts after his consecration

Having then been consecrated archbishop in the church of Canterbury by Roger, the bishop of London, his dean,[39] one saint by another, a theologian by a theologian, a virgin by a virgin, one who wore a hair-shirt by another of the same, on the Sunday when *Letare Ierusalem* is sung,[40] namely the 2nd April, in the presence of King Henry, thirteen bishops and a great multitude of magnates, that day the blessed Edmund solemnly celebrated mass with the pallium which the Lord Pope had dispatched to him without charge.[41]

Observe how that high office was reserved to the blessed Edmund by divine dispensation

Nor do I think we should omit the fact that the wonderful outcome in his case was preordained by God. For it was after three candidates chosen before his election had been quashed, namely John, the Prior of Canterbury, Ralph the bishop of Chichester, and Master John surnamed Blund, that that distinguished office was reserved for the blessed Edmund

---

38. See the *Vita S. Gregorii* by John the Deacon: *PL,* lxxv, p. 81.
39. Roger Niger, bishop of London, 1229–41. The bishop of London was ex officio dean of the Canterbury province, through whom the archbishop convened provincial assemblies.
40. The introit of the mass for the fourth Sunday of Lent.
41. Gregory IX confirmed the election on 22 December 1233, and dispatched the pallium on 3 February 1234: Auvray, i, pp. 907, 958.

by divine dispensation, as one preferred by many people. In this he was like Tobias the younger, to whom were pledged and given the embraces of Sarah, the daughter of Raguel, with the special help of the angel Gabriel, after many of her previous husbands had been strangled.[42]

Of events that chanced to fall out in his honour

It should also be noticed that it did not happen without divine providence that the blessed Edmund was consecrated archbishop of Canterbury in Lent, a time, that is, of penance, frugality and spirituality. And in Advent, likewise a time of penance, frugality and spirituality, after he had given a model and example of true penance and frugality, he was, as will later be said, canonized at Lyons by the Lord Pope Innocent. Both were occasions for joy and exultation. May whoever follow in his footsteps obtain, after practising penance and abstinence, the everlasting joy and honour signified by his consecration and canonization.

Of the increase of his sanctity

From that time he endeavoured to apply himself more earnestly than usual and with greater effectiveness to works of charity, especially those that concerned the kingdom and the magnates. He tried in a friendly way to get dissidents to make peace, anxiously having in mind that hatred and strife among magnates imperil subordinates. It was then, after earl Richard the Marshal had been slain, that the king raised difficulties over replacing him with Gilbert, his nearest brother, and admitting him to the Marshal's inheritance, on the grounds that earl Richard had been adjudged an enemy slain in battle against the king. The archbishop, who loved Gilbert – he was indeed a lovable man – and who was always tender hearted to those in distress, hurried therefore to the king, who was then at the royal manor of Woodstock. The king rose reverently and courteously to receive him with a kiss, saying 'Welcome, father. What has brought you here at such trouble?' To which he replied, 'A great matter, my lord; in fact, the safety of your soul and the salvation and prosperity of the kingdom.'

Then, basing his speech on the virtue of charity, of which he gave an elegant and eloquent exposition, with clasped hands and rising tears he devotedly implored the king on behalf of Gilbert, beseeching him that a brother should by no means expiate a brother's offence nor should the guilt

42. Tobias, vii. The angel, however, was Raphael not Gabriel.

of the offender rebound upon the innocent. Fortifying his arguments with theological authorities, in which he abounded, he persuasively begged him not only to put away all his anger, but even to extend his favour to the limit and grant him his inheritance along with the dignity of the office.

Moved to piety, the king answered him with a tranquil expression, 'O good archbishop, your prayers carry great weight; they possess some kind of more-than-human grace and effect; they have banished the anger from my mind and unexpectedly moved me to clemency and good-will.' And to speak in the common idiom and read out what the kind king declared, he said with a slight smile, 'How beautifully you know how to pray. Pray God for me in the same way and I do not doubt that, as God is kinder than me, He will listen to you. I in turn have now listened to you. Let it be done as you requested.' And summoning Gilbert, the king put aside all his indignation with him and restored his inheritance with the full dignity of the Marshal's office.

How he reconciled Hubert de Burgh and other nobles of the kingdom

Also the earl of Kent, Hubert de Burgh, whose misfortunes and unjust persecution would require a special treatise,[43] was mercifully reconciled to the king by Edmund, the most devoted and blessed bishop. His heart was touched by sorrow for the earl and he was moved to act by similar urgent entreaties. Shall I burden my hearers[44] and ask about Gilbert Basset and Stephen of Segrave and the other distinguished and powerful men in the kingdom, whom he not only pacified but made most friendly to the king? Acting with prudence and gentleness and not without great trouble and labour, he managed to put an end to the disturbance and damage they had been causing. O sinners, of whatever sort you may be, flee with confidence to the merciful breast of so great an intercessor. It is to persuade them of this that I have disclosed what has been said. Now without doubt you will obtain mercy, as the plea of souls wins more favour than that of bodies, and God is more open to entreaty than any earthly king if you address Him, as is fitting, with prayers for your salvation.

Thus, while engaged in warfare for God in this life, the blessed archbishop

43. This is one of Matthew's favourite expressions (*speciales tractatus exigerent*); cf. its use in connection with St Edmund in *Hist.Angl.*, ii, p. 442; iii, p. 27. Its use here suggests that Matthew may have contemplated writing a biography of Hubert de Burgh: cf. the sympathetic notices of the Justiciar in *Chron.Maj.*, iv, p. 243, and *Hist.Angl.*, ii, p. 477.
44. A reminder, among several, that Matthew assumed his work would be read aloud (the commonest way of even personal reading at this period) to an audience.

Edmund had compassion for all people and, so far as he could, lightened everyone's burdens and procured the honour and advantage of each and all. Being anxiously concerned for the cure of souls that had been committed to him and for the safeguarding of the spiritualities,[45] he gave sedulous attention either himself or through others to receiving the confessions of those whom he spiritually nurtured, so as to gain many for God. He dispensed alms to the poor in floods – streams that are said to extinguish sins – and he did so with such love and generosity that throughout the breadth of the province anyone who was starving would, on being informed of his arrival, fly to his open gates and be supported by a daily dole of food and drink. But those who were ashamed at having fallen into poverty, having been at one time respectable, he helped secretly and courteously with more luxurious food, more respectable clothes of linen and wool, and shoes. Thus by being informed and cheerfully taking pains he doubled the favour he bestowed. His early habits of abstinence were intensified daily, and although he frequently entertained noble guests at his table, he maintained his customary practice of sobriety without relaxation. He knew, though, how to conceal his hidden fasting with a serene face and holy dissimulation, and did so with wonderful prudence. When he was lunching, and delicious and attractive dishes were brought to him to eat, after first taking a tiny morsel, he ordered the food to be distributed either to his companions at table or to some stranger who was a guest or to the poor men called Friars, who were lunching in his presence.[46]

How he never took time for leisure

Blessed Edmund detested sloth and idleness. He was always occupied praying or meditating, correcting books, hearing confessions, resolving questions in the practice disputations of the Friars,[47] or giving judgement in legal disputes, lest the enemy of the human race should find him idle or

---

45. The phrase 'and for the safeguarding of the spiritualities' has been inserted by Matthew quite incongruously at this point in the text of Eustace. The insertion reflects Matthew's constant preoccupation with the encroachment of the temporal power upon the rights and privileges of the Church.

46. On the presence of Dominican friars in Edmund's household, see Trivet, *Annales*, p. 228, and W.H. Hinnebusch, *The Early English Friars Preachers* (Rome, 1951), pp. 446–7.

47. The phrase used here by Matthew Paris is *questionum collatarum*; these were informal disputations held among students for practice. The Dominican general chapter of 1259 decreed that 'collated questions are to be held at least once a week, where this can be conveniently done': Denifle & Chatelain, i, p. 386, no. 355, cf. A.G. Little & F. Pelster, *Oxford Theology and Theologians* (OHS, 1934), pp. 53–6. It is not clear whether the *collationes* mentioned here by Matthew took place between friars in the archbishop's household or in the priory of Canterbury.

resting from good works. If anyone chided him for overworking, he replied by repeating the saying of the Wise Man:

> Now read, now pray,
> Or toil in the sacred arts all day;
> So swift shall be time's flight,
> And toil itself be light.

Most of all, he exerted himself in long and frequent prayer, passing even the winter nights with very little sleep, watching, kneeling, weeping, and meditating until daybreak. Then he began the day prayers, which he called customary. But we who were torpid and sleepy were scarcely able to get to the end of his night office when it was time to begin Lauds.[48] When the customary hour of prayer was impeded by the pressure of daily business inherent in the office of a bishop, he varied the hour of prayer but his zeal for it was unchanged. He never spent time in leisure.

He never broke silence in church or during the night hours or after Compline, often quoting the text 'the effect of righteousness is quiet',[49] and 'he sitteth alone and keepeth silence, and shall raise himself above himself.'[50] We have thought it worthwhile to include in this little book an incident relating to this inviolable custom of his. One evening, when he was at Rome, after he had been some time in prayer, he was summoned by the lord Pope after Compline, and only went to him unwillingly and after those of his household had reproved him for his delay and hesitancy. And when speaking, he quoted that text of Samuel when summoned from the dead, and said to the lord Pope, 'O holy father, why did you trouble me at such an hour?' When he had fully explained the reason for what he had said, the Pope with an untroubled expression said jokingly, 'You would very well know how to be a monk.' To which he replied, 'How I wish I was a good monk and was rid of all these troubles. What a good and peaceful life monks have.'

A comparison between him and St Martin, whom he resembled

It was with Blessed Edmund as we read of St Martin: he was poor and modest in his demeanour, but magnificently rich in heavenly grace; a prelate, yet a servant to others; great in the sight of God, but of small account in his own eyes; conscious of the gravity of his office, but jovial in his looks, affable, and

---

48. The word used here by Matthew is *matutinas*. It is customary at this period to refer to the dawn office of Lauds as 'Matins'.
49. Isaiah, xxxii.17.
50. Cf. Lamentations, iii.28.

charming in his speech. He always rejected any gifts proffered by those seeking advantage; he knew how to be thankful and content with his own means. He was tireless in works of mercy. On becoming a bishop, he never faltered in the abounding goodness he always displayed towards the poor and afflicted. The abundant means and income he acquired with his office were barely enough to support the poor of Christ, to whom his helping hand was ever extended. For he would not suffer any beggar to leave his gates at any time empty-handed or forsaken. Lest anyone should be disturbed by my comparison of Blessed Edmund to St Martin, out of reverence for so great a saint, I shall examine in each of them their remarkably similar virtues.

For Martin, while he was still a catechumen, divided his cloak and clothed a shivering pauper, and in doing so, clothed Christ.[51] Edmund, to the best of his ability, clothed a numerous crowd of poor people every year, even before he had obtained a benefice. Many more he adorned with the garments of faith and doctrine. Martin revealed the glory of the Trinity to the heathen in the lands of the West. Edmund, as a renowned doctor of theology, gave the light of doctrine to the land of England, and by his preaching sowed far and wide a seed that bore fruit, leaving his writing for the profit of posterity. A holy contention arose over the desire to possess the body of St Martin. A holy contention arose over possession of St Edmund's body, as will later be told.[52] Martin was the shining flower of the Franks; Edmund the jewel of the English. Martin was distinguished as the archbishop of Tours, Edmund as archbishop of Canterbury. Martin, while yet living, by the power of the Trinity gloriously raised three people from the dead. Edmund, while still living, recalled three people to life from death, commanding no one to mention it during his lifetime. What else should I mention? Both fought their fight for one and the same King, and were sanctified by the one Spirit. Faithfully serving the one Lord, they merited to be 'made rulers over many things'.[53]

Concerning certain virtues of his

Let us therefore praise God who has thus glorified his saint. England is to be congratulated on having borne so great a denizen of heaven and on having fostered such a happy child in her bosom. Let France rejoice that she has merited to keep the tomb that holds the body of so great a patron.

---

51. Cf. Sulpicius Severus, *Dialogi,* ii, *PL,* xx, pp. 201–12. This forced comparison between Edmund and St Martin is from the Eustace Life.
52. A reference to the competing claims of Pontigny and the Templars of Coulours for possession of his body, which Matthew reports below, p. 159.
53. Cf. Matthew, xxv, p. 23.

Let the angels and all the knights of the court of heaven exult in the company of so great a fellow warrior.[54] For by his teaching he shone upon the earth like the sun, and the news of his deeds was like the perfume of incense, so that he fulfilled the saying of the Apostle, 'As you speak, so do.'[55] And like another John the Baptist in the desert of England,[56] having been made a preacher general,[57] he preached unceasingly, devoutly and effectively exhorting crowds of people – knights and townsmen, religious and clergy, and the faithful of either sex. Indeed he was for all a shining pattern of good living, an excellent mirror of sanctity, a zealous teacher of justice, a master of piety, the true form of doctrine, the consecration of learning, an example of religion. In him there is an ideal for every sex, age, condition or rank to choose; and from his holiness all receive a fullness of light. In him boyhood finds something to imitate, men see what to strive for and admire, the clergy are taught the ideal for which they should strive.

While his limbs grew weak, the strength of his soul increased. The beauty of his face became so pallid with fasting that it underwent a complete change. Sometimes he abstained so much from drink that the hair of his head and beard dropped out for lack of moisture to nourish it. This ugly loss of hair could not be concealed from his colleagues who were regent and practised in the art of medicine. Inquiring and arguing among themselves about the cause of it, they concluded from examination that it had come about from want of moisture. Also, through the desiccation of his bones and loss of bone-marrow his body was wasted and almost destroyed.

The testimony of the archbishop of York[58] to St Edmund's virtues

Among many who bore witness to his incomparable holiness, the archbishop of York wrote and spoke as follows:

As I firmly believe, and as far as human knowledge allows, I know that Edmund, the archbishop of Canterbury, was a man gloriously free from any lapse of the flesh. More than anyone I have known, he had a steadfast faith, strong hope and a most fervent charity. He was an eloquent speaker,

---

54. These phrases inserted by Matthew are derived from the bull of canonization.
55. James, ii.2.
56. 'The desert of England': the copyist has 'the desert, an angel' (*angelus* as opposed to *Anglie*).
57. i.e. a preacher commissioned to preach in several dioceses; a reference to Edmund's commission to preach the crusade.
58. Walter de Gray, archbishop of York, 1214–55.

abounding in good judgement, much given to abstinence, assiduous in prayer, frequently keeping vigil, a strenuous practitioner of mortification, an eminent teacher, an outstanding preacher and a discreet confessor. He always wore a hair-shirt. He rarely or never lay on his bed to rest, sleeping fully clothed and belted, scarcely ever removing his shoes. Nightly, except on major feast-days, he received flagellation, which we call the discipline, until his flesh was blue, sometimes to the point of bleeding, and if the person applying the discipline spared him, he chided him for his faint-heartedness. He was strongest in adversity, meek when his affairs prospered and affable to everyone; his talk was of religion, and albeit with due maturity he was always joyful and gay; he was compassionate towards the unfortunate, a benevolent alms-giver, and a consoler of those who were mourning, so much so that he could have said, like another Job, 'I was eyes to the blind, and feet was I to the lame, I was a father to the poor, a comforter of the wretched.'[59]

When I recall the indomitable faith that informed his acts, the extraordinary austerity of his life, his long struggle with the world and the Devil, I have no hesitation or doubt in asserting that this man endured a prolonged and almost insupportable martyrdom and received a martyr's palm, though his passion was not consummated by the sword, so that he could have said with the Apostle, 'for me to live is Christ, and to die is gain.'[60] Because he was taught by the heavenly unction of Him who appeared in tongues of fire and instructed the apostles so that they were fluent in speech and burning with charity, in a marvellous way his preaching pleased both by the authority of his judgement and the clarity and elegance of his language, so that it was in itself a kind of effective channel of heavenly grace.[61]

After meals and sleep, which he habitually took sitting down, he gave his attention to the sacred Scriptures or to honest and edifying conversation, making every effort to avoid idleness, lest 'the adversaries should see and mock his sabbaths.'[62] He rarely ate supper and very rarely drank after lunch, fulfilling that precept of Wisdom, 'Sobriety gives health to soul and body.'[63] After Matins, when his clerks and chaplains had retired to sleep, the archbishop, although he had clearly recited and had duly completed the office, remained alone in the oratory, both in winter and summer, and spent the rest of the night in meditation, tears and prayer. It was at these hours that he often had a visible struggle with the Devil, so that he was

59. Job, xxix.15.
60. Philippians, i.21.
61. Literally 'efficacious and in itself strengthening I know not what effect of heavenly grace.'
62. Lamentations, i.7.
63. Ecclesiasticus, xxxi.36.

heard as if rebuking someone. Moreover, he at some time saw the Devil between Wrotham and Otford in the likeness of a dragon, breathing out fire and alternately rearing up to the sky and cast down to the earth.

A true and short statement of Brother Robert surnamed Bacun concerning the sanctity of Blessed Edmund, the archbishop of Canterbury[64]

Brother Robert surnamed Bacun, of the Order of Preachers, being regent master in theology at Oxford, who was a particular scholar, auditor and colleague of the blessed Edmund, having taken the oath, states:

When the blessed Edmund was studying the liberal arts at Paris, his mother was wont to include a hair-shirt with the linen garments she sent him, begging him to use it. He gladly acceded to her request. When he came to Oxford after his mother's death, be began using the breastplate she had left him, which she had used in her lifetime. In Advent and Lent, it was his custom to use a garment of lead, and he was even in the habit of binding many parts of his body with cords. He never got into bed, especially one made up with linen sheets, but lay in front of the bed, clothed and belted. He used ankle-length robes that were closed all round, for it was his custom to give them to genuine widows or respectable girls. He did not use gloves or mitre. He very rarely or almost never washed his head. He ate practically no fleshmeat or fish. In Advent and Lent he took only vegetable pottage. He never bothered with spices or sweetmeats or with medicaments; indeed he considered them frivolities. He never wanted people to tell him on his own account what he was going to eat. Indeed, when someone praised food in his presence, he did not eat it, saying that the praise of it was food enough for him. In fact, he abstained so much that the hair dropped from his beard and head. On days when he celebrated mass, he ate no meat, nor did he eat it on Mondays nor in Septuagesima. He persisted with fervour in fasting, vigils and prayer. In church, he did not sit, but knelt on the harsh ground. He was merry and very charming to others, but very hard on himself, saying that the olive's own root is bitter, but its oil is sweet and gives light and refreshment to others. He did not carry a purse or other receptacle, but when he received money from his

64. This is the only extant text of this deposition by Robert Bacon, the distinguished Dominican theologian, who had been a colleague of Edmund in the Oxford schools. He also supplied the university with much of the material for the letter of postulation sent to the pope. The deposition became the source of many of the hagiographic anecdotes about St Edmund.

scholars, he was in the habit of placing it, or rather tossing it, in the window, as if it were available to everybody, and he would take some dust and say, 'Dust to dust, ashes to ashes.' Often it was carried off, presumably by a thief.

When he was regent in arts he heard mass every day before entering the schools, and in the same way he accustomed his pupils to hear mass with him. A scholar of his happened to have a disease on his arm, and went and showed it to Edmund, his master, who said some such words as 'May God heal you.' Next day the young man returned and announced he was healed; and, as Master Edmund reported to me, for some time afterwards he himself had the scholar's disease on his own arm.

At her death, his mother committed his two sisters to his care, with a sum of money so as to place them in a convent. He was anxious to do this, but was unable to accomplish it without stating what he was prepared to give with them by way of dowry, which he refused to do. At length, he arrived at Catesby. Although he was unknown to the prioress, before he had had any conversation with her she addressed him by his name, and declared the business on which he had come. She told him to send her the girls and she would make them nuns; and so it was done. He told me this himself.

Item. One day, when he was regent in arts and preoccupied with study, he forgot to say a certain prayer to the Blessed Virgin and St John the Evangelist, which it was his custom to say every day. The following night, the Blessed John appeared to him, carrying a rod, and said to him, 'Hold out your hand.' When he did so, St John threatened to strike him with the rod, albeit without a stern expression on his face. It seemed to him that such was the immensity of the threat that, had he wished to strike, he would have died. He said to him that he would not on any day thenceforth omit to say the prayer. This was reported to me by Master John de Wych,[65] to whom Master Edmund told it, and for whom he wrote out the prayer, which begins 'O intemerata' etc.[66]

When he was giving a quick lecture to his pupils in science and was constantly drawing diagrams in the dust, one night his mother appeared to him as he slept and said to him, 'My son, hold out your hand', and she wrote in his outstretched palm three circles, and said 'these three circles are three thrones of the Three Persons. From now on study these diagrams and no others.' Thus, after he had been regent in arts for six years with marvellous success, he transferred to hearing lectures on Holy Scripture. In this he bore much fruit, preaching, lecturing and conducting disputations.

---

65. Master John de Wych, who was possibly a relative of Richard de Wych, was a member of Edmund's archiepiscopal *familia* and was appointed one of his executors: *Close Rolls, 1238–42*, p. 280, and see above, Chapter 6.

66. For the earlier history of this prayer, which enjoyed great popularity in the twelfth century, see A. Wilmart, *Auteurs spirituels et textes dévots du moyen-âge latin* (Paris, 1932), pp. 474–504.

For many rich barons who heard him in mid-course were signed with the Cross, and leaving all things for the sake of Christ, subjected themselves to the perils of pilgrimage.[67] Some entered the cloister. Others, informed by the goodness of his life, gave themselves to the study of theology. One night when he was sleeping, it seemed to him that a great fire had broken out in his school and that seven burning brands were plucked from it. On the morrow, when he was seated in the master's chair and was teaching, the abbot of Quarr, of the Cistercian Order, entered the room. When the master had finished his lecture, seven of his scholars, urged it may be thought by the master as well as by the abbot, were fired by charity to take the monastic habit, and the abbot took them away with him. One of them was Master Stephen of Lexington, afterwards abbot of Clairvaux.[68] One day when he was preaching on the way to Wales, it happened that a heavy rain-cloud hung over the people who had come to hear him, threatening to pour down on them. But when he and they had prayed, it released its deluge on either side around, leaving them scarcely rained on at all. So he proceeded to preach in favourable conditions.

One day, he visited a scholar, a nobleman, who was sick. When he wanted to leave, the invalid held him back. When I asked the sick man why he had done this, he replied, 'While the master was with me, it seemed to me that the whole house was filled with fragrance.' When he was engaged in preaching, he was unwilling to talk to anyone, even a sick person, until he had preached.[69]

He always made a pact with his servants to the effect that if they were ever discovered to have fallen into a sin of the flesh, they would take the remuneration due to them and would leave him. He undertook the office of regent master in theology, as he did holy orders, unwillingly and under compulsion. He was wont to pray that no church in his gift should ever be vacant. It was his custom to kiss his Bible before he opened it. At Paris, even when he was hearing lectures on Holy Scripture, he sold the few books of Scripture that he had, and gave the price he got for them to poor scholars. While he was still regent in arts, one of his pupils happened to fall ill, and he had him carried to his own house, and he himself lay in the room with him almost every night for nearly five weeks and waited on him with a urinal and

67. The crusade was understood to be an armed pilgrimage. The crusade that Edmund preached set out for Palestine in 1227 under the leadership of the emperor Frederick II. There was a small but continuous flow of crusaders leaving England for Syria in these years.

68. Stephen of Lexington, abbot of Clairvaux, 1243–57. The Dunstable annalist places his departure from the Oxford schools in 1221: *Ann.Mon.*, iii, p. 67. He was abbot of Stanley by 1223: *Curia Regis Rolls,* xi, p. 251.

69. This statement is a *non sequitur.* The text appears to be corrupt at this point.

other necessities, as if he was a common servant. Nevertheless, on the following day he would lecture and conduct disputations. Often the pot fell from the invalid's hand on account of his light-head, but the fragile vessel was unbroken although it fell on a hard surface.

Archbishop Walter of York, who was very dear to Master Edmund and a well-loved friend, offered to have an entire glossed Bible written for him, but he declined with the answer that he feared the assignment of copyists for the task would burden abbeys and priories, and he preferred to lack books rather than burden religious in this way.

Once when he was harassed by a demon, he adjured him to say how he could cause him the greatest harm, to which he received the answer, 'by recalling the shedding of the blood of Christ.' He was himself accustomed to sign the parts of his body from head to foot daily with the sign of the Cross, saying as he signed each part, 'We adore you, O Christ, and bless you, because by your holy cross you have redeemed the world.'

Very renowned men and distinguished prelates of England, namely Stephen, the archbishop of Canterbury, and Walter, the archbishop of York, and other great men, knowing the holy man's reputation, hastened and vied with one another to enrich him with greater honours and a larger income. We thought you should be informed how and why these offers were received. Let one example serve for many. When the archbishop had sent him messengers offering him the rectorship of a church which customarily payed its rector about two hundred marks a year, after he had thought it over for some time, Master Edmund said in reply to the messenger, 'my friend, do you know how that church, which the archbishop is graciously prepared to confer on me, is furnished in chancel, vestments, books and other things that it is the rector's obligation to supply?' 'Certainly, very poorly, sir,' was the reply. On receipt of this information, he replied to the messenger, 'Convey my thanks to your lord. I accept the offer of income, lest perchance it should fall into the rapacious hands of the Romans or others like them, who seek nothing from the sheep of Christ except their milk and wool.'[70] He therefore appointed a faithful and diligent agent to extend, roof and decorate the chancel of that church, and paid out all the proceeds of the church for this, keeping nothing of it whatsoever for himself. And he continued to render this service for many years until all the defects of that church were made good. Afterwards he resigned all, lest an obligation to render account for souls and the worries of litigation should keep him away from the schools.

---

70. This speech, like others Matthew places in Edmund's mouth, clearly expressed Matthew's own views and prejudices on the subject of members of the papal Curia being provided to English benefices.

A miracle to note

As Blessed Edmund, the bishop, had a change of hair-shirts, it happened that when one of them was old and worn out, he took another, a new one which was harsher. The two faithful and intimate chamberlains, whom he kept for his private service, were ordered straightaway and secretly to burn the old hair-shirt, which was foul and torn and good for nothing. Obediently they lit a large fire in a suitable place and put the hair-shirt on it to burn. But the hungry flame failed to consume a single hair of it. The servants were astounded, but they did not dare to report it to their lord, for fear of seeming sycophantic. So they filled the shirt with as many heavy stones as it could hold and sank it in a deep pool to rot.

The beginning of many and various tribulations for the Blessed Edmund

Seeing that such a great man would be exceedingly useful to the Church of God, the common enemy of the human race was envious, and so as to prevent him from enjoying the peace of the prince as had been his wont, he chose many and mighty inciters of discord, through whom he sowed the detestable seeds of hatred in the hearts of the king and his courtiers. Then the monks of Canterbury, who were his special charge, zealous for justice in the bosom of his church, but acting without knowledge,[71] constantly demanded back certain liberties of theirs which pertained, as they said, to their convent, and which the archbishop's people were holding in their possession. The archbishop, inasmuch as he was their head and father, claimed these rights belonged to him and should be certified and recognized as pertaining to his household demesne. But the monks contradicted him to his face, and constantly appealed to stop him attempting any innovations prejudicial to them and to the ancient and proved custom of their church. For many were confident in their belief and had no doubt that these liberties pertained specifically to them, and showed charters and privileges to support their case. One of these, obtained, as they asserted, through the good offices of Blessed Thomas the Martyr, was improperly thought to be suspect and appeared to have been corrupted,

---

71. Matthew refers here to the opposition of the Canterbury monks to Edmund's plans to erect a collegiate church in the diocese to be endowed out of the properties of the see. The liberties were the *exennia* or dues that the archbishops had levied on a number of the priory's manors, see above, Chapter 7.

and for this reason it was burned on the advice of some of the brethren.[72] On account of this no small schism occurred in the community.

Now at this time Cardinal Otto, legate of the Roman See, was in England,[73] and went to Canterbury to deal with the damage caused by this shameful uproar and discord and restore peace; for the scandal of it exhaled its foul smell throughout the district. He entered the monks' chapter and, after making a careful investigation, he said to the convent, 'Dearest brethren, venerable monks of the most noble metropolitan church, of which there is none greater nor any peer in England, your case is weak and you are disunited. "Humble yourselves, therefore, under the mighty hand of God."[74] The members must obey the head. Obey your pastor and father, the most holy archbishop; and let this contagion be buried before further scandal can indelibly stain your reputation.'

Part of the community responded with good-will and acquiescence to this peroration of his. But when the archbishop returned not many days later and entered the chapter, he realized that there was a schism there and not all were of the same mind. Some wanted to humble themselves and give way. Others, believing their church was suffering an enormous injury, protested vociferously against it and lodged an appeal. On account of this discord the Lord's flock was scattered, and in order to pass their remaining days in peace many chose the Carthusian brethren or another order, and departed never to return.[75] Moreover some obstinate monks rebelled and with their secular friends reproached the archbishop for not merely disturbing his church and convent, but openly attacking them, and shamelessly oppressing those who had raised him from his very humble origins and had elected him to his high office, spurning, when they did so, very noble candidates and acting contrary to the requests of the king and many others.

---

72. Matthew here presents a laundered version of events at the cathedral priory. The charter of St Thomas had been separated from its seal and had been burned, but not before a replacement, with many 'improvements' in the favour of the priory, had been forged by Brother Ralph of Orpington on the instructions of the prior, see C.R. Cheney, 'Magna Carta Beati Thomae: another Canterbury forgery': *Medieval Texts and Studies* (1973), pp. 78–10, and above, Chapter 7.

73. Cardinal Otto di Monteferrato, *legatus a latere* to England, 1237–41. While in Rome Edmund obtained a papal mandate instructing the legate to visit Canterbury and examine the charters of the priory, sending any that were suspect to the pope: *CPL*, i, pp. 173–4.

74. 1 Peter, v.6. Like many speeches that Matthew attributes to people, this one is probably an invention, though it may have a general basis in his information about the legate's visit. The flattering preamble of the legate's address to the monks obviously expresses Matthew's own ideas about their status.

75. Here again, Matthew's partiality for his monastic brethren has led him to gloss over a discreditable incident. In fact, the prior, John of Chetham, and others involved in the forgery of the charter were disciplined by the legate and forced to enter the Carthusian Order to do penance. That Matthew knew the true facts is evident from his account in *Chron. Maj.*, iii, p. 492.

Out of pity the archbishop makes concessions to the wishes of his convent

Not a little grieved by the disturbance of the convent and church, the archbishop sighed deeply in the bitterness of his spirit. One day, therefore, to prevent an imminent scandal, he entered the chapter with the greatest humility and by reasoning and restraint curbed the disquiet that had been aroused, not wanting to seem forgetful of the favours the monks had bestowed on him; for he was very fearful of being accused of ingratitude in any way. He therefore condescended so far to their wishes that all strife was quelled and peace was joyfully restored. One and all of the monks submitted with good grace, rendering thanks for this to God and the archbishop. In order to confirm this agreed form of peace with apostolic authority, the archbishop announced he was going to Rome. It was also the purpose of his journey to procure the settlement of another dispute between his church and the cathedral church of London, which had arisen in the time of Bishop Roger of holy memory, and of other difficult matters relating to his church and his office. He therefore made the necessary arrangements and crossed the Alps as early as possible.[76] And when he got to Rome, lo and behold, on the first day of his arrival, he found some of the monks who, following the deceptive advice of their lawyers, had dashed off and with indecent haste arrived before the archbishop. To his great surprise and that of his party, they unexpectedly and impudently appealed against the form of agreement mentioned above, which the archbishop had been happy to confirm. Much confused by this, the archbishop declared it was an insult to him, a scandal, and an injury to his church, but the lawyers, who are only interested in gain, incited the monks to hold their ground and contradict the archbishop to his face. Execrating their tergiversation and foolishness, he said to them, 'There is no peace for the wicked, says the Lord'.[77] What else? In the end, since the monks obstinately declined to depart in any way from the advice of their hired lawyers, the archbishop imposed the sentence of excommunication on all those who were upsetting the agreed form of peace. From then onwards, displeasure grew daily between the archbishop and his individual adversaries.

---

76. In the margin of the Great Chronicle Matthew noted that Archbishop Edmund left for Rome during the week before Christmas, 1237: *Chron.Maj.*, iii, p. 470. An act of the archbishop is dated at Canterbury on 19 December 1237: Lambeth Palace, MS 582, fo. 58, thus fixing Edmund's departure between 20 and 24 December.
77. Isaiah, xlviii.22.

Adversaries of the archbishop grow in numbers everywhere

In fact, besides all those who appeared to be sons of his own church, Roger, the bishop of London, the convent of Rochester, Hugh earl of Arundel, Hubert the Justiciar of England and earl Simon of Leicester, turned against the archbishop and initiated serious actions against him. He sustained the attacks of these people, which seemed to be based upon reasonable grounds, and they cost him no little trouble and expense. For along with the great who rose against him, there were also lesser folk who knocked him. At length, after he had had a private discussion about these matters with the lord Pope, a commission was sent to judges in England to find on the rights of these questions. Afterwards, when the (archbishop's)[78] suffragans met together at the king's command to consider the needs of the Church, contention arose between the king and the Church, which, by the instigation of the Devil, daily grew worse. Many days were fixed to negotiate a restoration of peace, but, thanks to the author of discord, after frustrating postponements, those in dispute parted from each other with their differences unresolved. Then, after renewed vexations and repeated insults, the archbishop arose and, proffering himself as a wall about Israel, with the advice of his suffragans, repeated, renewed and extended the sentence of anathema against those who disturbed the peace of the Church. Moreover, the man of God, being firmly planted upon the rock which is Christ, could be neither softened by blandishments nor intimidated by threats to deviate from the path of righteousness.

Otto, the legate, desired to please the king, and when he saw the king's heart was completely alienated from the archbishop and that the adversaries of the latter were multiplying everywhere, he was keen to fall in with the crowd. So by the authority vested in him he quashed the acts of the archbishop, absolved those individuals whom he had excommunicated, and anathematized those whom he had at some previous time absolved. What else? He evaluated and reckoned all his acts as worthless. What is more, after the archbishop's death, the monks of Canterbury lost no time in petitioning absolution at Rome, and with the help of the king and legate they obtained it without difficulty. Those to be absolved were sent to England to Richard, the prior of Dunstable, and John, the archdeacon of St Albans, who forthwith absolved them by papal authority.[79] The monks

---

78. This appears to refer to an assembly of the bishops at Westminster on 13 January 1240, when Edmund presented an itemized list of complaints to the king about the infringement of ecclesiastical liberties, and the bishops renewed the anathemas against those who were in breach of Magna Carta: *Chron.Maj.*, iv, p. 3.

79. *Ann.Mon.*, iii, p. 156.

did not obtain this favour without pouring out a great deal of money. Moreover, by the same authority sentence was given against him and for the convent of Rochester.[80] Also, Simon, the earl of Leicester, was permitted to keep his wife in peace, despite the fact that the archbishop had himself fully informed the Pope about the solemn vow (of chastity) she had taken in his presence. In other cases, too, he was pitifully worn down to the point of almost draining his treasury, worsted and oppressed in various ways.

Everything goes wrong for the archbishop and his acts are misinterpreted

The wicked tried to obscure this change of the right hand of the Most High[81] with a malicious interpretation. They asserted that the higher life he lived was over-scrupulous, that his zeal for justice was cruel, that his affability was the garrulity of a buffoon. They attributed the advantages he procured for the Church to avarice. They lyingly pretended that his contempt for the approval of the world was a desire for vain glory. His noble courtesy was made out to be self-aggrandizement. That he followed the dictates of a will instructed by heaven was said to be a mark of arrogance. In sum, he could say or do nothing that was not maliciously misinterpreted and vilified. If much of this disturbed and offended him, as it should, what he most passionately complained of in private was this: when the first-born of our lord, the king of England, the heir of all things, was baptized, it was Otto, then the legate, who was chosen to baptize him, after putting himself forward for the office. He who was in deacon's orders, a foreigner, a man of inferior character and a pretty poor theologian,[82] was given precedence over the archbishop of Canterbury and primate of all England, who was well known to be a priest, of native birth, a man of conspicuous holiness and a famous teacher learned in many disciplines. He was indeed present at that event, but the principal office was performed by the legate, while the bishop of Carlisle immersed the infant in the font. He

---

80. Matthew's account of the archbishop's troubles ignores the chronology of events at this point. In the case against Rochester Cathedral Priory judgement was given against the archbishop in 1238: Auvray, n. 4197; and so was the judgement in favour of Montfort's marriage: *ibid.*, nos. 4330, 4889.

81. Cf. Psalms, lxxvi.11. The wording of this passage, derived from Eustace, is taken from the Life of St Thomas Becket by John of Salisbury: *Materials for the History of Thomas Becket*, ed. J.C. Roberson & J.B. Sheppard (RS, 1875–85), ii, pp. 309–10.

82. In accordance with canonical protocol, the legate was correctly given precedence over the archbishop at the baptism of the Lord Edward in June 1239.

was, however, allowed to confirm the child after baptism. From this everyone concluded he was useless, and held him in the utmost contempt. What was there left for him to do but abandon everything?

Surrender

The man of God saw, therefore, that the proper thing to do was to surrender and absent himself, as the poet has it,

> When madness is in spate, let madness take its course.[83]

One night he prayed more earnestly that the Angel of Great Counsel should direct his course and reveal to his heart what it would be best to do and what would be most fitting and healthy for his soul in this predicament. And lo, while he was praying and greatly fearful of yielding, it was revealed to him what to do in this way, by a voice from above: 'Trust the circumscription on your smaller seal, and follow him whose martyrdom is represented in the centre of it.' Now the inscription on his privy seal was this: 'Let my death teach Edmund to be fearless', and in the centre was an elegant carving of Thomas the Martyr and the knights dashing out his brains.[84]

The counsel of Blessed Thomas

Having been clearly informed by heaven what to do, the archbishop therefore endeavoured from then on to follow in the footsteps of Blessed Thomas the Martyr. For it was given him in spirit to recognize that the voice was that of Blessed Thomas his predecessor, advising and consoling him. Although he had been in the habit of frequently and devoutly invoking the martyr when in trouble, from that time he prayed for his help with increased frequency and devotion, requesting that just as St Thomas had migrated in glory to eternal peace after enduring the trials and tribulations of this world, so he too might flee away to the God of all consolation and peace, after manfully suffering the oppression of the world and worldly men. So the archbishop was comforted in the Lord, and cloaked the anxiety of his heart

---

83. Ovid, *Remedium Amoris*, p. 119. It is improbable that Matthew had in mind the original context of this verse.
84. Matthew noted the details of the archbishop's seal in the margin of the Liber Additamentorum: *Chron. Maj.*, vi, p. 124 n. The scene of Becket's martyrdom is shown on the reverse of the seal; a perfect example is preserved in Magdalen College Oxford, Durrington charter, no. 2.

under a serene expression. O what marvellous patience of the man of God, deserving everlasting commemoration! As often as he was defeated in litigation and the lawyers obtained judgement against him, he promptly fell to prayer, and with clasped hands and eyes turned to heaven said, 'Lord Jesus, who prayed saying "Father, not my will but yours be done",[85] I pray in the same way, let it be done not as I will, but as you will; and let the outcome be as it shall be your will in heaven. Only would that my church might obtain what ought in law to be hers, and that, despite her adversaries, she might possess all that belongs to her.'

What wonder, when he constantly heard that many of his adversaries obtained what they asked for? Otto the legate, in effect another pope, was a powerful adversary of his. Yet the constancy of the holy man was never once moved to allow bitter words to pass his lips, nor was his countenance changed. Assuming the persons of the holy Job, he said, 'It has been done as it has pleased the Lord. Blessed be the name of the Lord.[86] It has been so decreed by men learned in the law. It must be presumed that so many great and discerning men have not erred and could not have been deceived.'

As oppression increases, the archbishop goes into exile

At length, as his tribulations multiplied at the hands of the mightier persons of the kingdom whom, out of reverence for pope and king, I consider it neither proper nor safe to accuse by name, the archbishop pondered acting upon the Gospel precept 'When they persecute you in this city, flee into another.'[87] Since he was unable to exercise freely the office of pastoral care committed to him, though he desired to do so, he decided to give up and depart, following the acts and advice of Blessed Thomas, previously referred to.

He crosses the sea

He therefore commended himself, his servants and the cause of his church, to God, to the glorious Virgin, his lady and spouse, and to Blessed Thomas, his predecessor and leader, and had a ship secretly and quickly made ready, and from the island in eastern England called Thanet[88] he was borne by a favourable wind to a port across the sea. He reduced his

---

85. Luke, xxii. 41.
86. Job, i.21.
87. Matthew, x.23.
88. Eustace, who accompanied Edmund on the journey, says they sailed from Sandwich: Lawrence, *St Edmund*, p. 217.

household which was not a little burdened by debt. In order to imitate the acts of the martyr faithfully and follow unerringly in his path, he hastened his steps towards Pontigny. He intended to stay there privately and in peace, with time to pray and meditate, and wait a few days until the dawn from on high visited him and the English kingdom, and the burden of his debts was lightened.

Concerning the honour shown him by Blanche, the Queen of France

When the archbishop reached France, he had an intimate and lengthy conversation at Senlis with the Lady Blanche, mother of the king of France, who is well known to be a strong-minded woman of great counsel. Her sons, whom she had brought with her, were present, and commending herself and them to his prayers, she asked him to give them his blessing; and with clasped hands she pressed him with great earnestness to pray God devoutly and tirelessly for the state of the French kingdom and the safety of the king. This request he granted and he undoubtedly fulfilled it. Hence we believe – and I consider it right to believe it – that his blessing restored the king's health and life when he was later gravely ill and was said by many to have died,[89] and that it afterwards brought him honour and prosperity, as was verified by subsequent events.

The queen pressed her request all the more persistently because she had heard that he had been distinguished by many signs of sanctity, and that he was following unerringly in the footsteps of Blessed Thomas the Martyr. She therefore offered him at his pleasure a special refuge of peace and tranquillity in the kingdom of France, where he might stay with great honour at the expense of the lord king, her son; and the king himself and his brothers devoutly implored him to accept this. The archbishop, though, declining to prolong his stay, thanked them profusely, and with this permit made his farewells. He hastened on his journey to Pontigny, where he was received with due honour and reverence. He was assigned a house not far from the cloister and church, which according to the monks had been the secret residence of Blessed Thomas in his exile, and with it he was assigned honest chamberlains who could be trusted with secrets. This the archbishop gratefully, and indeed joyfully accepted.

89. The illness of Louis IX occurred in December 1244, see Guillaume de Nangis in *Receuil*, xx, p. 344.

How he conducted himself at Pontigny

There he stayed peacefully for some days, occupying himself with prayer, contemplation, preaching and other good works, with such intensity that he instructed all who lived there and increased their devotion. They marvelled to see such devotion in a secular clerk. He reduced his diet beyond measure and persisted, though some of the brethren protested, saying 'Holy father, St Bernard, the abbot of Clairvaux, one of our doctors, says "curb your body, do not kill it; repress it, do not oppress it"; and at prayer the Church's usage teaches us, "let your service be reasonable,"[90] and so does the master's comment, "Provide food, burden and a rod for the beast, that is, the body."'[91] The archbishop yielded to their persuasion and mitigated the rigour of his abstenance in many respects, but without entirely satisfying them. So the monks were shamed and condemned their own weakness and sloth, despite the fact that they were leading the austere life of the Cistercians.

How he received confraternity in their chapter [92]

One day the archbishop went into the chapter at the request of the abbot and community and delivered them a sermon. His teaching on life and his learning touched their hearts. He spoke with intense fervour, briefly, succinctly and eloquently in Latin and in the French vernacular. After his sermon he sought and obtained the lot and spiritual privileges of a monk, requesting a special association with the whole house. From then on, he was made one of their company as if he was a monk of the selfsame monastery, though he did not wear the cowl, and he confessed himself to be their confrater. Also he gratefully refreshed them with meals that we call pittances.[93]

How he was ill and prepared himself for death

When he had stayed a little time at Pontigny, he was taken ill with a sickness which, although it gave him no little pain, little affected his

---

90. Romans, xii.1.
91. Apparently from the Glossa Ordinaria on Ecclesiasticus, xxxiii.25.
92. The privilege of confraternity was a form of association open to individual benefactors, clerical or lay. The recipient was made a participant in the spiritual benefits of the monastery, and on his death the community celebrated for him the office of the dead as it did for its own monks.
93. Pittances were extra dishes, often delicacies, that supplemented the two main cooked dishes prescribed by the Rule of St Benedict; they were served on festivals and the anniversaries of benefactors, who bequeathed funds for the purpose.

understanding or the old vigour of his reason. In order to have a breath of purer air, more like that of his native land, he took the advice of his doctors to leave Pontigny for a time, so as to come back restored in health. When he yielded to the persuasion of his own party – for he was nothing if not amenable – and was about to set out on the journey, the brethren of Pontigny made an outcry and wept, saying, 'Why are you abandoning us, father? Whom are you leaving us for? Why are you in such haste to depart from us, who are your devoted servants? We were so consoled by your venerable presence that now we are all the more saddened by your departure. You see, we have been allowed to taste only so much of your sweetness, with which, alas, we have not deserved to be filled. It is much to be feared that it is our sins that have incurred this punishment.'

Note that he had the spirit of prophecy

The archbishop felt sympathy for them as they wept and howled, and to console them he said, 'Don't be saddened by my departure, brethren. By God's grace I shall come back to you on the feast of St Edmund, king and martyr.'[94] So it came about. As is known, on that very day the body of the blessed confessor was brought to Pontigny, as will be more fully reported in the proper place. Now when the saint, with deep sighs and groans, had with difficulty reached Soisy, a house of the canons regular, contrary to the hope and judgement of the doctors his illness grew daily worse. On a certain day, knowing in the spirit that the day of his dissolution was imminent, he had the eucharist brought to him with due veneration. Before receiving it, he confessed all the articles of faith. He spoke with such fervent faith and showed such devotion that, to the bystanders who were watching, it seemed that the Lord's passion was being re-enacted before them in the flesh. The fervour of his faith and the intensity of his devotion beggar description. Among other declarations he made, he said these and similar words: 'It is you, Lord, in whom I have believed, whom I have loved, of whom I have preached and taught. You are my witness that I have sought nothing on earth save you.'

Some wise men were astonished by these words. But these words were manifestly uttered by the prompting of the Holy Spirit to strengthen veneration for so great a sacrament in the hearts of the faithful. For the Most High, who has since made his saint glorious by innumerable signs, has Himself validated these words with the seal of irrefutable truth. By reason of which, the Catholic faith is beautifully renewed, the obstinacy of

94. viz. 20 November.

the Jews is confounded, the cunning of heretics is rejected, pagans in their blindness tremble, faint-hearted sinners recover hope, and the Church universal has gained increased honour.

Some wonderful things he said and did when close to death

After being fortified by the viaticum of salvation, he began to seem a little better, and became merry, as though he had been fed to repletion by the celestial banquet. Supported by a pillow so that he could sit up, he looked serene and he joked with those standing around, telling them this proverb in English: 'Men seth gamen gooth on wombe. Ac ich segge, gamen gooth on herte; which is to say, play enters the belly; but now I say play enters the heart.' The meaning of this epigram is: it is commonly said that a full belly makes men joyful and ready for play; but it is my opinion that a heart fed by a spiritual feast produces a serene conscience, freedom from anxiety and joyfulness. In fact, he displayed such joyfulness and hilarity that those who were with him were quite astonished. Anyone wanting to explain the meaning of this joyfulness would have to find suitable words to describe the spiritual joy of heaven or he would overstep the truth. That delightful tearfulness or tearful delight, that grieving laughter or laughing grief, that sad cheerfulness or cheerful sadness, are even now resolved into a thanksgiving that transcends human nature, so that it seemed he was surely experiencing the joy of paradise. Lest I should be accused of any negligence by witholding or omitting from what I have written the immense goodness of his which affected all whom we have seen, I think it right to insert one of his works of mercy in this little book.

When his servants, all of whom were honest and kept under a strict regime, saw that he was approaching the gates of death, they began to wail and lament, saying, 'O God, what will become of us? Where shall we go when our dearest lord has died? We are left exiles in a far-away place, penniless, and even without any victuals. These clerks get all kinds of revenues from members of the Curia to make them rich; but we are utterly penniless and left by our master to beg. Alas, "to beg we are ashamed, and to dig we are not able."[95] We are not used to business, and our penury makes it impossible. If we return home we shall be odious to the king and the magnates on account of their hatred for our lord. What is left for us but a miserable death?'

Hearing this, the archbishop was moved in his indescribable goodness, and calling one of them who seemed more miserable than the others, he

95. Luke, xvi.3.

said, 'My friend, I will write to a loyal friend of mine on your behalf. He will not fail me when I write, nor will he fail you in your need.' And asking for the necessary implements, he wrote as follows:

The archbishop's last letters

Edmund, by the grace of God archbishop of Canterbury and primate of all England, to our venerable brother in Christ, William, by the same grace bishop of Norwich,[96] greetings and sincere love in the Lord. Although it is commonly said that death bears all things away, the love which is rooted in charity is neither broken by adversity nor parted by death, for 'charity never fails.' With this love that we have long had for you, we embrace you, brother, most warmly, knowing from past experience that we likewise are embraced by your affection and kindness. Being afflicted with grave bodily infirmity and at the point of death, we appeal to you and humbly beg you of your constant and loving kindness to pray for us and have us prayed for throughout your diocese.

Also, we humbly ask you of your generosity if you would be so kind as to retain in your service our beloved Robert of Essex, the bearer of these letters. By experience we have found him commendable for his faithfulness and his honest service. Thus through him, whom we have long loved for his merits, you may often be reminded of us. Lastly, since the dead usually have few friends, especially in the realm of England, we commend to your perfect love the will, drawn up by us and sealed with our seal, and our executors named therein, begging you, for the love of Him who richly rewards good deeds, to give the said executors your advice and assistance.

Given at Soisy, 14th November, in the 7th year of our pontificate.[97]

That he had certain foreknowledge of his death

When he had performed a similar kind service for the others, he handed each of them the letters he had written, all of which by God's grace produced a most pleasing result; and he said to them, 'This handwriting of mine in which I have written for your benefit, is known to my loyal friends and it is more advantageous and more effective than any seal.' Thus the anxiety of many of his poor servants was set at rest. I have said this so

96. William Ralegh, bishop of Norwich, 1239–43.
97. The manuscript has, incorrectly, '8th year'.

that any reader of this little book may know the fervour of the charity possessed by Blessed Edmund, the archbishop of Canterbury. But I thought this letter should be stuck to this page so that any reader should realize how sure our holy father Edmund was that he was then leaving his fleshly abode, for he urgently implores the friend to whom he is writing to give his conscientious assistance to the execution of his will.

Of his bearing and devotion when receiving extreme unction

As his natural strength ebbed and his illness increased in gravity, he asked for the sacrament of extreme unction which, as is well known, had its origin in the holy instructions of St James the apostle,[98] and assumed customary form through the admonition of the Holy Spirit. Who could adequately describe in writing the tears, groans and trembling of God's saint as he was anointed by the priest who duly performed this office? For as his eyes and hands were ever turned toward heaven, his spirit seemed already to be winging its way heavenwards and to resent its longer detention in the prison of the flesh. Then, when the sacrament had been administered with due reverence, the holy man seized the cross from the hand of the minister, and with wonderful devotion pressed the places of the nails, which were coloured blood-red, to his mouth and eyes, constantly and sorrowfully kissing them and moistening them with copious tears. Above all, for a long time he sucked and licked the gaping wound in the side of the figure, saying with sighs, 'With joy shall you draw water out of the wells of the Saviour.'[99] The manner of his devotion produced no little astonishment in the bystanders, not least on account of its novelty.

That the spirit of prophecy was in him

At the urgent request of those about him, he cast away any feelings of resentment he had towards the monks of Canterbury, and relaxed his sentence in the case of those willing to submit and render satisfaction. With hands clasped he asked forgiveness from all who were present and assigned his body to the house of Pontigny. Before he had finished saying this, the prior of the house,[100] who was very dear to the archbishop and who was present, said, 'Alas, alas, are you leaving us altogether and

98. James, v.14.
99. Isaiah, xii.3.
100. i.e. the prior of Soisy.

deserting us?' But he replied, 'By no means. My heart and my love are with you always.' And they did not understand his words. But after his death his body was eviscerated and his heart and entrails were buried in that place. Then their eyes were opened and they understood his words.[101] This was done as his body had to be borne to Pontigny, which is about twenty leagues or at least a two-day journey from Soisy, where he died.

Concerning a cloak and a panel

Nor, although at the point of death, did the good brother forget his two sisters who were living as nuns at Catesby. For he sent them his ash-grey cloak, made of the cloth commonly called 'camelot', with a mantle of lamb's wool, and a silver panel on which was carved a figure of Blessed Mary with her Son on her lap, and the passion of Christ and the martyrdom of Blessed Thomas. On account of these relics which are preserved and venerated at Catesby, even until the present day the Lord performs miracles in that place that are worthy of everlasting remembrance.

How he found release in a very holy death

Taxed and wearied by these labours, he became silent. Then he fell into his last sleep, and like one who slept he sank into the peace of death without any of the signs that are usual in the dying such as a murmur in the throat or a struggle, and so took his leave of his brethren and this world. Thus, untroubled by a lingering agony, he gently fell asleep in the Lord, and he, who had always been a maker of peace, departed peacefully into the peace that is eternal. For to those like him it is given to have an easy passing. In this way then, on the 15th November,[102] Blessed Edmund, the archbishop of Canterbury and the glorious confessor of the Lord, happily fled from his fleshly abode to the palace of heaven, from exile to his homeland, from the darkness of this world to the glorious light of the heavens. On the 21st of the same month his body was buried according to the law of the human condition in the church of St Mary at Pontigny. There in that place the saint manifestly demonstrates that he is alive in Christ and plainly testifies that he is in glory, much to the consolation of the living, for the frequency of signs and miracles, that it would take us too long to enumerate, makes it look as if we have returned to the age of the apostles.

---

101. Luke, xxiv.31. Cf. the whole paragraph with the identical passage in the margin of the Great Chronicle: *Chron.Maj.*, iv, p. 73.
102. The manuscript has *xvii Kal Dec.* i.e. 15 November; the copyist should have written *xvi Kal.Dec.*, i.e. 16 November.

England should rejoice, therefore, to have produced from the bosom of Abingdon such and so great a patron. Pontigny should rejoice exceedingly at having received in its midst the remains of so great a bishop. France, which opened its gates and offered a refuge to an exile, should be thankful. Those who at some time gave him service or the solace of companionship should be gladdened. Those who caused him vexation or troubled him by detraction should be converted and repent; and those who harassed him and out of ignorance or insolence inflicted on him the wrongs he endured, should at least honour him now that he has triumphed. God has avenged him, and those who disparaged him shall come to him and adore his footprints. For your knights who fight for justice and truth conquer, O Christ, at last, and their triumph is everlasting glory.[103]

What was done immediately after his death

On the morning of the first day after he had fallen asleep, he who performed the office of chancellor[104] sealed the aforesaid letters, which were sealed with his last seal, and handed them to those who had been granted them by the saint, to take to his friends. Having obtained these, the staff of the household bade farewell to the clerks who had stayed with the body, and weeping and sobbing immediately took their leave. Then, when everyone had been called together, in their presence the seal was broken, as is the custom, on account of the risk of fraudulent counterfeit or legal quibbling. It had carved on it, as has been previously described, the figure of his predecessor, the Blessed Thomas, with his brains dashed out, in whose footsteps Blessed Edmund had followed and whose company he merited to share in heaven. The same day, his body, clothed with honour in episcopal vestments, was borne from Soisy to Trainel, and it was followed with great devotion and songs of praise by an innumerable multitude of the faithful spread out far and wide in long columns. The further it was borne, greater and greater grew the crowds that followed, like a flood that is swollen by torrential rains. All are attracted by the sight of the body, crushing one another to follow the saint on foot. Now they are impeded and checked by the narrowness of the way, and as the ministers shout and chide them, they push together in a rush, falling over themselves as each strives to get in front of another. For any who boast of

---

103. This paragraph seems to have been intended by Matthew as a grand finale to his Life of St Edmund. What follows is an addition containing a narrative of the funeral procession to Pontigny supplied by Eustace, with additional details probably supplied by Edmund's chancellor, Richard de Wych.

104. Richard de Wych. The oblique manner of reference suggests that the report was penned by himself.

having touched the body regard themselves as having been blessed and having expiated their sins; nor was this without justification, since very many people obtained alleviation and help in their troubles.

On this side are women carrying sick children, over there are others labouring under various afflictions, shouting loudly, 'Bearers, why are you in such a hurry? Why do you not let us enjoy the presence of this holy body at least for a short while? Although we are sinners and held to be unworthy of such a great favour, everyone knows that it is not those who think themselves to be well who need a doctor, but those who are sick.' Anyone who thought he had not either touched or kissed the bier, the hands or the feet, felt sorry for himself, similarly if he had failed to get a sight of the sacred body or had not had a chance to show his reverence at such a great funeral. We were a numerous throng of clerks and religious, the priests wearing sacred dress, namely surplices, albs and copes, proceeding with measured and rapid steps in processional order. There were also many monks with us, whose habits were thought to add distinction,[105] among whom was the abbot of Pontigny, who had come to meet us.

When the abbot saw the crush of people and the wonderful devotion and reverence shown the body by clergy and people, having first removed outsiders from the place, he addressed God's saint in this way, as though he was still living, saying, 'Good father, in that you are a brother of the church of Pontigny you owe me obedience. I make bold to speak to you. I am your abbot, and you are a monk of mine. I speak not to the archbishop as his superior, but to the monk. Obey and hear my requests: I beseech you to perform no more miraculous signs of this kind until you arrive at the place of your rest, that is Pontigny.' Indeed, on account of some signs already performed and well publicized, the abbot was very fearful that the body of the glorious confessor would be violently seized and taken off or stolen. He therefore sealed the bier with his seal, in the presence of him who wrote this and of many others.

What was done with his sacred body on the second day

The abbot claimed the holy body with all the more assurance because, while the archbishop was staying at Pontigny, he one day entered the chapter to give a sermon, and having finished it, with much devotion he petitioned them of their charity to grant him the bond of confraternity.[106]

---

105. This is a typical interjection by Matthew in his source – the suggestion that the monks added a touch of distinction to the lower orders of clergy.
106. This repetition of the event already described above, p. 151, is a reminder that Matthew is here copying a report of the funeral procession which he has added to the Life. He retains the use of the first person singular, which was used by Eustace, who was an eye-witness.

This was granted him. For this reason the abbot often said playfully to the secular clerks, 'What have the remains of my monk got to do with you?' And by way of more effective argument, he added, 'For sure, no one has the power to oppose or contradict the ordinance of St Thomas and the prophecy he made to us long ago. This is he whom he once promised us. This is he who will repay all the debt the martyr owed to our poor house of Pontigny. You English have the martyr. We are keeping our monk and confessor.' This was the talk that went on between us that night, as we argued about who had the better right to possession of the body. A careful watch was kept, and having posted guards, we passed an anxious night, fearing that because of our sins some mishap would happen to us with the body.

On the morning of the second day, as we were carrying the sacred body through Villeneuve-l'Archevêque, a crowd of men and women came to meet it with joyful cries of acclamation and noisy applause. With marvellous devotion they kissed the bier which was held in the tightly wedged procession. Despite our annoyance, no argument could restrain their devotion or prevent them from carrying the body off by force to the church and placing it upon the high altar. Some people rush into the church; others, because of the dense crowd, wait for the body to be brought out. We judged it to be a wonderful presage of his glorification.[107] At length, after a long wait, the elders of the town were persuaded by certain persons of note to disperse the people with clubs. We therefore received back the body, and with many people preceding and following us, it was carried on the same day as far as the house of the Templars at Coulours.[108] When the holy man had passed this on his way back from Pontigny, he asked someone whose house it was, and receiving the answer 'of the Templars', he remarked 'I shall lie at that house on my return.' And so it was done. For we passed the night with the holy body in that house in continuous psalmody. While there, we heard murmurs from the brethren of the house in council and we were not a little afraid that the body would be taken from us by violence; for they said that the saint himself had declared with a prophetic spirit that he wished to rest there. We steadily contradicted them, but it was only by pointing out the intention that the saint had expressed both orally and in writing that we were able to put down their shamelessness. Indeed in our bitterness we warned them that if they used force they would feel the anger and

---

107. i.e. the placing of the bier on the altar anticipated Edmund's elevation to the altars of the Church through his canonization.
108. Coulours (Aube). I have not been able to trace a house of the Templars at this place. The order had a commandery at Provins: V. Carrière, *Histoire et cartulaire des Templiers de Provins* (Paris, 1919).

vengeance of God and the saint. For the saint only said this in reference to taking his rest there on that night. So we got away, though with great difficulty.

What was done with his sacred body on the third day

As we proceeded from there on the third day, as on the day before innumerable people of both sexes ran to meet us, shouting and wailing, 'Where is the holy body? Where is the body?' Here are the phalanxes of clergy chanting psalms, here are the religious in orderly procession, the cross-bearers and those in sacred vestments singing dirges, and, running to meet us, peasants from the fields, who as if crazy had even left their oxen yoked to the plough, a numberless concourse of people, like a great army, that flowed from fields, townships, villages and streets.

Two of our people, who were greatly astonished by the unusual concourse and astounded by the size of the crowds, said to one another, 'What does this unheard of demonstration mean?' For it seemed to them to be both excessive and irrational. One of them said to another, in what spirit God knows, 'It seems that the monks of Pontigny have preached great things about this body, so as to invent a saint for themselves and gain profits from the offerings. The people are clamouring "Let us go and meet his most holy body, escort it, look at it, touch it, and venerate it in every way we can." And they vie with one another and crush one another in their haste. Yet men agree that nothing has been seen or written about his sanctity.' One of those who was conversing, or rather condemning, replied, 'If he was a saint and worthy to be counted among the real saints, he would not have cared to be buried and remain entombed in a Cistercian house. Almost all the glorious saints lie in houses of the order of black monks, few or none in houses of the Cistercians.'[109] To confirm what he had said and for the sake of example, he listed the houses of Canterbury, St Albans, St Edmund's, Durham, and many others in the realms of both France and England. A disagreement arose over this and they and many others were divided in their opinions, according to the text of Isaiah, 'I will lead the blind in a way they know not, in a path that they have not known I will guide them.'[110] But within a few days, after glorious signs, the prophetic saying that follows became shiningly clear: 'I will turn the darkness before them into light, the rough places into level ground.'

109. Another of Matthew's dramatic dialogues expressing his own feelings. Edmund's eccentric wish to be buried at Pontigny offended his patriotism and touched his pride in his own Benedictine order.
110. Isaiah, xlii.16.

How some of our clerks and laymen still did not believe in his sanctity

There were some of our clerks and laymen, namely household officers, real doubting Thomases, who, although they had frequently seen the saint in his lifetime, did not believe in his great sanctity. Inexcusable in their unbelief and slowness of heart, they were unwilling to admit that he was such a special friend of the Most High as was clearly demonstrated by the subsequent testimonies of God. To these sceptics must be added even some of the monks of the Canterbury convent. Heaven grant that the offence of some members does not rebound upon the whole community. As the poet rather urbanely puts it,

> Be careful all are not swamped by the fault of the few.[111]

Just so it is not fitting that the incredulity of some who gainsay should recoil upon the saint's entire household. In men of the present age the smallest spark of charity grows cold and turns to ash. And is it any wonder? Even of the disciples of the Saviour, who had imbibed the rudiments of faith from his own teaching and had the best of all masters, we find it written that Jesus appeared to them and 'reproved their incredulity and hardness of heart, because they did not believe those who had seen him after he had risen from the dead.'[112] How much more are those of the present, the impure children of a vile age, blind and hard of heart! We are become like owls and bats which are not permitted to see the light of day. How hard it is in these times to discern a hypocrite apart from a saint, to distinguish between a true lover of God and a dissembler! I say this because even men of discretion and worldly wisdom did not judge Edmund to be a blessed confessor of God. But 'man looks on the outward appearance, but the Lord looks on the heart.'[113] I therefore think it salutary advice for a man to venerate someone after he has manifestly been glorified by God, and to accept God's reproof and instruction.

Concerning his burial

Four days later, by which time a throng had assembled as big as is commonly seen gathering to transact business at fairs, on the feast of St Clement, that is on the 23rd November,[114] the body of our blessed and

---

111. *Ars Amatoria*, iii.9.
112. Cf. Mark, xvi.14.
113. Cf. 1 Kings, xvi.7.
114. Manuscript has *undecimo Kal. Decembris*, i.e. 21 November.

glorious father Edmund, archbishop of Canterbury and confessor, was buried in the church of Blessed Mary the mother of God, in the house of the Cistercian Order at Pontigny, in the presence of prelates, monks, clergy and lay people. His funeral was attended by important men of authority — bishops, abbots, priors, monks and magnates, with bells, lights and vestments, devoutly celebrating the various parts of divine service. In this place, and in other places where the sweet memory of the saint is cultivated to the honour of God, manifest miracles are proclaimed, worthy of eternal remembrance, the like of which have not been seen in our time nor distantly heard of, for the verification and strengthening of the Christian faith.

Of miracles proclaimed at Catesby

In order that the favours of the blessed Edmund might be spread more widely and the odour of his sweetness fill many regions, in England also, which merited to be mother and nurse of so great a bishop, there is an unheard-of coruscation of miracles at the house of nuns at Catesby. It was there that the two sisters of Bishop Edmund, both women of outstanding piety, had taken the veil of perpetual chastity. By reason of their blood relationship and their holy innocence, he warmly loved his admirable sisters, and when he was about to depart from this world, as a token of his charity, he sent them his cloak, and a painted or carved panel depicting the passion of Christ, which are kept to this day in the church of Catesby in memory of the saint. And these things have enriched and beautified that house, which was once poor, by the multiplication of miracles and of favours bestowed on it in this country and overseas, to the honour and glory of the realms of England and France, through the gift of Him who lives and reigns for ever and ever.

How his canonization was delayed through ill-will

Blessed Edmund of glorious memory was postulated (for canonization) by men of the highest authority, that is by the lord Pope in the first place, and by other important and holy prelates, and they procured his solemn canonization in the Council of Lyons. But his earthly honour was impeded by the carping of envious people, whom it is unsafe to name. Even after his death they tried to rend him with obloquy, as the Jews did Christ, and to detract from his virtues, which were apparent to the whole world. Yet heaven conferred this honour upon him at an opportune time. It was thus determined by Him who 'reaches mightily from one end of the earth to the other and orders all things sweetly,'[115] so that 'a city set on a hill could not be hid.'[116] Those who pursued him with inexorable hatred, when they realized from unimpeachable signs that he was manifestly made a friend of God, were all the readier to repent of their ignorance and pursue the saint with their veneration.

Here begins the official edict of the canonization of Blessed Edmund, the confessor [117]

Innocent, bishop, servant of the servants of God, to our venerable brothers, archbishops, bishops, and to our beloved sons, the abbots, priors, deans, archdeacons, provosts, archpriests and other prelates of the churches, who shall receive these letters, greetings and apostolic blessing.

With great gladness we report the new joy of mother Church as she celebrates a new saint. With exultation of spirit we proclaim a great festival that is being kept by the company of heaven which has gained a new member. The Church indeed rejoices to have produced so great a son, to guide others by the example of his holy life and to give them a sure hope of salvation by having himself won the prize of beatitude. She, whom all must proclaim and venerate, is exceedingly joyful to have received lustre from such a distinguished son, and she plainly declares that those who confess the Church as their mother by faith and works are to be admitted to a share in an eternal inheritance, and that none can enter the glory of heaven except through her, as she holds the keys of the kingdom of heaven. The celestial homeland rejoices at the arrival of a noble inhabitant and union with a new settler tried in faith. The citizens of heaven rejoice to be joined by a distinguished fellow-citizen. The saints sing with psalmody who have lately received a worthy consort. Arise, therefore, you who are zealous for the faith, and together with the Church, your mother, be glad for the grandeur and exaltation of a brother. Come together with joy and take sure hope from a neighbour who has been made a compatriot of the land of heaven. Rejoice with immense joy because you have gained a new patron with the Lord, because there stands in His presence a gentle

---

115. Wisdom, viii.1.
116. Cf. Matthew, v.14.
117. Matthew refers to this copy of the bull in *Hist.Angl.*, iii, p. 135. He kept a copy of it in the Liber Additamentorum: *Chron.Maj.*, vi, pp. 120–5. Original copies, addressed to the church of Lyons and the English baronage, are in the muniments of Sens cathedral, nos. 31, 32. Copies are very numerous, see Potthast, ii, 12392, and printed text in *Bullarium Romanum* (Turin, 1858), iii, 522.

intercessor for our salvation. See with what loving zeal the blessed archbishop Edmund, wisely reflecting that the creature is directed by natural affection towards its creator and that fallen nature ought to acknowledge its restorer, sought his own creator and redeemer. Therefore, straightly directed by the light of his mind, he advanced step by step to Christ, the finisher of our works, by the splendour of his life and the brilliance of his teaching showing others the path to salvation. Wherefore, distinguished as he was by a threefold charisma of true faith, sure hope and fervent charity, by perseverance in these three things in harmonious conjunction namely purity of mind, perfect living and virtuous speech, he vanquished the three enemies of the world, the flesh and the Devil, and was worthy to receive the palm of victory prepared for him with a place of honour in the heaven of the Most High Trinity with the threefold order of the elect – the virgins, the continent and the married people.

Let us then relate something of his acts. The more fully his life is described, the more it enchants the narrator and the more it delights the spirits of those who hear it. He loved the Son of God from his tender years and did not cease later to keep Him in his heart, for the stilus of contemplation inscribed Him upon the soft tablet of his mind. Rather, indeed, the more he advanced in age, the fuller the knowledge that fired his love. And lest the fervour of his spirit should be extinguished by the heat of the flesh but rather fired by its mortification, he tamed it harshly by constant use of a hair-shirt, binding its desires with the bonds of strict abstinence, so that it was not under the constraint of his vows but in the freedom of his spirit that he inclined to what was right and prudently avoided what was wrong. For he afflicted his body with severe fasting. To the observance of the ancients he added a new austerity that he imposed upon himself: despising the delights of delicate food and content with the meals of humble people, at the periods of general fasting he chose to abstain even from the foods that were permitted, and on other days of the week he abstained still more. He hated excessive sleep; he was given to prolonged vigils and subjected his body to the demands of unremitting prayer. For, despising the softness of a bed and fearing to be made soft by luxurious rest, he indulged his limbs only by reclining quietly, and then refreshed by the briefest sleep, he rose straightaway and on his knees devoted himself to prolonged prayer. From the beginning of his ways until the end he was zealous for purity, and thus he avoided the snare of the world and the mire of sensual pleasure, and shone with the brightness of purity. He wasted the frail vessel of the flesh in order to preserve with greater care the treasure of the soul entrusted to him.

A distinguished teacher and an excellent preacher, he flooded the minds of his hearers with the light of knowledge and planted the seeds of virtue in the hearts of the faithful and tore out the thorns of vice. He had sublime humility, was strong in patience, kind and affable, compassionate and ready to forgive, and to help the needy he poured out alms in abundance. To summarize his many deeds in brief, he knew Jesus with so firm a faith and loved Him so deeply and so fixed all his desire upon the Beloved, that he held the world and the things in it to be of little worth, and all his care was for the things of heaven. He strove to make his deeds conform to his name, to prove that, being called Edmund, he was pure and free from reproach and separated from the world. Thus, like a man wholly of the spirit, untouched by the contagion of the flesh, when he was dying and the body of Christ was brought to him, Edmund uttered these marvellous words, which we should mark most attentively, 'Thou art he whom I have believed, whom I have preached, whom I have taught. Thou art my witness, Lord, that I have sought nothing on earth except thee. As thou knowest, I want nothing except that which is thy will. Thy will be done.' Truly, having in his lifetime illuminated the Church of God by his shining merits, in death he has not deprived her of the rays of his glory. For it was not the will of the Lord that the holiness of so great a man should be lost to the world, but that it should be manifest by divers miracles, as it had been by his numerous merits. For he has restored sight to the blind and, which is more glorious, he has infused clear vision and banished the darkness of one who was born blind. He has cleansed a leper with a sudden and wonderful ablution that caused the scales of leprosy to fall off. To another, who was naturally tongue-tied he has given the power of speech. He has fortified the trembling limbs of one who was paralysed by giving him solid sinews. He has helped those with contracted limbs by extending them. He has reduced and cured a dropsy and restored the health of an aged and bent hunchback so that he could stand up straight and raise his face. The flame of his glory has shown itself in these and many other manifest miracles, the list of which we did not consider it proper to include in this letter. By these the Catholic faith has been strengthened, the obstinacy of the Jews has been shamed, the deceitful teachings of heretics have been confounded and the ignorant pagans have been amazed. Let the church of Canterbury, therefore, sing a song of praise to the Lord because among her other adornments she has in modern times been embellished by venerable patrons with a crimson hue by one who was a martyr and with the pure whiteness of one who was a confessor. Let fertile Canterbury be full of joy for having dispatched from the threshing-floor of her church so pure a grain to the barns of the supreme king. Let the monastery of Pontigny rejoice that she merited the honour of having the presence of such great fathers, one of whom long resided there and ennobled her by the manner of his life, and the other on coming there, after rendering his soul to heaven, has enriched her with the treasure of his body, so that what the glorious martyr Thomas is claimed to have said after a long stay in that monastery at the time of his exile, might be fulfilled. Since he was unable to repay the great honour and charity shown him by the monks to the extent he wished, he said a successor of his would render them worthy recompense.

Since it is fitting, then, that those whom God has magnified in heaven with a crown of eternal glory should be venerated by men on earth with the greatest zeal and devotion, that by solemnly commemorating the saints the faithful may be more deserving of their patronage, we therefore, after careful and solemn inquiry and strict examination, have reached full certainty regarding the holiness of life and the truth of the miracles of the same Saint Edmund; and with the common counsel and assent of our brethren and of all the prelates then present at the Apostolic See, on the Sunday of Advent on which *Gaudete in Domino* is sung,[118] we thought it our duty to inscribe him in the catalogue of the saints, or rather to proclaim that he was already so inscribed. Therefore we advise and earnestly exhort you all, and by apostolic letters we command you, devoutly and solemnly to celebrate his feast on the 16th November, the day when his happy soul, freed from the prison of the flesh, ascended the skies and came to the halls of heaven, there to enjoy the bliss of paradise. Do you, brother archbishops and bishops, cause it to be celebrated by Christ's faithful with fitting veneration throughout your cities and dioceses, so that by his intercession you may be delivered from present perils, and may in the future obtain the reward of eternal life.

But in order that Christian people may come in greater crowds and with greater fervour to his venerable tomb and that the solemn festival of the saint may be observed with greater magnificence, to all those truly penitent and confessed, who come thither annually with reverence on the feast day to seek his intercession, we, trusting in the mercy of Almighty God and in the authority of the Blessed Peter and Paul his apostles, remit a year and forty days of the penance enjoined on them, and forty days to those coming in any year to the said tomb within the octave of the festival.

Given at Lyons on the 11th January in the 4th year of our pontificate.

Clear testimony to the state of his body when it was translated

Richard, by the grace of God bishop of Chichester[119] to his venerable friend Reginald abbot of Bayham,[120] greetings. In order to provide you with more certain information about the elevation and condition of the most holy body of Blessed Edmund, I am writing to notify you that on the

118. The introit of the mass for the third Sunday of Advent, which in 1246 fell on 16 December.
119. Richard de Wych, St, bishop of Chichester, 1244–53. Cf. the text of this letter in the Additamenta: *Chron.Maj.*, vi, pp. 128–9.
120. Reginald, abbot of Bayham, attests several acts of Archbishop Edmund. He appears to have served him as an estates steward.

morrow of Holy Trinity last, namely in the year of grace 1247, on the 27th May,[121] in the evening, when the tomb of our holy father Edmund was first opened in the presence of a few people, we found his body complete and intact and it exuded a most sweet perfume. His head with its hair and his face were shining, and the body was complete with all its members and was redolent with a heavenly scent surpassing that of any balsam or thyme. Only the nose had suffered a slight abrasion from the weight of the metal lid pressing upon it. The entire body, particularly the face, was found unharmed and looked as if it was suffused with oil. We interpreted this as a favour merited by the intact virginity he promised and afterwards kept when he espoused the statue of the Blessed Virgin with a ring. We can properly take the oil to signify the grace that abounded in his behaviour and his teaching and his excellent learning, for in lecturing, disputation, preaching or teaching 'grace was poured upon his lips';[122] 'therefore God hath anointed him with the oil of gladness above his fellows.'[123]

We found other signs of his virtues which the protracted length of events prevents us from setting out in writing, but which, given time and opportunity, we shall report to you privately and in full. But have no doubts, my lord, about the matters we have mentioned, for we speak that which we know and testify to that which we have seen, and we have been made certain beyond any doubt of the things to write. We have also touched the sacred head with our own hands, and have reverently and joyfully combed and composed the firm undamaged hair.

On Sunday before the feast of St Barnabas,[124] the translation of our blessed father the archbishop of Canterbury and confessor was celebrated at Pontigny by the divine will with exultation and indescribable glory, in the presence of the lord king of France, his mother and his brothers, many counts and great persons, assisted by two cardinals, that is the cardinal of Albano and the legate of France, with archbishops, bishops, abbots, priors, and a great many venerable prelates whose number we were unable to count. It added not a little to the honour of our nation.

Farewell, your holiness. Best wishes for your health and preservation for a long time to come.

---

121. Either Matthew or the copyist confused the entry: the MS. has *xv Kal Iunii*, i.e. 15 May, but in 1247 the morrow of Trinity fell on 27 May.
122. Psalms, xliv.3.
123. Psalms, xliv.8.
124. In 1247 this would be 9 June. The medieval English Church observed the feast of Edmund's translation on this date. But in the chronicles Matthew gives 7 June as the date of the solemn translation of the relics: *Chron.Maj.*, iv, p. 631.

Appendix I
The Alleged Exile of Archbishop Edmund

For many years the self-imposed exile of Archbishop Edmund formed part of the accepted account of his career. The incident provides an excellent example of the psychological gulf that separates the medieval hagiographer from the modern historian. For the historian tends to be unsympathetic towards such acts of fugitive virtue, and the plain fact suggested by the story was that the archbishop ran away from his responsibilities. Thus, in a century of great ecclesiastical leaders, St Edmund was assigned the role of a gentle, saintly but ineffectual reformer, overwhelmed by forces that he was not strong enough to resist. But the thirteenth-century hagiographers had different criteria. In their view, the archbishop's exile was a flight from iniquity which vindicated the rights of the Church. It formed a dramatic consummation of his career, as meritorious as martyrdom. As they eagerly pointed out, his exile and residence at Pontigny offered an obvious parallel to events in the lives of St Thomas Becket and Stephen Langton. On this occasion, Pontigny, now the traditional refuge for fugitive archbishops of Canterbury, was handsomely rewarded with the bones of a saint.

On closer inspection, however, the parallel between Edmund and his distinguished predecessors looks less impressive. Becket, after all, escaped into exile because he could not remain in England without surrendering fundamental principles. Langton was forced to stay abroad because King John would not have him. But it is difficult to discover any important issue that could account for Edmund's resignation and withdrawal to France in the autumn of 1240. The difficulty has, I think, been felt if not squarely faced by modern historians, and has given rise to rather general and varied explanations.[1]

The thirteenth-century hagiographers themselves are curiously vague on the subject. The earliest account is to be found in the first Life, composed by Edmund's chaplain, Eustace of Faversham, between 1242 and 1244.

---

1. Cf. F.M. Powicke, *Henry III and the Lord Edward* (1947), pp. 141, 262: 'The archbishop worn out by disputes with his monks of Christ Church and greatly distressed by the new influences at court, left England to die in the odour of sanctity near Pontigny' and 'his fretful and conscientious life of conflicts had come to its close in voluntary exile at Pontigny'; and A.B. Emden, *An Oxford Hall in Medieval Times* (1927), p. 97: 'Unwilling to submit to claims and policies which he regarded as harmful to his church and country, he decided to make the one impressive protest open to him.'

Eustace, who accompanied the archbishop on his last journey, has, strangely enough, chosen to describe the events leading up to the archbishop's departure in conventional words borrowed from John of Salisbury's Life of Becket. He sums the matter up like this:

> Since he could not freely exercise the pastoral office, although he had stretched out his hand to liberate the Church, he decided to surrender the field to wickedness, wishing in this to imitate the glorious martyr Thomas.[2]

This account was substantially repeated by the author of the Pontigny Life, and was incorporated by Matthew Paris into his Life of St Edmund. Matthew, on the other hand, writing ten years or more after the event, infused some historical facts into the sonorous platitudes of Eustace. He pointed to the rebellious conduct of the monks of Christ Church, as Eustace had done, but he mentioned also the archbishop's failure in litigation with the chapter of Rochester, his failure to prevent the irregular marriage of earl Simon de Montfort with the king's sister, the overbearing conduct of the papal legate, Cardinal Otto, and the vexations that the archbishop suffered at the hands of 'the mightier of the kingdom whom, out of respect for pope and king, I do not consider it proper or safe to accuse by name.'[3]

If these vague and guarded allegations are inspected more closely, it will be found that none of them offers a really satisfactory reason for the archbishop's retirement. There is, for instance, the matter of the legate, Cardinal Otto. There is no evidence that the legate was regarded with hostility by the English bishops, or that relations between him and the archbishop were bad. Recent research had tended to reveal his work in a more favourable light, and to emphasize the care and restraint with which he wielded his great powers.[4] The assumption that his presence was a source of annoyance to Archbishop Edmund rests on the *ex parte* statements of Matthew Paris, whose prejudices regarding the agents of Rome are notorious. There is, in fact, plenty of evidence that Edmund and the cardinal worked harmoniously together. Eustace, in his deposition before the canonization commission, stated that the legate had the archbishop's complete confidence; and his statement is borne out by the support the cardinal gave to Edmund in his dispute with the monks and his approval of, and active help with, his plan for a new collegiate church in the diocese of Canterbury. It is, too, a striking fact that when Edmund left

---

2. Lawrence, *St Edmund*, p. 217.
3. Above, p. 149.
4. See Dorothy Williamson, 'Some aspects of the legation of cardinal Otto': *EHR*, lxiv (1949), pp. 145–73.

for Rome at the end of 1237, he instructed his official and his own brother, whom he had left in charge of affairs at Canterbury, to turn to the cardinal for assistance should they encounter any serious difficulty during his absence.[5] Matthew's suggestion, therefore, that the hostility of the legate was one of the motives for the archbishop's withdrawal from England in 1240, is unsupported by the known facts and lacks inherent probability. In any case, it would be strange if the archbishop, after enduring the legate's presence for three years, should have left the country at the very time when the legate's own departure was known to be imminent.

Matthew's other explanations of the archbishop's conduct are no more satisfactory. He points out that Edmund lost his case against Rochester cathedral priory, whose monks had, contrary to the archbishop's rights of patronage, elected themselves a new bishop, and that he was unsuccessful in preventing the sacrilegious marriage of the king's sister. It seems improbable, however, that failure in litigation at the Curia would have persuaded the archbishop to throw up his responsibilities. The Rochester judgement had, in fact, guaranteed his rights in the see for the future. In any case, both these judgements were given against him in the spring of 1238, while he was in Rome.[6] If he wished to register a protest in this curious and novel form, why did he return to England in the summer of that year and remain at his post for the next two years? The obvious procedure, surely, would have been to remain abroad. He seems to have accepted the Rochester judgement with good grace and to have consecrated Richard of Wendover without undue delay.

When speaking of misunderstandings between the archbishop and the king, Matthew Paris adopts the vague and guarded phrases of Eustace, possibly without recognizing that they were drawn from the Life of Becket. There is no doubt that relations between the king and the bishops were strained in 1240, for Henry III's proceedings at Winchester were causing much anxiety. In his efforts to get a relative elected to the bishopric, he had resorted to the unprecedented step of appointing a new prior to the cathedral monastery and to packing the chapter.[7] This crude attempt to manipulate the electoral procedure, together with a number of other grievances, were the subject of a formal protest presented to the king by the bishops in assembly in January 1240.[8] No doubt feelings were exacerbated by other incidents that touched the archbishop more closely. Trouble had arisen over the wardship of the estates of Ralph fitzBernard,

5. The archbishop's instructions are cited in a letter addressed to the legate by Robert of Abingdon and Nicholas of Burford, the Official: PRO, Ancient Correspondence, xi, p. 159.
6. *CPL,* i, pp. 172, 174. *Annales Roffenses,* ed. Wharton, *Anglia Sacra* (1691), i, p. 349.
7. *Chron.Maj.,* iii, pp. 490–1.
8. *Ibid.,* iv, p. 3.

one of the archbishop's tenants, who was also a tenant of the Crown. On his death in 1238, the prerogative wardship of the whole estate was claimed by the king.[9] The archbishop was not prepared to surrender the wardship of Ralph's three Kentish fees without a struggle, and excommunications were launched against royal bailiffs.[10] It appears to be this incident which the hagiographers describe in their perfervid language as an unjust attack upon the temporalities of the church of Canterbury.

Such minor incidents could engender ill feeling, but they were, after all, commonplace in the life of a thirteenth-century bishop charged with the duty of defending a large territorial estate. The king's attitude in the Winchester affair provided grounds for deeper anxiety, but the suggestion that it persuaded the archbishop to throw up his duties and retire from the country is, to say the least, unconvincing. Edmund had given an impressive demonstration of strength in the crisis of 1234 when, by his fearless criticism of the administration, he had forced the king to reconstruct his council. The way in which he handled the rebellion of Richard the Marshal and the threat of civil war does not suggest that he was the man to abandon his post when his presence was most needed.

Perhaps the least plausible of the explanations for the archbishop's voluntary exile is that he was broken by the rebellion of his chapter. The dispute had its origins in the forgery of a charter of privileges by one of the monks and the consequent resignation of the prior, who was disciplined by the cardinal legate. When the archbishop entered the chapter to discuss the appointment of a new superior, the monks affronted him by walking out of the chapter-house and then, after an interval, proceeded to elect a new prior without his consent, and in so doing, placed themselves in an indefensible position. In the effort to bring them to submission, Edmund resorted by degrees to the most severe censures, suspension *in sacris*, excommunication, and finally interdict.[11] Not only the weight of canonical opinion but time was on his side. His interdict lay heavily on Canterbury. The cessation of pilgrim traffic to the shrine of St Thomas the Martyr had serious economic repercussions, and neither the monks nor the townspeople could afford to put up with the situation indefinitely.[12] The suggestion that, having done his worst, the archbishop ran away, offends common sense. Constitutional conflicts between bishop and chapter are not uncommon in the thirteenth century, but no case can be cited of a fractious chapter breaking a bishop's nerve to the extent of driving him into exile.

9. *Close Rolls, 1237–42*, pp. 59, 92. The Kentish fees of the archbishopric in question are listed in *The Red Book of the Exchequer*, ed. H. Hall (RS), ii, pp. 472, 725, 727.

10. *Ann.Mon.*, iii, p. 150.

11. The sequence of events is described by the continuator of *Gervase of Canterbury*, pp. 139 ff.

12. See the protest of the townspeople recorded by Gervase: *ibid.*, ii, p. 173.

If we lack any completely satisfactory explanation for the archbishop's voluntary exile, we are met, more curiously, by a conspiracy of silence on the part of the contemporary chroniclers. The one exception is the chronicle of St Albans, and to this we shall later return. The self-imposed exile of the archbishop of Canterbury and his assumption of the monastic habit at Pontigny were surely matters for comment; yet, Matthew Paris apart, the contemporary annalists do not even notice it. Thus the Rochester annalist makes no mention of Edmund's departure, although his church was at that time undertaking fresh litigation with the archbishop at Rome.[13] Richard of Morins, the Dunstable annalist, who was a papal judge-delegate in various cases concerning the archbishop and one of the best informed commentators of his time, simply ignores the archbishop's departure. He does, however, record Edmund's death in Burgundy and his burial at Pontigny, remarking only that before leaving, he had excommunicated the monks of Christ Church. This annal was evidently written later than March 1241, for Richard goes on to mention that he was one of those deputed by the pope to relax the archbishop's sentence.[14] The continuator of Gervase of Canterbury, who recorded in detail the course of the conflict between his brethren and the archbishop, notices Edmund's departure and says that on his disembarkation at Gravelines, he was seriously ill, and that he pursued his journey to Pontigny, where he died.[15] He says nothing, however, about the archbishop's reasons for leaving the country. The Oseney annalist says that the archbishop crossed the sea about the feast of All Saints, that he was taken ill at Pontigny, and that continuing on his way to Soisy, he died at that place.[16] The writer excusably assumed that the village of Soisy-en-Brie was south, not north of Pontigny. He evidently believed that Pontigny was only a stage in the archbishop's journey to some other destination, and not his ultimate goal.

None of these writers, who were writing up their annals year by year, saw anything in the archbishop's departure that called for special comment. However, two writers referred in passing to the purpose of Edmund's travels, a purpose so natural and commonplace that the other chroniclers did not trouble to mention it. The first, the writer of the unpublished annals of Hailes abbey, writes in the annal for 1240

> Master Edmund, the archbishop of Canterbury, crossed the sea on the way to the Roman Curia, and while on his journey, died at Pontigny, where God is performing many miracles for him.[17]

---

13. *Anglia Sacra*, i, p. 349.
14. *Ann.Mon.*, iii, p. 156; *CPL*, i, p. 194.
15. Gervase, ii, pp. 179–80.
16. *Ann.Mon.*, iv, pp. 87–8.
17. BL, Cotton MS., Cleopatra D III, fo. 43ʳ.

The other writer is the Tewkesbury annalist, who tells us that

> The lord Edmund, the archbishop of Canterbury, died around the feast of St Edmund, on his journey to Rome.[18]

As a matter of fact, these two notices represent the statement not of two independent authorities, but of one. Textual collation shows that both are based upon a common source no longer extant, which was apparently a Tewkesbury chronicle. The version of Edmund's departure given by the Hailes annalist is clearly the original form of the entry derived from the lost source. The writer had heard report of miracles at Pontigny, for Edmund's chaplain and his old associates were already propagating his reputation for sanctity in the spring of 1241.[19] But canonization proceedings were not yet in the wind, for the annalist was content to describe the late archbishop simply as 'Master Edmund'. We conclude then that the author of the lost Tewkesbury chronicle wrote the annal for 1240 either in 1241 or in 1242, and that at that date he had, in common with other well informed chroniclers, heard nothing about the archbishop's 'exile', and believed the archbishop to be on his way to Rome at the time of his death.

Apart from its inherent probability, the statement of the Hailes-Tewkesbury chronicler explains the absence of any reference to an exile or resignation in the many letters that were written to postulate Edmund's canonization. The point would presumably have been one worth making when arguing the archbishop's heroic sanctity. The Pontigny letter, it is true, makes ambiguous references to the archbishop's enemies who avoided him when he was alive and who were now confounded by his miracles. This letter was written rather later than the others, some time after June 1243,[20] and it may be that here already we have the myth of the exile germinating. But this may be to read too much into words that can bear a simpler and more straightforward explanation.

Reasons for the archbishop's visit to Rome are not far to seek. The profession of obedience that he made on receiving his pallium laid on him the obligation of making a triennial visit *ad limina* – to the Apostolic See,[21] and Edmund was the man to take this undertaking seriously. If he was to be punctilious in observing it he would need to present himself at the Curia in the spring of 1241. In any case, he had reasons of his own for waiting on the pope. The proctors of the Canterbury chapter were busy at the Curia

18. *Ann.Mon.*, i, p. 116.
19. Gervase, ii, p. 182.
20. The letter is addressed to Pope Innocent IV: *M.D.Thes.*, iii, col. 1,902.
21. See the profession made by Archbishop Edmund in *Le Liber Censuum de l'église romaine*, ed. P. Fabre and L. Duchesne (Paris, 1910), i, 286b, 449a.

pursuing an appeal against his interdict, while the king's proceedings over the vacant see of Winchester gave him a compelling reason for seeking an audience with Pope Gregory. But more insistent than all these reasons was the fact that, in common with the other prelates of Europe, he had received papal letters summoning him to a general council. The summons was issued on 9 August 1240, and the council was to meet the following Easter.[22] An archbishop with fish of his own to fry, would be well advised to arrive early to get his business dealt with before the council began to assemble. This would have indicated an autumn departure in order to accomplish the passage of the Alps before the winter months made the journey too hazardous.

Unfortunately it is impossible to fix the precise date at which Edmund left England. The Patent Rolls for the years 23 and 24 Henry III were already missing in the fourteenth century, so there is no record of a safe-conduct issued to the archbishop. The two annalists who date his embarkation differ by as much as three months. Thus the Tewkesbury annalist places it in August, and the Oseney annalist places it around the feast of All Saints – 1 November. No act of Edmund's given on English soil has come to light dated later than one given at Wingham on 23 July 1240,[23] but this does not mean that none exists. The last episcopal consecration that was certainly performed by him was that of Hugh Pateshall to the see of Lichfield, which took place at Newark on 23 July 1240. Wykes says that this was some time (diu) before the archbishop crossed the seas. A copy of the *Flores Historiarum* made at St Paul's notes that Edmund was present on 1 October, when Bishop Roger Niger consecrated St Paul's cathedral.[24] Although this is a later copy, its provenance gives it some title to consideration on this point. On this evidence there is something to be said for placing the archbishop's departure in about the third week of October.

On the evidence supplied by Matthew Paris, Edmund took with him his chaplain, Eustace, his chancellor, Richard de Wych, and some at least of the clerks of his secretariat, together with an unstated number of domestic servants. The route he took was the one we should expect him to have taken if he was on his way to Rome. He embarked at or near Sandwich and landed at Gravelines; this was the best port for the abbey of St Bertin, where he had broken his journey to Rome in 1238. From there he made his way to Senlis, where he encountered the French court and was

---

22. *Les registres de Grégoire IX*, ed. L. Auvray (Ecole française de Rome, 1896–1910), nos. 5,420–5,633. Matthew Paris records the departure of a number of English prelates for Rome in December 1240.

23. *Cartulary of the Priory of St. Gregory, Canterbury*, ed. Audrey Woodcock (Camden Soc., 3rd series, lxxxviii, 1956), p. 159.

24. *Flores Historiarum*, ed. H.R. Luard (RS), ii, p. 237 & n.

graciously received by Louis IX and the Queen Mother, Blanche of Castile. The party then proceeded to Pontigny, which lay midway between Auxerre and Tonnerre, a few miles north of the Grand Chemin Tonnerois leading to Langres. In view of its associations with Canterbury, as well as its size and eminence, it was a natural resting place for the archbishop and his household. It is highly probable that Edmund had stayed there before on his way back from Rome in 1238, for the Pontigny archives contained an *inspeximus* and grant which he made to the abbey in that year.[25]

We cannot be sure how long he stayed at Pontigny. Matthew Paris tells us that his stay lasted only a few days. Possibly Edmund thought it prudent to wait until the situation in north Italy had been clarified, for the emperor Frederick II had made it known that he would not allow any prelates across his territory to reach the pope. If his last sickness had not been upon him, he would presumably have continued his journey to Rome either by land or sea. As it was, after a period of rest, he was obliged by his illness to turn back. His itinerary northwards through Coulours to Soisy suggests that the party was making for Provins, and probably home. But on reaching Soisy, he was too weak to proceed further, and there, under the roof of a small Augustinian priory, he died on 16 November.

If this account of St Edmund's departure from England and death is more in accord with the known facts and with common sense, it remains to be seen how the story of the exile originated. The earliest references to it are to be found, wrapped up in rhetorical and ambiguous language, in the Life by Eustace, the chaplain, which we cited at the beginning. He applies to Edmund the phrase borrowed from the Life of Becket: 'he decided to surrender the field to wickedness'. Although the word 'exile' is not used here and the possibility of a journey to Rome is not completely excluded, the phraseology clearly implies that the archbishop had decided to throw up the unequal struggle and go into retirement.

What Eustace had stated by implication was gladly seized upon and elaborated by the hagiographers who followed him. Although the records of the canonization process contain no such allegation, the writer of the Anonymous 'A' Life developed Eustace's statement as follows:

> He decided to surrender the field to wickedness, and since he could not freely exercise the pastoral office . . . he chose to be banished and an exile outside the kingdom of England . . . and crossing the sea, he proceeded under the guidance of the Lord to Pontigny, the place of refuge for all prelates in exile from the realm of England for the sake of justice.

---

25. *Le premier cartulaire de l'abbaye cistercienne de Pontigny*, ed. M. Garrigues (Paris, 1981), nos. 241, 245.

Thus the story of the archbishop's self-sought exile was fairly launched.

By the time that Matthew Paris came to write his Life of St Edmund, using the work of Eustace as a literary base, the story already had a literary history and was well established. Matthew's dependence on Eustace explains the presence of the exile story in the Great Chronicle of St Albans and in the *Historia Anglorum* – the shorter history of his times begun by Matthew in 1250. The admission of the story to the Great Chronicle is to be explained by the fact that the annal for the year 1240, containing the notice of St Edmund's death, was not written up in its existing form until some years after Eustace's account had been put into circulation.[26]

How, one is inclined to ask, did Eustace come to perpetrate what appears at first sight to be a literary fraud? But this is to mis-state the question. If his Life of St Edmund is read continuously it is possible to see how he came to describe the archbishop's last journey in terms of an exile without any preconceived plan of distorting the truth. In writing of Edmund he made frequent and extensive use of John of Salisbury's Life of St Thomas Becket. As he approaches the end of Edmund's life, he draws increasingly on this source for his phraseology. He seems to feel the lack of a dramatic finale like that which ended Becket's career, and he argues that Edmund too had, in his own way, merited the crown of a martyr. The cumulative effect of these passages is unmistakable: the writer is trying to show that Becket's mantle had fallen on St Edmund. It must be remembered that Eustace was a monk of Christ Church Canterbury, where the cult and the shrine of St Thomas the Martyr were focal points in the devotional life of the community. The brief stay of Edmund's party at Pontigny must have kindled fresh memories of Becket's exile. The analogy with Becket must have been irresistible. It is unnecessary to accuse Eustace of deliberate deceit. The attempt to depict St Edmund as a *pedisequus* of Becket, treading in his footsteps, was neither a literary conceit nor an elaborate effort at deception. The accidental parallels of place and circumstance only provided the writer with outward corroboration of what for him was evidently a substantial reality. He believed that the spiritual likeness between Becket and his master was a real one, and that was what he wished to convey. Above all, it suggested strong grounds for canonization. But historically the service that Eustace performed for the archbishop's memory was a dubious one.

---

26. It is doubtful when the annal for 1240 was written up as it stands in the B text of the Great Chronicle. From a reference to the death of Gilbert the Marshal (who died in 1245) in the annal for the year 1239, it has been concluded that this part of the text of the chronicle was not written earlier than 1245, see R. Vaughan, *Matthew Paris* (1958), pp. 59–60. It is not, however, absolutely clear that the references to the Marshal under the annal for 1239 will bear that interpretation.

Appendix II
An Itinerary of Archbishop Edmund

Numbers cited as evidence refer to the *acta* of Archbishop Edmund catalogued in Lawrence, *St Edmund*, pp. 303–14.

Year	Date	Place	Evidence
1234	January	South Malling	No. 1
	2 February	Westminster	Attended council: *Chron.Maj.*, iii, pp. 268–70
	2 April	Canterbury	The day of his consecration: *Early Charters of St Paul's Cathedral*, ed. M. Gibbs (CS, 3rd series, lviii, 1939), p. 141; *Chron.Maj.*, iii, p. 272
	9 April	Westminster	Attended council: *Chron.Maj.*, iii, p. 272
	10 April	Westminster	*Charters and Documents relating to Selbourne Priory*, ed. W.D. Macray (Hampshire Record Society, iv, 1891), p. 13
	13 May	Leominster	No. 2
	15 May	Hereford	No. 3
	18 May	Gloucester	*Cal.Pat.Rolls, 1232–47*, p. 45
	23 May	Gloucester	PRO, Charter Roll, 29 (20 Henry III)
	25 May	Gloucester	*Cal.Pat.Rolls, 1232–47*, p. 75
	8 June	Gloucester	*Close Rolls, 1231–34*, pp. 566–7
	19 June	Shrewsbury	*Ibid.*, p. 564
	21 June	Middle	Negotiating with Llewelyn: *Cal.Pat.Rolls, 1232–47*, p. 59
	26 June	Leominster	No. 4
	14 July	Westminster	*Chron.Maj.*, iii, pp. 294–5
	25 July	Rochester	*CChR*, iii, p. 361
	26 September	Marlborough	*Cal.Pat.Rolls, 1232–47*, p. 70
	30 September	London	No. 6
	14 October	Westminster	HMC. *Report, Wells* I, p. 495
	18–27 October	Wrotham	Lambeth Palace, MS. 1212, fo. 45
	9 December	Reading	*Cal.Pat.Rolls, 1232–47*, pp. 45, 46, 48
1235	20 January	Westminster	Attended council: *Close Rolls, 1234–37*, pp. 160–1
	26–28 January	Westminster	PRO, Charter Roll, 28 (19 Henry III)
	19–20 February	Westminster	*Ibid.*
	1 May	Westminster	*Ibid.*
	9–10 May	Canterbury	*Ibid.*
	8 June	Windsor	Westminster Abbey, Dean & Chapter muniment no. 32676 (Archbishop E. attests the king's confirmation of a gift to the abbey)
	9 June	Windsor	PRO, Charter Roll, 28 (19 Henry III)
	17 June	Reading	No. 8 (consecration of Robert Grosseteste to Lincoln)

Year	Date	Place	Evidence
1235	18 June	Woodstock	PRO, E326/B11402 (Kilwardby's *inspeximus* of Archbishop E.'s charter in favour of the nuns of Catesby)
	23 June	Farnham	No. 9
	8–10 July	Westminster	PRO, Charter Roll, 28 (19 Henry III)
	17–19 August	Westminster	*Ibid.*
	2 October	South Malling	BL, Cotton MS., Otho A II, fo. 49v
	21 October	Westminster	*Close Rolls, 1234–7*, p. 202
	3 November	Woodstock	*Ibid.*, p. 203
	24 November	Aldington	No. 10
	10 November	Aldington	No. 11
1236	14 January	Canterbury	*Chron.Maj.*, iii, p. 336
	20 January	Westminster	*Ibid.*, iii, p. 337
	21–30 January	Merton	Attending council: *Close Rolls , 1234–7*, pp. 337–9; PRO, Charter Roll, 29 (20 Henry III)
	21 February	South Malling	No. 13
	5 March	South Malling	No. 14
	4 April	Croydon	No. 15
	19 May	Slindon	No. 16
	1 June	Slindon	No. 17
	11 July	Tewkesbury	*Cal.Pat.Rolls, 1232–47*, p. 153
	23 July	Worcester	PRO, Charter Roll, 29 (20 Henry III)
1237	20 January	Westminster	*Close Rolls, 1234–7*, p. 543
	28 January	Westminster	*Magnum Registrum Album of Lichfield*, ed. H.E. Savage (1924), p. 100
	30 January	Westminster	PRO, Charter Roll, 30 (21 Henry III)
	22 April	Wingham	No. 19
	4 May	Maidstone	No. 20
	9 June	Canterbury	Lambeth Palace, MS. 1212, fos. 85–6
	c. 17 July	Dover	To meet the papal legate, Cardinal Otto: *Chron.Maj.*, iii, pp. 395–6; cf. *Close Rolls, 1234–7*, p. 541
	13 October	Worcester	At the enthronement of Walter Cantilupe as bishop of Worcester: *Ann.Mon.*, iv, p. 428
	18–21 November	London	Attending the legatine council at St Paul's: *Chron.Maj.*, iii, p. 415; *Ann.Mon.*, i, p. 105
	18 December	Canterbury	Nos. 21, 22
	19 December	Canterbury	No. 23
	19 x 24 December	Crossed the Channel for Rome, resting at St Bertin, Flanders	*Chron.Maj.*, iii, p. 470; PRO Ancient Correspondence, xi, 159, refers to his stay at St Bertin's abbey
	12 March	Rome	BL, Add.Ms. 15264 (Pontigny Life), fo. 107ra
	20 March	Rome	*Annales Roffenses*, ed. Wharton, *Anglia Sacra* (1691), I, p. 349
1238	July	Returned from Rome (Dover)	*Ann.Mon.*, i, p. 110, which dates his return on 15 August; a copy of his *inspeximus* of a Dover

Year	Date	Place	Evidence
1238			charter (No. 30) in Lambeth Palace, MS. 1212, fo. 177, is dated July 1238
	17 November	Canterbury	Gervase, ii, p. 134
	21 November	Canterbury	Consecrated Richard of Wendover to the see of Rochester: *Annales Roffenses*, p. 349
	c. 3–9 December	Aldington	Gervase, ii, pp. 138–9
	11 December	Canterbury	No. 35
	13–15 December	Canterbury	Nos. 36, 37, 38
	23 December	Canterbury	Gervase, ii, p. 141
	23–*c.* 27 December	Wingham	*Ibid.*, ii, p. 141
1239	2–5 January	Canterbury	*Ibid.*, ii, pp. 142–5
	5–6 January	Teynham	*Ibid.*, ii, pp. 145–6; Nos. 41, 42
	10 January	Hadlow	No. 43
	14–15 January	Hadlow	*Ibid.*, ii, pp. 150–1; No. 44
	20 January	Lambeth	No. 45
	7 February	Tunbridge	Gervase, ii, p. 155
	4–6 March	London	Attended meeting of the bishops summoned by the papal legate: *ibid.*, ii, p. 159; *Chron.Maj.*, iii, p. 524
	18 March	South Malling	Gervase, ii, p. 160
	12 April	South Malling	No. 48
	17 April	London	Meeting with the papal legate: Gervase, ii, p. 166
	24 April	Teynham	*Ibid.*, ii, p. 166
	24 April	Shalmsford	*Ibid.*, ii, p. 166
	24–27 April	Wingham	*Ibid.*, ii, pp. 166–8; Nos. 49, 50, 51
	1 May	Canterbury	Edmund preached at St Sepulchre's: *ibid.*, ii, p. 168
	20 June	London	For the baptism of the Lord Edward: *Chron.Maj.*, ii, p. 539
	31 July	London	At meeting with the papal legate: *Chron.Maj.*, iii, p. 567
	25 September	London	Consecrated William Ralegh to the see of Norwich: *Ann.Mon.*, iv, p. 86; *Chron.Maj.*, iii, p. 617
	5 October	Wingham	No. 52
	3 November	London	*Roberti Grosseteste Epistolae*, ed. H.R. Luard (RS, 1861), p. 254
	16 November	Teynham	No. 53
1240	2 January	Lyminge	No. 54
	13 January	London	Attended council: *Chron.Maj.*, iv, p. 3
	4 March	South Malling	No. 56
	7 March	South Malling	No. 57
	15 March	South Malling	No. 58
	1 July	Newark	Consecrated Hugh Pateshall to the see of Lichfield: *Ann.Mon.*, iv, pp. 86–7
	9 July	Aldington	No. 59
	23 July	Wingham	Nos. 60, 61
	? 1 October	London	According to the *Flores*, Edmund was present at

Year	Date	Place	Evidence
1240			the consecration of St Paul's by Bishop Roger Niger: *Flores Historiarum*, ed. H.R. (RS, 1890), ii, p. 237 & n.
	October	Embarked for Rome; disembarked at Gravelines, proceeded via Senlis to Pontigny	*Ann.Mon.*, i, p. 116; iii, p. 88. See the Life by Matthew Paris, chapter xxxv
	c. 5–10 November	Pontigny	The Lives by Eustace and Matthew Paris: Lawrence, *St Edmund*, pp. 217, 263–4
	13 November	Soisy	No. 64
	14 November	Soisy	No. 65
	16 November	Soisy	Day of his death: the *Vitae*; *Bullarium Romanum* (Turin, 1858), iii, p. 522

Index